Perspectives on Rules of Origin

Perspectives on Rules of Origin

Analytical and Policy Insights from the Indian Experience

Ram Upendra Das
and
Rajan Sudesh Ratna

palgrave
macmillan

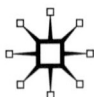

First published 2011 by
PALGRAVE MACMILLAN

Palgrave Macmillan in the UK is an imprint of Macmillan Publishers Limited, registered in England, company number 785998, of Houndmills, Basingstoke, Hampshire RG21 6XS.

Palgrave Macmillan in the US is a division of St Martin's Press LLC, 175 Fifth Avenue, New York, NY 10010.

Palgrave Macmillan is the global academic imprint of the above companies and has companies and representatives throughout the world.

Palgrave® and Macmillan® are registered trademarks in the United States, the United Kingdom, Europe and other countries.

ISBN 978–0–230–21729–4   hardback

This book is printed on paper suitable for recycling and made from fully managed and sustained forest sources. Logging, pulping and manufacturing processes are expected to conform to the environmental regulations of the country of origin.

A catalogue record for this book is available from the British Library.

Library of Congress Cataloging-in-Publication Data

Upendra Das, R.
Perspectives on rules of origin : analytical and policy insights from the
  Indian experience / Ram Upendra Das and Rajan Sudesh Ratna.
      p. cm.
    ISBN 978–0–230–21729–4 (hardback)
1. Certificates of origin.   2. Commercial policy.   3. Commerce.
   4. Certificates of origin—India.   5. India—Commerce.   6. India—
  Commercial policy.   I. Ratna, Rajan Sudesh, 1961– II. Title.
HJ6617.U64 2010
382'.910954—dc22   2010023756

10   9   8   7   6   5   4   3   2   1
20   19   18   17   16   15   14   13   12   11

Printed and bound in Great Britain by
CPI Antony Rowe, Chippenham and Eastbourne

Dedicated to Our Parents
As More than Our Best Teachers

Contents

List of Tables, Figures and Boxes

Tables

Figures

Boxes

Foreword

The global trading regime has witnessed a proliferation of regional trading arrangements (RTAs) in both the developed and developing worlds. Recently, there has also been an intensification of India's economic engagements with other countries. These are primarily manifested in the signing of preferential trading agreements (PTAs), free trade agreements (FTAs) and comprehensive economic partnership agreements (CEPA) with the Association of Southeast Asian Nations (ASEAN), Thailand, the Southern Common Market (MERCOSUR), etc. and also in the frameworks of SAFTA and the Bay of Bengal Initiative for Multi-Sectoral technical and Economic Cooperation (BIMSTEC). India is already engaged with Nepal and Sri Lanka under bilateral trading arrangements. There are some economic partnership arrangements between India and other countries that are also in the offing such as the European Union, South Kore, Japan, and China.

The framework of rules of origin (ROO) being an integral part of RTAs has emerged as one of the most controversial issues in any trade negotiations. India has adopted a comprehensive approach thus far, in terms of laying down originating criteria for its preferential imports. However, various divergent views have emerged in the academic and policy circles in terms of the efficacy of ROO. The Indian industry is apprehensive of trade deflection and has voiced its concerns and advocated for ROO as a possible safeguard instrument against deflected imports. On the contrary, some of India's trading partners view it as a non-trade barrier and instruments of trade-distortion.

The proposed study aims at presenting an objective viewpoint of the ROO. This would be taken up by critically examining the analytical debate on the subject and the associated economic rationale for having it or dispensing with it. Even more so, it is imperative that a comprehensive study is undertaken to help evolve India's overall position *vis-à-vis* the application of the ROO under different trading agreements so that it does not lead to a 'spaghetti-bowl' phenomenon.

The scope of the book thus includes an objective assessment of analytical arguments along with an empirical exploration into the issues, which could help bring out the policy insights, facilitating a consensus on the Indian framework of ROO to be applied during the economic engagements of India with her partner countries.

Acknowledgements

This book has evolved over years as a result of our academic work. Since we were intensively engaged in various studies and negotiations of India's RTAs, it is only natural that the study benefited immensely from both Indian and foreign experts and negotiators. We would like to place on record our gratitude to Nagesh Kumar, R. Khullar, U. S. Bhatia, S. S. Kapur, Rajeet Mitter, P. K. Dash, A. Khatua, Paul-de Voucher, Walter Scott, Rebecca S. Maria, Khun Chana Kanaratnadilok, Y. Lucas, Saman Kelagama, Binod Karmacharya, P.R.V. Ramanan, K.C. Rout, Anant Swarup, K.N. Singh, Anoop Swarup, V.L. Kantha Rao, Shashank Priya, Ajay Shrivatava, Geetu Sidhu and Santha Thampi.

As members of the Expert Group on Preferential Rules of Origin (PROO), constituted by the Government of India, we would also like to acknowledge various inputs and suggestions that were provided during the RTA negotiations of India and several rounds of stakeholder consultations of which we were a part.

Valuable guidance was received on various occasions from Sunanda Sen, Muchkund Dubey, Shiv Shankar Menon, L. K. Ponappa, Deepak Chattrejee, S.N. Menon, G.K. Pillai, Hardeep Puri, Nirupama Rao, Lakshmi Puri, Meera Shankar, Ashok Sajjanhar, Pradeep Kapur, Sudhir Vyas, Kheya Bhattacharya, T. S. Triumurty, Preeti Saran, Rajiva Mishra, Rajiv Kher, and B. S. Bishnoi.

We were inspired by the rigorous work that had been undertaken on the subject and related aspects by Jagdish Bhagwati, Antoni Estevadeordal, O. Cadot, Vermulst, Stephenson, James, Rugman, A. Panaghariya, Kala Krishna, V. R. Panchamukhi, K. Kalirajan, Hoeckman, Kati, A. Mattoo and the Australian Productivity Commission.

One of the challenging aspects while writing this book related to the adjustments in our personal lives as most of the time that would have otherwise been devoted to the families was dedicated to this endeavour as well as to respective official commitments. This book would not have been possible without the support and encouragement of our families. We thank our families who gave their support without question. Upendra would like to thank Anuradha, Sanjana and Utkarsh for anything and everything. Rajan would like to thank his wife Sonali and loving children Harshit and Urvashi for fully supporting and helping during this period, and the constant source of encouragement given by

Mrs and Mr M.N. Sahay, Simpa and Rajesh, Ranu and Sanjeev and their children during the difficult times.

We must also acknowledge the contribution of several rounds of coffees that were served to us while writing this book at the Café Coffee Day, located at the crossing of Lodhi Colony in Lutyen's Delhi. The place was our big *adda* for solving intricate issues of trade and development policy pertaining to this book. During our saturation points it were these coffees in a warm and modern ambience and the views of traffic and people through the glass panels that were indeed refreshing and gave us the time to recharge ourselves. It was this that always kept reminding us to keep the 'people' at the centre of all our developmental analysis in the book. The waiters there, were really hospitable who would bear with us while we were occupying a small corner for long hours while writing this book. We find it very difficult to thank them but they will always be cherished in our memories.

The Palgrave professionals need to be thanked for their care and cooperation at every stage of the publication, specially, Ruttaman, Taiba, Alec, Gemma and Ann.

Last, but not the least, we are extremely grateful to the anonymous referees for their constructive comments.

Ram Upendra Das
Rajan Sudesh Ratna
Deepavali (Festival of Lights)
New Delhi

List of Abbreviations

ACP	African, Caribbean and Pacific countries
AFTA	ASEAN Free Trade Area
AGOA	African Growth and Opportunity Act
ANZCERTA	Australia New Zealand Closer Economic Agreement
APTA	Asia-Pacific Trade Agreement
ARO	Agreement on Rules of Origin
ASEAN	Association of Southeast Asian Nations
ATC	Agreement on Textiles and Clothing
ATPDEA	Andean Trade Preference Programme
BIMSTEC	Bay of Bengal Initiative for Multi-Sectoral Technical and Economic Cooperation
CBTPP	Caribbean basin Trade Programme
CEPA	Comprehensive Economic Partnership Agreement
CEPT	Common Effective Preferential Tariff
CIF	cost, insurance, freight
COOL	Country of Origin Labeling
CRO	Committee on Rules of Origin
CTC	Change in tariff classification
CTSH	Change in Tariff Sub-heading
CTH	Change in Tariff Heading
EEZ	Exclusive Economic Zone
EFTA	European Free Trade Association
EPA	Economic Partnership Agreement
ESCAP	United Nations Economic and Social Commission for Asia and the Pacific
FOB	free on board
FTA	Free Trade Agreement
FTAA	Free Trade Area of the Americas

GATT	General Agreement on Tariffs and Trade
GI	geographical Indications
GSP	Generalized System of Preferences
GSTP	Global System of Trade Preferences
HS	Harmonized System
LDC	Least Developed Countries
MERCOSUR	Southern Common Market
MFN	Most-favoured Nation
NAFTA	North American Free Trade Agreement
NTB	Non Tariff Barrier
PROO	Preferential Rules of Origin
PSR	Product Specific Rules of Origin
PTA	Preferential Trading Agreement
RDI	Rules of Origin Development Index
ROO	Rules of Origin
RTA	Regional Trading Agreement
SAA	Statement of Administrative Action
SAARC	South Asian Association for Regional Cooperation
SAFTA	South Asian Free Trade Area
SAPTA	SAARC Preferential Trading Arrangement
SGA	selling, general and administrative
TCRO	Technical Committee on Rules of Origin
VC	Value Content
WCO	Customs Cooperation Council/World Customs Organization
WTO	World Trade Organization

1
Introduction

The global trading regime is witnessing today a proliferation of regional trading arrangements (RTAs) in both the developed and developing worlds. Recently, there has also been an intensification of individual country's economic engagements with its other trading partners. These are primarily manifested in the signing of Preferential Trading Agreements (PTAs), Free Trade Agreements (FTAs) and Comprehensive Economic Partnership Agreements (CEPA). The developed, as well as the developing countries, are participating in these RTAs very actively. At present, the number of agreements notified to the World Trade Organization (WTO) is more than 200, a sixfold rise over just two decades. Given the rush to conclude RTAs, it is expected that the number will reach 300 in about 2 years' time. Today, with the exception of Mongolia, all the WTO Members are participating in one or more RTA negotiations.

It is not difficult to explain how important Rules of Origin (ROO) are, especially in the context of preferential trading relations of a country. It is a set of instruments, a lack of consensus on which, has delayed the implementation of various RTAs. This has been particularly true of the Indian experience. A lack of consensus on this issue delayed the implementation of the Framework Agreement on the India–Thailand FTA. The SAFTA treaty has also kept this issue open for further negotiations for a long time. Absence of provisions relating to ROO under the India–Nepal FTA raised concerns about imports from Nepal into India, which had adverse implications for some Indian domestic sectors. The problem was tackled by setting in place these rules during subsequent negotiations. Similar problems have been experienced in the India–ASEAN FTA, among many others, which led to scrapping of the Early Harvest Programme. Similarly, the deadlines to conclude FTA negotiations with

1

ASEAN, Thailand and BIMSTEC have been missed. This is mainly due to lack of consensus on ROO.

Even within the ambit of negotiations on non-preferential rules of origin (NPROO)under the WTO framework, consensus on this issue has proved to be an illusive one. The obvious question is why ROO are so important that they have such a strong bearing on the outcome of international economic negotiations? The answer lies perhaps in the conceptual ambiguity that envelopes this trade policy instrument in developing countries.

Whether or not a product has originated in a particular country is decided on the basis of the fact that the product has undergone substantial transformation. There are three prime ways of determining this. First, the change in tariff heading test implying that the tariff heading of the final product is different from the tariff headings of its non-originating inputs. Secondly, a percentage test is applied according to which a minimum percentage of total value addition should be achieved with the help of domestic inputs. Finally, specified process tests require a product to undergo certain stipulated processes.

However, agreement on the implementation of these tests is often difficult. For instance, the extent of 'substantial transformation' for different products would depend on the level of dis-aggregation (i.e. at 4- or 6-digit Harmonized System [HS] level) on which tariff-shift is envisaged. Similarly, the fixing of percentages of minimum value addition varies from product to product, depending on the prevailing labour costs and the product-specific import dependence of the country in terms of intermediates. These policy-conflicts can be resolved only if the role of ROO is understood clearly.

One of the prime functions of these rules is to prevent trade deflection in trading arrangements. In any FTA, members set their own external tariffs but give preferential tariff treatment to each other. The divergence between external tariffs of the members and the preferential tariffs becomes a potential source of trade deflection. In the absence of any ROO within the FTA, the country with lowest external tariffs is likely to serve as an entry point into the partner's market for the goods of the non-member countries. In this sense, ROO are important tools for checking trade deflection from one member country to another of third country goods.

The three modalities of determining origin of a product aim at substantial transformation in inputs. They together facilitate value-addition in the country of manufacturing and play a developmental role. Such requirements, which limite the import content of value addition, have the potential for generating backward and forward linkages in a country adhering to the rules. Thus, a member country is prevented from becoming a mere trading country as these requirements act as a deterrent to assembly production activities. However, ROO should be designed in a manner that is not trade-restricting. They should not become trade barriers merely because of their complex methods of implementation. Developed countries use the ROO for developmental purposes, though in some cases they do act as NTBs. The North American Free Trade Agreement (NAFTA) is a case in point, where for the automotive sector different percentages of the regional value content are laid down for various phases, for instance 56 per cent between 1998 and 2002 and 62.5 per cent thereafter for some categories of motor vehicles. In the case of textiles and clothing, there is a 'triple-transformation test' that requires fabrics or clothing items to be spun from yarns or fibres produced in North America as well as to be cut and sewn within the FTA.

It is clear from above that ROO, if designed adequately, should not only prevent trade deflection possibilities but also act as a catalyst to value-addition efforts in members of an FTA. Their implementation should, however, not swing to the other end of the spectrum where its effects are similar to NTBs. This remains as a policy challenge, especially in FTA negotiations in the developing world.

Little analytical attention has so far been devoted to the issue of ROO in the context of services and investment agreements. This chapter explores this largely uncharted territory by advancing a few thoughts on a range of economic and legal considerations arising from the way in which various agreements seek to determine as to who benefits from services trade and investment liberalization. It focuses on the practice of preferential and non-preferential services trade liberalization found in various bilateral and regional trade and investment agreements as well as the WTO General Agreement on Trade in Services (GATS). It addresses a range of conceptual issues relating to services trade that impinge upon the design and implementation of ROO for services. The discussion draws attention to a number of salient characteristics of trade in services that limit the usefulness of concepts and approaches to origin developed in the context of trade in goods. Attention is also drawn to a number of economic considerations that should inform the design of ROO for services trade to minimize the potentially adverse effects of trade and investment diversion, and maximize the economy-wide gains in allocative efficiency that well-designed services liberalization can entail (Cadot *et al.*, 2006).

Against the above backdrop, in Chapter 1, the subject is introduced and the context for the analysis is set by highlighting the conceptual ambiguity that envelopes this trade policy instrument in developing countries in general and India in particular.

In a somewhat novel way, Chapter 2 builds a conceptual economic basis for ROO. It discusses both the non-preferential and preferential rules involved. While discussing the harmonization work programme in WTO, it explains the specific issues where there is yet to be a consensus among members. The chapter dwells upon the legal and interpretational aspects of the Agreement on Rules of Origin (ARO) of the WTO. In so doing, ROO disputes in the WTO have been taken up as a case study in order to bring about clarity in different concepts and terms used in the ARO. It underscores the importance of ROO and argues how if properly formulated they can play a developmental role in the context of RTAs, an aspect often omitted from the analysis on the subject. The economic effects of ROO are brought out at varying dimensions of trade flows especially of the goods in different categories. This has been argued and concluded by including in the analysis the positive effects of ROO through three channels, i.e. (i) preventing trade deflection, (ii) facilitating value addition, and (iii) augmenting intra-regional trade. The chapter also refers to the aspects of balancing export interests and preventing undue import competition as well as the prospects of enhancing the feasibility of welfare-inducing FTA. This chapter also contributes to laying the foundations of ROO analysis with the help of a gravity model that also offers new methodologies to measure trade deflection. In this context, the book presents a new concept of a development index of ROO as opposed to the well-known restrictiveness index on the subject.

Chapter 3 goes into the detail of assessing the merits and demerits of ROO. The intricacies surrounding the concepts of wholly-owned and not wholly-owned criteria are unravelled along with the imperatives of understanding the nuances of change in tariff classification with respect to the level of determination of 'substantial transformation'. Against this background, the chapter offers new insights by answering the usually unasked question of whether change in tariff classification (CTH) and change in tariff sub-heading (CTSH) are substitutes or complements? Similarly, the chapter examines the various contentious dimensions of the percentage test and the specific process test and concludes that an optimum mix is needed of these tests in a country-specific context. Further, the ambiguities relating to the minimal processes and different types of cumulation are addressed.

In Chapter 4, ROO, as practised in different RTAs, are analysed, including divergences across RTAs on the treatment of select sectors. An objective analysis of ROO in India's RTAs is then presented in Chapter 5. Apart from tracing the evolution of ROO in India's RTAs in Chapter 5, we dwell upon some of the case studies of infringement of ROO in the India's RTAs; assess Indian industry's perception; and analyse the trade effects of ROO formulation with the help of detailed data analysis, gravity modelling and trade deflection ratio calculations. It is worth highlighting that the empirical analysis has been undertaken with the help of the developmental index that this book introduces as a completely new concept.

This book provides a comprehensive treatment of ROO in the realm of trade in services in Chapter 6, given the fact that trade in services is assuming greater importance and is being increasingly included in RTAs. This chapter first brings out the differences between trade in services and trade in goods – then highlights the uniqueness of trade in services followed by the distinct approaches towards ROO in different RTAs. The chapter further sets in place a conceptual framework for ROO relating to trade in services in RTAs. Subsequently, dimensions of ROO in the Asian context including India's RTAs are analysed and, finally, certain policy suggestions have been made to improve the efficacy of ROO for services trade.

Lastly, Chapter 7 offers various policy prescriptions and options in order to make ROO serve the dual objectives of preventing trade deflection on one hand and playing a developmental role on the other. The policy dimensions are not only discussed for ROO relating to trade in goods and services but also include issues relating to investment, geographical indications, need for consistency and harmonization, issues for implementation, and labelling requirements. The chapter finally addresses the issue of how ROO can be formulated as a trade policy instrument and a tool for development.

The broad conclusions and insights of the book are summarized in Chapter 8.

2
Conceptual Basis for Rules of Origin

This chapter introduces the broad contours of concepts relating to rules of origin. It explores why ROO are so important in having such a strong bearing on the outcome of international trade negotiations. The chapter aims at setting the context for the analysis by highlighting the conceptual ambiguity that envelopes this trade policy instrument in developing countries in general and India in particular. It offers fresh insights into the conceptual foundation of ROO and departs from the conventional approach towards the subject, by putting the developmental aspects to the core of its analysis as a commercial policy instrument.

2.1 Rationale for Rules of Origin

The term 'Rules of Origin' speaks for itself – rules that determine the origin of a product in international trade. Because of varying definitions that have been used, ROO are perceived as a technical and incomprehensible set of rules governing international trade. Determining the origin of a product is necessary in both the preferential as well as multilateral (non-preferential) regimes. In the multilateral context this fact was recognized during the Uruguay Round negotiations of the General Agreement on Tariffs and Trade (GATT) wherein it was felt that ascertaining the country of origin of imported products is necessary in applying basic trade policy measures such as tariffs, quantitative restrictions, anti-dumping and countervailing duties and safeguard measures, etc.

Countries that offer zero or reduced duty access to imports from certain trade partners often apply another and different set of preferential rules of origin (PROO) to determine the eligibility of products to receive preferential access. The justification for PROO is to prevent trade deflection, or simple trans-shipment, whereby products from non-participating countries are redirected through a free trade partner to avoid the payment of customs duties. Hence, the role of PROO is to ensure that only goods originating in participating countries enjoy tariff or other preferences. Therefore, they are integral parts of preferential trade agreements such as bilateral and regional free trade agreements and the non-reciprocal preferences that industrial countries offer to developing countries.

The general approach that most of the countries have followed in operationalizing their FTAs or PTAs is based on well–recognized principles that govern the working of PROO the world over and also their industry's perceptions of the disadvantages and opportunities from such trading arrangements.

The global trading regime is witnessing today a proliferation of RTAs in both the developed and developing worlds. Recently, there has also been an intensification of individual country's economic engagements with its other trading partners. These are primarily manifested in signing of PTAs, FTAs and CEPA. The developed as well as the developing countries are participating in these RTAs very actively. At present, the number of agreements notified to the WTO is more than 200,[1] a six-fold rise over just two decades (Figure 2.1). Given the rush to conclude RTAs, it is expected that the number will reach 300 in about two years' time.

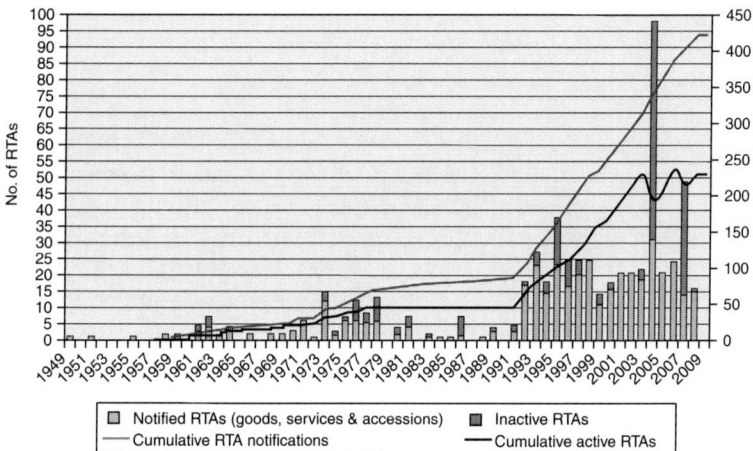

Figure 2.1 RTAs notified to the GATT/WTO, 1948–2009 (cumulative).

Today, with the exception of Mongolia, all the WTO members are participating in one or more RTA negotiations.[2]

The boom in RTAs reflects changes in certain countries' trade-policy objectives, the changing perceptions of the multilateral liberalization process, and the reintegration into the global economy of countries in transition from socialism. This last category accounts for many of the new agreements signed in the early 1990s, when countries in Eastern Europe and the former Soviet Union negotiated RTAs with Western Europe [both the EU and the European Free Trade Association (EFTA)] and with each other. This fact can be illustrated from Table 2.1.

It may be pointed out that on an average, each country belongs to 6 RTAs, though there is considerable variation across regions and levels of development. Northern countries have participated to the greatest extent, each signing, on average, 13 agreements. A substantial number of developing countries (45) have signed bilateral preferential agreements with a Northern partner. Since 2000, several major new trends have emerged in the pattern of regional trade agreements. One unifying characteristic is that these take RTAs well beyond agreements between adjacent countries. For example:

- The EU's move toward bilateral market access FTAs and Economic Partnership Agreements (EPAs) with the African, Caribbean and Pacific (ACP) countries;
- The shift in the US position toward bilateral preferential agreements; and
- The effort of a handful of developing countries to open markets through RTAs.

An important feature of the rise in the number of RTAs is the growing number of overlapping agreements and the so-called 'spaghetti bowl' that has emerged from the proliferation of bilateral/ regional agreements. A web of differing trade arrangements can entangle administrative procedures – customs procedures, technical standards, ROO, and so on – and thereby raise the costs for both enterprises and governments. Figure 2.2 illustrates the so-called 'spaghetti bowl' or, possibly a more fitting term for Asia and the Pacific, 'noodle bowl' view of the preferential trade routes in this region. It shows the entanglement of bilateral and regional free trade and other types of agreements that are in force. There are about 40 more that are being negotiated, and many more that are considered in either political or policy circles.

Table 2.1 RTAs: Overall scenario

	East Asia and Pacific	Europe and Central Asia	Latin America and the Caribbean	Middle East and North Africa	South Asia	Sub-Saharan Africa	North	Total
(No. of countries)								
	32	36	39	21	8	48	25	209
North–South bilateral								
Countries belonging to at least one RTA	4	12	6	10	0	2	10	44
Average number of RTAs per country	2	1	2	1		1	4	2
Maximum number of RTAs per country	4	4	4	3	0	1	24	24
All others								
Countries belonging to at least one RTA	24	22	33	20	8	47	10	164
Average number of RTAs per country	2	6	8	5	4	4	8	5
Maximum number of RTAs per country	3	12	17	12	9	9	15	17
Total								
Countries belonging to at least one RTA	26	26	35	20	8	48	11	174
Average number of RTAs per country	2	6	8	5	4	4	11	5
Maximum number of RTAs per country	7	12	19	13	9	9	29	29

Note: Bilateral agreements are defined as an RTA with two members. North is OECD 24 plus Lichtenstein, and South is all other countries.
Source: World Bank (2005), *Global Economic Prospects*, Washington, D C

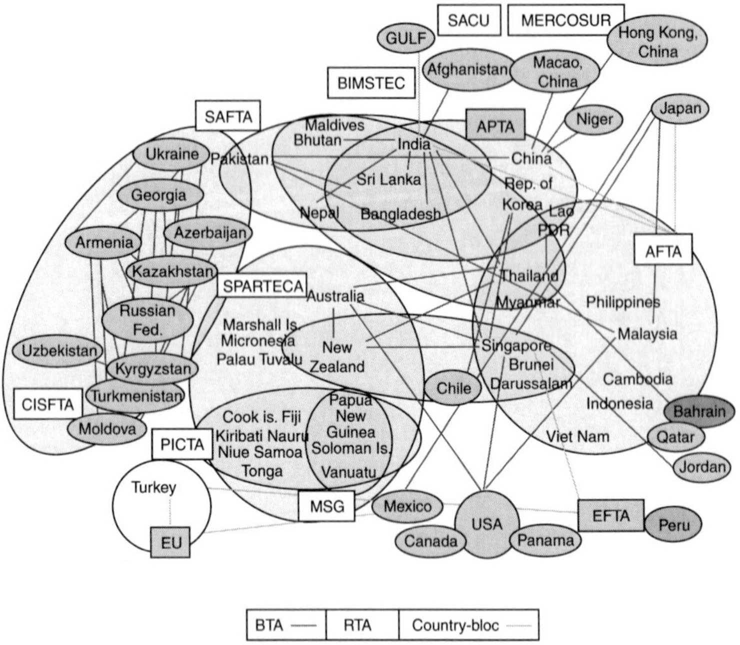

Source: Mikic, Mia (2007): Mapping preferential trade in Asia and Pacific.
Figure 2.2   The 'spaghetti-bowl'.

Many agreements between country pairs are duplicated by other agreements to which the same two countries are parties. With conflicting rules, these agreements would lead to fragmented markets and increase the transaction cost of trade, thus adversely affecting the volume of trade as well as global and national welfare. Therefore, to achieve significant benefit in terms of lower administrative costs and more effective implementation, it would be necessary to rationalize the current structure of such 'spaghetti-bowl' agreements.

Figure 2.2 shows how regional trading arrangements have proliferated and made the trading linkages more complex. At a time when increasing numbers of companies are globalizing their parts procurement and production networks, the significant differences in national ROO can work to disrupt the free flow of trade. Unnecessary complications and confusion arise when the same product may have several different countries of origin depending on the country for which it is destined. Needless to say, this greatly diminishes the exporter's predictability of trade, which creates a scenario where these ROO will contribute or further aggravate the 'spaghetti-bowl' effects of RTAs. In addition, a change in the ROO of a particular country may force globalized producers to add certain manufacturing processes in that country, resulting in substantially higher costs.

As a result of this, criticisms are often made of RTAs that they necessarily lead to the proliferation of PROO and so add complexity to the trading system and potentially make harmonization more difficult. This issue, therefore, needs to be approached in an objective manner, for which the issue of ROO harmonization first between the different PROO needs to be addressed. The RTAs described here do not seem to support this observation unambiguously. Subsequently, the issue of harmonizing the PROO NPROO would also need to be taken, even though their objectives are different. This is necessary in the broader context of making them facilitate trade rather than using it as a non-tariff measure to impede trade.

2.2 Preferential vs Non-Preferential Rules of Origin

In general, rules of origin have not been adequately addressed at the international level. For many years, the GATT contained no specific provisions on rules of origin other than Article IX, which deals with marking requirements (i.e. 'marks of origin'). ROO are only covered by the GATT's general provisions, such as Article I (most-favoured nation [MFN] treatment) and Article 5, the latter of which requires that free trade areas shall not increase restrictions on trade with members who are not part of the free trade area or parties to the customs union.

Aside from the GATT, the International Convention on Simplification and Harmonization of Customs Procedures (the Kyoto Convention), concluded under the aegis of the Customs Cooperation Council (commonly called "WCO", abbreviated from "World Customs Organization"), contains an Annex on ROO. Although binding on parties that accept it, the range of permitted options is so wide that the Annex imposes no effective restrictions. The ability of the Annex to serve as a set of international rules is thus severely limited from the outset.

The imposition of ROO should properly be a technical and neutral matter. However, because there are no common international standards, it has been increasingly common for the rules to be formulated and administered in an arbitrary fashion in an attempt to achieve protectionist policy objectives. To remedy the trade problems this has caused, countries are now in the process of formulating harmonized

NPROO under the terms outlined in the Agreement on Rules of Origin, an Annex to the WTO Agreement.

2.3   Non-preferential Rules of Origin[3]

At this stage the entire evolution of NPROO needs to be traced to place the issues in a balanced perspective. Looking back historically, it can be seen that it was in 1923 that an International Convention relating to the Simplification of Customs Formalities outlined various steps to simplify the procedure and formalities connected with verification of the origin of goods. It also dealt with the issues relating to issuance and acceptance of certificates of origin. It is worth mentioning that the Convention allowed private entities as well to issue certificates of origin. It also allowed provisional clearance of goods pending production of certificates of origin. The original signatories to this Convention included Germany, Austria, Belgium, British Empire, etc., which was signed at Geneva on 3 November 1923.

In the original GATT 1947, there were no multilateral rules for determination of origin of goods except for a reference to production of certificates or origin in the Notes and Supplementary Provisions under Ad Article VIII:

> It will be consistent with paragraph 1 if, on the importation of products from the territory of a contracting party, the production of certificates of origin should only be required to the extent that is strictly indispensable.

It is evident that the reference to origin determination was considered so unimportant that it was referred to only in the *Notes and Supplementary Provisions* and was required only in a situation wherein it was *strictly indispensable*. Again historically, the provisions of the Convention (1923) were functioning adequately as signatories were free to determine the origin of goods. This was possibly due to the fact that the countries would have faced hardly any legal hindrance or intervention during origin determination.

This situation continued for almost half a century up until 1973, when in Kyoto, Japan a separate Annex D was created, which dealt with origin determination, but it was a small part of the International Convention on the Simplification and Harmonization of Customs Procedures commonly known as the Kyoto Convention. The unbinding nature of honouring a certificate of origin by an importing country, like the 1923 Convention, continued and this is evident from the general principles and procedural provisions:

> Customs authorities are not bound to accept the documentary evidence of origin produced to them and retain the right to control the origin of the goods when they consider the circumstances warrant it.

Subsequently, over the years, especially in late 1980s, due to the predominance of multinational and transnational corporations and their incumbent production networks, the use of multi-country products made determination of origin complex and difficult. This was one of the important reasons the nations at the Uruguay Round agreed to negotiate a framework for harmonizing the NPROO as doubts regarding non-uniformity in the determination of origin and the consequent trade restrictive effects as a non-tariff barrier were expressed.[4] This resulted in an Agreement on Rules of Origin (ARO) as an integral part of the WTO in 1995. Some salient features of this Agreement are discussed later.

The ARO emanated from the fact that at the initial level discussions countries were not clear on whether ROO were necessary and what it should it cover. At a later stage, an agreement was reached to negotiate a framework agreement laying down certain basic principles that could be applied by the GATT contracting parties; the harmonization work programme could proceed later to cover the non-preferential trade. Though the negotiations for harmoniszng the NPROO were to be held under the WTO, because the WCO had considerable experience in evolving the Harmonized System of Nomenclature for classification of goods, it was decided to form two committees, viz. (i) the Committee on Rules of Origin (CRO) at WTO and (ii) the Technical Committee on Rules of Origin (TCRO) at the WCO. All WTO members are members of these two committees.

In the multilateral context, in ascertaining the origin of imported products measures like tariffs, quantitative restrictions, anti-dumping and countervailing duties are applied. In addition, the issue of originating status of an imported product assumes importance in application of safeguard measures, for requirements relating to origin marking, public procurement and for statistical purposes. These objectives are met through the application of NPROO. The CRO, constituted in the WTO, looks after the work of harmonization of ROO.

The WTO ROO Agreement (ARO) provides for the following four (4) basic principles (see Annex A for the text of ARO):

(1) *Non-discrimination:* RoO must apply equally for all purposes of *non-preferential* treatment;

(2) *Predictability:* RoO must be objective, understandable and predictable;
(3) *Transparency:* RoO must not be used directly or indirectly as instruments to pursue trade policy objectives; and
(4) *Neutrality:* RoO must not, in and of themselves, have a restrictive, distorting or disruptive influence on international trade.

At the same time, Annex II[5] of the Agreement sets down a number of disciplines applicable to RoO in preferential regimes, which provide that RoO should clearly define requirements for conferring origin; based on a positive standard; published in accordance with GATT Article X:I; and applied prospectively. It is important to note that the Agreement distinguishes (if not focused on one) between PROO and NPROO. This is relevant taking into consideration the difference of the two general types of ROO.

2.3.1 Disputes relating to Non-Preferential Rules of Origin

The Agreement on ROO (ARO) resulted in the Uruguay Round, and there are certain jurisprudences relating to ROO. A study of these is important in understanding the legal underpinnings of ROO formulation and implementation.

2.3.1.1 *ARO provisions prescribe what members cannot do*

It is clear from reading the Article 2(b)–(d) of the ARO that they prescribe negative list of disciplines whereby members enjoy 'considerable discretion in designing and applying their rules of origin'. This needs to be explained further since this is an important dimension with immense policy implications. As per these provisions it is easily discernible that the ARO sets out what ROO should not do. This is captured in terms of the stipulations that they should not pursue trade objectives directly or indirectly; they should not themselves create restrictive, distorting or disruptive effects on international trade; they should not pose unduly strict requirements or require the fulfilment of a condition unrelated to manufacturing or processing; and they should not discriminate between other members. In other words, these provisions do not prescribe what a member must do with respect to ROO (Panel Report on *US – Textiles Rules of Origin*, paras 6.23–6.25 WT/DS/243R). The Panel has further observed:

> By setting out what Members cannot do, these provisions leave for Members themselves the discretion to decide what, within those bounds, they can do. In this regard, it is common ground between

the parties that Article 2 does not prevent Members from determining the criteria which confer origin, changing those criteria over time, or applying different criteria to different goods.

Accordingly, in assessing whether the relevant United States rules of origin are inconsistent with the provisions of Article 2, we will bear in mind that, while during the post-harmonization period Members will be constrained by the result of the harmonization work programme, during the transition period, Members retain considerable discretion in designing and applying their rules of origin.

Having clarified this, it is still possible to misinterpret or misunderstand some of the important provisions of ARO as referred to above. One such provision is that 'rules of origin should not pursue trade objectives directly or indirectly'. Should it be interpreted as that ROO should not be used as a trade policy instrument both for pursuing developmental goals or restricting imports or does this mean that ROO should not be so burdensome that it creates unnecessary obstacles to trade? This is discussed below.

2.3.1.2   ROO should support trade policies

The correct interpretation of this provision is that ROO should not be trade-restrictive with the objective of protecting the domestic industry or favouring use of domestic goods over the imported goods. While interpreting the Article 2 (b) of ARO the Panel (Panel Report on *US – Textiles Rules of Origin*, paras 6.43 as well as 6.84 WT/DS/243R) observed that Article 2(b) is intended to preclude Members from using rules of origin 'to substitute for, or to supplement, the intended effect of trade policy instruments':

> In our view, Article 2(b) is intended to ensure that rules of origin are used to implement and support trade policy instruments, rather than to substitute for, or to supplement, the intended effect of trade policy instruments. Allowing Members to use rules of origin to pursue the objectives of 'protecting the domestic industry against import competition' or 'favouring imports from one Member over imports from another' would be to substitute for, or supplement, the intended effect of a trade policy instrument and, hence, be contrary to the objective of Article 2(b).

This raises a fundamental question about the very definition of 'pursue trade objectives'. Unless there is some degree of clarity about this, it would be difficult to derive inferences about the exact function of the ROO.

2.3.1.3   Meaning of 'pursuing trade objectives'

As is evident from Box 2.1, in the India–US dispute on ROO for textiles and clothing, India claimed that both Section 334 of the United States

Box 2.1 India–USA dispute on ROO on textiles and clothing

India sought consultations with the USA concerning the USA ROO on textiles and clothing. India requested establishment of a panel which was set up in June 2002 with the following terms of reference: 'To examine in the light of the relevant provisions of the covered agreements cited by India in document WT/DS 243/5/Rev. 1, the matter referred to the DSB by India in that document and to make such findings as will assist the DSB in making the recommendations or in giving the rulings provided for in those agreements.' The major points made by India were that ROO set out in Section 334 and as modified by Section 405 and the relevant customs notifications:

(a) are being used by the United States as instruments to pursue trade objectives, thereby violating Article 2(b) of the RO Agreement. Section 334 is being used as an instrument to protect the United States' textile and apparel industry. Section 405 is being used as an instrument to favour imports of the products of concern to the European Communities;

(b) create restrictive, distorting and disruptive effects on international trade and are, therefore, inconsistent with the United States' obligations under Article 2(c), first sentence, of the RO Agreement;

(c) require the fulfilment of a certain condition not related to manufacturing or processing and pose unduly strict requirements and are, therefore, inconsistent with Article 2(c), second sentence, of the RO Agreement; and

(d) with respect to Section 405, discriminate between Members and, in particular, discriminate in favour of the European Communities and are, therefore, inconsistent with the United States' obligations under Article 2(d)of the RO Agreement.

Box 2.1 Continued

Due to these reasons, India considered that the US ROO for textiles and apparel products are inconsistent with paragraphs (b), (c), (d) and (e) of Article 2 of the ARO. Leaving aside complex legal points and textual interpretations, the major economic issue raised was the possible use of ROO as a trade policy instrument, specifically to provide protection to domestic industry. The desire to use this instrument to subdue the competitive effect of MFA dismantling is *prima facie* clear. The restrictiveness in trade flows in this case is coming out of the quota regime of ATC due to which India had argued that it had suffered disadvantage. Specifically, India cited its export of grey fabric to Sri Lanka for manufacture into bed linen. India had argued that Section 334 caused a major setback to this trade, because the products were considered as Indian and not of Sri Lanka, as a result of which Indian quota got exhausted. India also argued that since section 405 was a product of bilateral settlement between EU and USA, this is discriminatory to India, as it unduly favours the EU and, therefore, violates Article 2(b) and 2(d). Basically, the point was that settlement took into account products of export interest only to the EU.

US response

USA responded to all these points, in addition to its own as to why India's contention was not valid. Legally, it raised the point that as a complainant, it was India's responsibility to provide the burden of proof which India had not done. USA maintained that ARO allows changes in the ROO during the transition period and the changes made are, in the ordinary meaning of Article 2, consistent with the ARO. It argued that 'a finding that the US regime is inconsistent with Article 2 leads to an impossible result under the ARO: that the United States should have no ROO and instead simply make case by case determination of origin or that the WTO dispute settlement system can assign origin determination for specific products'. The USA argued that Section 334 does not have the objective of protecting domestic industry, as the Statement of Administrative Action (SAA) reveals.

The USA also argued that even if Section 405 was the result of bilateral consultations, the Section was not discriminatory as it

(Continued)

Box 2.1 Continued

is applied to all WTO members on an MFN basis. The concept of *de facto* advantage was not applicable in this case. On the issue of providing protection to domestic textiles trade, the USA argued that 'Section 334 has facilitated an enormous increase in trade and textiles product, to the US market. Accordingly, a conclusion that Section 334 was enacted to protect the US textile industry and is, therefore, a trade objective in the context of Article 2(b) would not be based on any legal or factual foundation'.

Findings

The Panel (2003) concluded:

(a) India has failed to establish that Section 334 of the Uruguay Round Agreements Act is inconsistent with Articles 2(b) or 2(c) of the RO Agreement;

(b) India has failed to establish that Section 405 of the Trade and Development Act is inconsistent with Articles 2(b), 2(c) or 2(d) of the RO Agreement and

(c) India has failed to establish that the customs regulations contained in 19 C.F.R. ± 102.21 are inconsistent with Articles 2(b), 2(c) or 2(d) of the RO Agreement. (20)

1. Article 2 of the ARO provides a fair amount of discretion to members, as to the determination criteria which confer origin, changing those criteria overtime, or applying different criteria to different goods. (pp. 71–2)

2. The objectives identified by India, i.e., the objective of protecting domestic industry against import competition and favouring imports from one member over imports from another may, in principle, be considered to constitute trade objectives in pursuit of which ROO may not be used. (pp. 73–4)

3. As to India's claim that section 405 is inconsistent with Article 2(b) as it favours imports from the European Communities, the Panel observed that since the 'section 305 applies equally to qualifying goods from all Members, we do not see how section 405 is being used as an instrument to pursue the objective of favouring EC imports ...' ... setting a bilateral

Box 2.1 Continued

> trade dispute does not imply an intention on the part of the disputing parties to disfavour members who are not parties to a settlement agreement'. (pp. 91)
>
> ## Conclusions
>
> India's decision to take the USA to the Dispute Settlement Board possibly arose out of the concern that the unilateral determination of rules of origin during the transition period might bring unexpected and undesirable consequences to its export interests. The long delay in the work programme of the Committee on ROO strengthened this threat perception. Had India won the case, that would have set restraints on such future actions by other member states. India has already felt the adverse impact of the NAFTA rules of origin, especially the triple transformation rule, on India's exports of textiles and clothing to USA. As the NAFTA experience as well as almost total collapse of India's grey fabric exports to Sri Lanka reveal, ROO can effectively deny market access to textiles and clothing exports from India, especially till the time the ATC quotas are in place. However, the dispute, despite all its legal complexities, does not have much substantive long-term implications for two reasons. First, the dispute arose out of the quota regime of the ATC which will become inoperative by 2005, with the complete integration of the T&C trade. Secondly, non-preferential rules of origin will have to be harmonized under the work programme of the Doha Development Agenda. That cannot be indefinitely postponed, even if there are delays as of now.
>
> From the legal stand point, two points are important. First, this as well as some other current disputes tend to substantiate the view that since under the WTO's dispute settlement system, the WTO rules can be consequentially enforced only if there are formal challenges, the body of case law may get developed in a skewed form, depending upon the interests of important members who are willing to use the DSM to push the envelop in their own interest. Secondly, the Panel Report brought into sharp focus the importance of trade data, in addition to the legal interpretation of the Agreements in arriving at findings. The Panel has observed with reference to at least two claims made by India on the inadequacy of empirical evidence

(Continued)

Box 2.1   Continued

submitted. This shows that trade economists along trade lawyers should be involved in preparing a country's substantive and legal position. Finally, from a systemic standpoint, the rapid rise in the number of disputes being brought to WTO, despite this being a sign of the robustness of the mechanism, calls for a review of the current system, to ensure that it does not collapse because of its own success.

Source: WTO, WT/DS 243/5 Rev. 1.

Uruguay Agreement Act and Section 405 of the United States Trade and Development Act of 2000 are inconsistent with Article 2(b) of the ARO. The Panel (Panel Report on *US – Textiles Rules of Origin*, para. 6.36 WT/DS/243R) agreed with both India and the United States that the operative clause of Article 2(b) includes the obligation that ROO must not be used as instruments to pursue trade objectives:

> *The Panel agrees with the parties that the operative part of Article 2(b) is the phrase 'rules of origin are not [to be] used as instruments to pursue trade objectives directly or indirectly'. It is clear from this phrase that in order to establish a violation of Article 2(b), a Member needs to demonstrate that another Member is using rules of origin for a specified purpose, viz., to pursue trade objectives.*

The Panel addressed India's claim that United States ROO provisions were to pursue the trade objective of favouring imports from the European Communities over imports from other countries, and particularly imports from developing countries such as India. However, the Panel ruled that *an incidental effect should not be inferred as a trade objective* (Panel Report on *US – Textiles Rules of Origin*, para. 6.117 WT/DS/243R):

> [W]e note, finally, that even if section 405 had the practical effect of favouring goods imported from the European Communities over competitive goods imported from other Members, that effect might be incidental rather than intentional. In other words, we do not think that the mere effect of favouring European Communities imports over imports from other Members would in itself justify the

inference that creating such an effect is an objective pursued by the United States.

This is an important ruling, as while dismissing India's claim of the US pursuing trade policy objectives of favouring EC's exports into the US market, in a way sided with a trade practice that was preferential in nature but non-discriminatory *vis-à-vis* third parties. This is a classic case of favouring a PROO provision, albeit not in the ambit of a formal trade agreement, with the help of interpreting ROO provision under the non-preferential trade flows. This is also clear from the US response to India's claims.

In this context, taking recourse in interpreting the term *themselves* in Article 2 (c) becomes extremely relevant. The Panel discussed the term 'themselves' as follows:

> [W]e consider that, in the first sentence of Article 2(c), the pronoun 'themselves' is used mainly to emphasise the preceding term 'rules of origin'. By emphasising the term 'rules of origin', the pronoun 'themselves' brings out very clearly that the first sentence of Article 2(c) is concerned with a Member's rules of origin, as distinct from something other than rules of origin, and that it is rules of origin, as opposed to something other than rules of origin, that must not 'create restrictive, distorting, or disruptive effects on international trade'.

It is clear from the above that any trade policy other than ROO *per se* could still be pursuing trade policy objectives but it cannot be achieved by ROO themselves. This is further explained by the Panel:

> [T]he term 'themselves' is meant to highlight that, although there may be commercial policy measures which create restrictive, distorting, or disruptive effects on international trade, the rules of origin used to implement and support these commercial policy measures must not create restrictive, distorting, or disruptive effects on international trade additional to those which may be caused by the underlying commercial policy measures. Similarly, in cases where an underlying commercial policy measure does not cause any restrictive, distorting, or disruptive effects on international trade, the word 'themselves' would serve to underscore that rules of origin must not create any new restrictive, distorting, or disruptive effects on international trade." (Panel Report on US – Textiles Rules of Origin, paras 6.136–6.137 WT/DS/243R)

The term *create* ensures that there should be a 'causal link' between a certain ROO and a prohibited trade effect for that ROO to be considered inconsistent with the first sentence of Article 2(c). The terms *restrictive, distorting or disruptive effects* are explained in terms of the each being independent of the other and neither of them should be a resultant effect of ROO on international trade:

> Turning to the prohibited effects – i.e., 'restrictive, distorting, or disruptive effects' – the Panel notes that these effects constitute alternative bases for a claim under the first sentence of Article 2(c), as is confirmed by the use of the disjunctive 'or'. Accordingly, independent meaning and effect should be given to the concepts of 'restriction', 'distortion' and 'disruption'. In this regard, we note that the ordinary meaning of the term 'restrict' is to 'limit, bound, confine'; that of the term 'distort' is to 'alter to an unnatural shape by twisting'; and that of the term to 'disrupt' is to 'interrupt the normal continuity of'. Thus, the first sentence of Article 2(c) prohibits rules of origin which create the effect of limiting the level of international trade ('restrictive' effects); of interfering with the natural pattern of international trade ('distorting' effects); or of interrupting the normal continuity of international trade ('disruptive' effects).

Finally, within the meaning of pursuing trade policy objectives it is important to understand the interpretation of *effects on international trade*.

2.3.1.4 *Understanding effects on international trade*

The Panel explained that the term 'effects on international trade' could not be interpreted as covering adverse effects on trade in *different* goods:

> [W]e cannot assume that Members intended to bring adverse effects on different types of goods within the ambit of the prohibition set out in the first sentence of Article 2(c). Indeed, as the Appellate Body has said in a different context, '[t]o sustain such an assumption and to warrant such a far-reaching interpretation, treaty language far more specific [...] would be necessary'. We consider that the same could be said of Article 2(c), first sentence.
>
> Therefore, we consider that it would not be appropriate to interpret the phrase 'effects on international trade' as covering adverse effects on trade in different (but closely similar) types of finished goods. We construe the phrase 'effects on international trade' to cover trade in the goods to which the relevant rule of origin is applied (e.g., cotton bed linen).

The above may be understood in the context of interpretation of the term 'unduly strict requirements'.

2.3.1.5 Interpreting unduly strict requirements

The meaning of the phrase 'unduly strict requirement' was also examined by the Panel:

> First, we need to examine what kind of 'requirements' are covered by the obligation that Members must ensure that their rules of origin not 'pose unduly strict requirements'. In this regard, we note the view of the United States that the clause 'as a prerequisite for the determination of the country of origin' qualifies also the phrase '[rules of origin] shall not pose unduly strict requirements'. While the English version of Article 2(c) may be susceptible of such an interpretation, the equally authentic French version is not. Nevertheless, the clause 'as a prerequisite for the determination of the country of origin' is part of the immediate context of the term 'requirements'. Considered as relevant context, the clause at issue lends force to the argument that the 'requirements' which must not be unduly strict include the kind of requirements which must be fulfilled as a prerequisite for the determination of the country of origin. Article 2(a) of the RO Agreement provides further contextual support for such an interpretation. The first sentence of that provision states that the 'requirements to be fulfilled' must be clearly defined. It is clear to us that these requirements include the substantive requirements which must be met for a good to be determined to originate in a particular country. For these reasons, we read the term 'requirements' in the second sentence of Article 2(c) as encompassing the substantive origin requirements that must be met for a good to obtain origin status.
>
> Another issue presented by the phrase 'unduly strict requirements' is the interpretation to be given to the adjective 'strict'. The most pertinent dictionary definitions of the term 'strict' are 'exacting' and 'rigorous'. Thus, a 'strict' requirement is an exacting or rigorous requirement. In the specific context of Article 2 of the RO Agreement, and also bearing in mind our interpretation of the term 'requirements', 'strict' requirements are, therefore, those requirements which make the conferral of origin conditional on conformity with an exacting or rigorous (technical) standard.
>
> The second sentence of Article 2(c) only precludes Members from imposing requirements which are 'unduly' strict. The dictionary

meaning of the adverb 'unduly' is 'more than is warranted or natural; excessively, disproportionately'. Accordingly, an origin requirement can be considered to be 'unduly' strict if it is excessively strict.

The Panel observed that the 'strictness' of requirements is to be assessed from the perspective of countries wanting to obtain origin status, rather than from the perspective of countries wanting to lose origin status. In nutshell, the interpretation of 'unduly strict requirements' is that the ROO provisions should be clearly defined but should not be exacting or rigorous requirement that are excessively strict.

2.3.2 Harmonization of the ROO relating to non-preferential treatment

Recognizing that harmonization of ROO is a highly technical task, accomplishment of which could not fit into the time frame of the Uruguay Round, therefore, the contracting parties agreed to embark on a three-year work programme after the conclusion of the Uruguay Round. Work on the harmonization of ROO formally began in July 1995 and at present, negotiators are considering (i) ROO in the context of individual items and (ii) general provisions containing general rules that will be applied widely to various items. Although the ARO specified a deadline of three years for the harmonization programme (i.e. July 1998), the CRO decided on 29 May 1998 that this deadline would not be met.

As mentioned earlier, two intergovernmental organizations, i.e. the WTO and the WCO, are presently engaged in the work programme and, as of January 2000, the WTO had held twenty-eight committee meetings and the WCO seventeen technical committee meetings. By referring to the HS Code, negotiators are considering rules of origin relating to individual items, based on the following three standards, i.e. (i) the 'Wholly Obtained Criteria' which applies to goods that are domestically produced only in a specific country; (ii) the 'Minimal Operation Criteria' for little processing that is negligible in origin determination; and (iii) the 'Substantial Transformation Criteria' where, more than two countries are involved in the production of goods and their origin will be conferred upon the country where the last substantial transformation has been carried out. In light of the Substantial Transformation Criteria mentioned in (iii) above, the Agreement allows negotiators to introduce the "Change in Tariff Classification Criteria" and, as a supplementary criteria for the Substantial Transformation Criteria, the "*Ad Valorem* Criteria" and the "Manufacturing or Processing Operations Criteria" in order to determine whether the Substantial Transformation has been occurred.

In addition, negotiators are considering the following items that are to be mentioned in Annex III of the Agreement, i.e. (i) a final composition of the ROO relating to individual items and (ii) general provisions containing general rules applied widely to various items. The procedures call for the WCO to perform technical studies for individual items. When the WCO reaches a consensus on an item, it is referred to the WTO for endorsement, and is only considered formally agreed upon after this endorsement is obtained. Should the technical arguments be exhausted and the WCO still be unable to reach a consensus, the item is referred to the WTO for decision. The WTO then becomes the forum for consideration, studying the item in light of the sensitivities and concerns of individual countries. The technical studies undertaken by the WCO have been completed as of the seventeenth meeting held in May, 1999. The items on which the WCO could not reach consensus, therefore, are being discussed by the WTO.

At this time, WTO approval and formal agreement had been reached on only about 1,750 HS subheadings (out of a total of 5,113 HS subheadings). The WTO is planning intensive studies in order to complete the programme as soon as possible.

PSR of origin evolved during the negotiation that put forward specific criteria for substantial transformation with the predominant issue as to *what will* or *will not* qualify for substantial transformation. While on a large number of products a consensus is emerging, on a few items it is the national trade interests rather than common economic principle that is holding the consensus. It is precisely for this reason that the Harmonization Work Programme of WTO has not been completed.

The work done under the Harmonization Work Programme on ROO, in the CRO on the product-specific ROO is ongoing, however, the items on which consensus has not been reached are reflected in square brackets as they have not yet been adopted by the Committee. The proposals indicated there only reflect the proposals by the Chairperson of the Committee. In this regard in it may be pointed out that the General Rules, definition 2 of Appendix 1, and rules of Appendix 2 as well as product-specific rules of origin of chs 84–90 have not yet been endorsed by the Committee. Some of the specific issues are discussed below.

2.3.2.1 Wholly obtained goods

2.3.2.1.1 Scope. As per the latest information available on this subject from the WTO, the following text as contained in Table 2.2, for the wholly obtained goods has been proposed by the Chairman:

Table 2.2 Wholly obtained goods: agreed text

Definitions	Notes
1. The following goods are to be considered as being wholly obtained in one country:	
(a) Live animals born and raised in that country;	In definitions 1 (a), (b), and (c) the term "animals" covers all animal life, including mammals, birds, fish, crustaceans, molluscs, reptiles, bacteria and viruses.
(b) Animals obtained by hunting, trapping, fishing, gathering or capturing in that country;	Definition 1 (b) covers animals obtained in the wild, whether live or dead, whether or not born and raised in that country.
(c) Products obtained from live animals in that country;	Definition 1 (c) covers products obtained from live animals without further processing, including milk, eggs, natural honey, hair, wool, semen and dung.
(d) Plants and plant products harvested, picked or gathered in that country;	Definition 1 (d) covers all plant life, including fruit, flowers, vegetables, trees, seaweed, fungi and live plants grown in that country.
(e) Minerals and other naturally occurring substances, not included in definitions (a)-(d), extracted or taken in that country;	Definition 1 (e) covers crude minerals and other naturally occurring substances, including rock or solar salt, crude mineral sulphur occurring in free state, natural sands, clays, stones, metallic ores, crude oil, natural gas, bituminous minerals, natural earths, ordinary natural waters, natural mineral waters, natural snow and ice.

(f) Scrap and waste derived from manufacturing or processing operations or from consumption in that country and fit only for disposal or for the recovery of raw materials;

Definition 1(f) covers all scrap and waste, including scrap and waste resulting from manufacturing or processing operations or consumption in the same country, scrap machinery, discarded packaging and household rubbish and all products that can no longer perform the purpose for which they were produced, and are fit only for discarding or for the recovery of raw materials. Such manufacturing or processing operations include all types of processing, not only industrial or chemical but also mining, agricultural, construction, refining, incineration and sewage treatment operations.

(g) Articles collected in that country which can no longer perform their original purpose there nor are capable of being restored or repaired and which are fit only for disposal or for the recovery of parts or raw materials;

(h) Parts or raw materials recovered in that country from articles which can no longer perform their original purpose nor are capable of being restored or repaired;

(i) Goods obtained or produced in that country solely from products referred to in (a) through to(h) above.

Source: WTO, Doc no. G/RO/W/111 Rev.4.)

[handwritten: Fish caught in international waters are origin of the Sea vessels flag nationality]

From Table 2.2 it can be seen that the text is not in square brackets and, therefore, it can be presumed that the consensus has evolved on the scope of wholly obtained goods at the technical level. It is most likely that the CRO may approve the same once other unresolved issues reach a consensus.

Some of the dimensions where divergent opinions exist due to different country-positions are discussed below (WTO Document G/RO/W/111/ Rev.4, August 2009). These include issues relating to the Exclusive Economic Zone (EEZ) and certain important processes that may or may not entail substantial transformation.

2.3.2.1.1.1 Issue relating to catching of fish within the Exclusive Economic Zone. The issue of products of sea-fishing and other products taken from the sea including minerals extracted from the sub-soil in the EEZ) remains unresolved. This is due to the fact that different countries treat the issue of 'territoriality' differently. For example, fish caught in the territorial waters (not exceeding 12 nautical miles) of a country would be considered to be originating in the country itself. Fish caught in the high seas would be considered to originate in the country whose flag the vessel has on its mast.

As regards the EEZ, the WTO basically offered two proposals. One suggested that the country of origin of the fish and other products taken from the EEZ should be the country of the flag of the vessel (at par with the criteria prescribed for high sea fishing). This proposal was mooted by Canada, China, the EC, Egypt, Japan, Korea, Mexico, Norway, USA, etc. The other countries suggested that the country of origin of such fish and other products should be the coastal state. This was due to the fact that proponents felt that the EEZ is a territory of a particular coastal state. The proponents were India, Argentina, Australia, New Zealand, Brazil, Philippines, Cuba, Pakistan, etc. There is also a third proposal that the importing country may determine the origin of such products according to its own standpoint of the Law of the Sea. The Chairman of CRO had also proposed an alternate text to resolve this issue. The text still remains in square brackets (Table 2.3) though on this issue a consensus text evolved during the informal Working Group to the CRO on 6 February 1997 (WTO Document: G/RO/M/ 9 Paragraph 3) wherein the following was proposed:

Products of sea-fishing and other products taken from the sea outside a country are considered to be wholly obtained in the country of registration of the vessel that carries out those operations.

Table 2.3 Wholly obtained goods: square-bracketed text

Definitions	Notes
2. [(a) Products of sea-fishing and other products taken from the sea outside a country are considered to be wholly obtained in the country whose flag the vessel that carries out those operations is entitled to fly.	
(b) Goods obtained or produced on board a factory ship outside a country are considered to be wholly obtained in the country whose flag the ship that carries out those operations is entitled to fly, provided that these goods are manufactured from products referred to in subparagraph (a) originating in the same country.	
(c) Products taken from the sea bed or subsoil beneath the sea bed outside a country, are considered to be wholly obtained in the country that has the rights to exploit that sea bed or subsoil in accordance with the provisions of the UN Convention on the Law of the Sea.[6]]	

Source: WTO, Doc no. G/RO/W/111 Rev.4).

2.3.2.1.2 Process

2.3.2.1.2.1 Slaughtering of live animals. The issue of slaughtering of live animals, whether it is a substantial transformation or not, was under debate. On one hand countries like India, US, Argentina, Australia, Brazil, Canada, etc. held the view that production of meat by slaughtering of live animals is substantial transformation; on the other hand, countries like the EC, Egypt, Japan, Korea, Thailand were of the view that slaughtering can confer origin only with a certain period of fattening of animals (e.g. 4 months). The proponents of the earlier proposal felt that the products that come out of slaughter plant bear no resemblance to the live animals that enter the plant and that there would be no way that the sum of the parts would ever be able to reconstitute live animals; the latter felt that the quality of meat depends on the conditions in which the animals are raised as well as on the period of time under such conditions. They thus felt that at least 4 months period for fattening should be allowed. A decision on the ROO criteria is pending before the CRO.

2.3.2.1.2.2 Coffee creamer. There were several proposals made on this product. Countries like Australia, New Zealand, Philippines, Singapore, Thailand, etc. proposed that since coffee creamer is made from skimmed milk powder and milk fat and water, to which emulsifiers and stabilizers are added, which is then sterilized at a specific temperature and cooled it should be considered as a substantial transformation and the country of origin of such a product should be the country where such conversion takes place. However, countries like Argentina, Brazil, Canada, the EC, India, Japan, Korea and USA felt that since the process required is not a particularly complex one and the product obtained is also not specially different than inputs, therefore, the proposed criteria of CTSH is not proper. They proposed that the country of origin should be the country in which the milk is obtained in its natural or unprocessed state. This formulation is waiting the CRO's approval.

While it appears that views have converged in the case of 'Milk and cream, not concentrated nor containing added sugar or other sweetening matter' (HS 04.01) with the criteria that the origin will be the country where the milk is obtained in its natural or unprocessed state, the same eludes consensus for "Milk and cream, concentrated or containing added sugar or other sweetening matter" (HS 04.02).

2.3.2.2 Non-wholly obtained: disputes on processes – minimal vs substantial

2.3.2.2.1 Processed cheese. The issue for grant of origin for processed cheese if manufactured from natural cheese has also been debated for a long time. Countries like Argentina, Australia, Mexico, New Zealand, Singapore, etc. proposed for CTSH, but this was not acceptable to Brazil, Canada, Egypt, the EC, India, Korea, Thailand and USA as they felt that the process for obtaining processed cheese is a simple one as various sorts of cheese are first mixed and then melted by heating or using emulsifiers. They thus proposed for CTH criteria. The proposal is yet to be finalized.

2.3.2.2.2 Roasted coffee. Countries are also divided on this issue of processing. The coffee-growing countries like Chile, Ecuador, Guatemala, Kenya, Mexico, Philippines, Uruguay, etc. proposed that roasted and blended coffee should retain the origin of the country where the plants grew. On the other hand, countries like Canada, Egypt, Korea, the EC, New Zealand, Thailand and USA wanted the origin to be that of the country where coffee was roasted and blended. India, Argentina and the EC made a compromise proposal under which the country from where 85 per cent of the coffee beans came from would determine origin. If no country meets this requirement then the country roasting the coffee would be the country of origin. The present text which is in Table 2.3 and is in square bracket states that "the origin shall be the country where the plant grew" for some sub-headings and CTSH for the rest. Likewise, the proposal relating to roasting and blending of coffee is yet to be adopted.

2.3.2.2.3 Fats and oils. Determining the origin for fFats and oils (chapter 15, HS) is also pending for a majority of HS headings. Countries like Australia, the EC, India, Japan, etc. proposed that refining, bleaching and deodorizing of fats and oils are to be treated as substantial transformation and proposed CTH or change by refining. However, several other countries like Argentina, Brazil, Canada, Sri Lanka, USA, etc. felt that the essential character of fats and oils does not change by refining and hence there should be no change of origin because of refining and so they proposed CTH.

2.3.2.2.4 Refining of sugar. Origin criteria for refined sugar, if manufactured from raw sugar, is yet to be finalized and is pending for a decision from the CRO. Australia, Canada, Cuba and New Zealand felt that refining of raw sugar should be considered as substantial transformation and the country of refining should be the country of origin. However, several other countries like the US, the EC, Korea, India, Argentina, Brazil, Mexico, Thailand, etc. did not consider refining of sugar to be substantial transformation and proposed CC. The proposal for CC is in square brackets.

2.3.2.2.5 Fruit juices. During negotiations, the US, the EC, India, Brazil, Egypt, Canada, etc. proposed CTH because they considered there was substantial transformation for fruit juices. However, countries like Australia, Philippines did not agree and were of the view that the country of origin of the juices should be the country in which the fruits were harvested. At present, the proposals relating to CC and CTH on different headings are pending a decision.

2.3.2.2.6 Producing wine from grapes. Countries like Australia, Canada, Egypt, India, Japan, Thailand, the USA, etc. consider production of wine from grapes to be substantial transformation and proposed CTH criteria. However, Argentina, Brazil, the EC, New Zealand, etc. felt that the country of origin for wines should be where the grapes grew. They argued that wine was a special product, whereby the concept of *quality* (emphasis added) was a crucial element in the differentiation of wines. The distinctive features of a wine are defined by the quality and thus the origin of the raw material, the grapes, in combination with certain vinification techniques. Of these two criteria, the origin of the grapes is by far the most decisive factor in forming the character of a wine. The particular soil and the particular climate in a given region determine the quality of the grapes. When wine is prepared in a country different from the country the grapes come from, the origin is determined by the country where the grapes grew. This issue is also being debated further to confirm the origin criteria. At present the proposal that is being considered by the CRO is CTH and for 'wines in container having more than 2 liters' an alternate proposal of "origin where grapes are grown" is pending.

2.3.2.2.7 Crushing/grinding of spices. Argentina, Canada, Singapore and the US proposed that crushing/grinding of spices be considered as substantial transformation on the grounds that this process increases the surface area thereby enhancing the transfer of flavouring agents as well as releasing essential oils from inside the seeds. But many other countries like Brazil, the EC, Egypt, India Japan, Korea, etc. did not consider it to be substantial transformation and would prefer the country of origin to be the one in which the plants grew. They feel that crushing and/or grinding are not substantial transformations as all the characteristics of the spices of Chapter 9 of HS or of the abovementioned plants and parts of plants are determined when they are growing, thereby crushing and/or grinding merely release properties already present in those products. Consequently, the origin is the country where the plants grew.

At present various options are available to the CRO including CTSH or granting the origin to the country where the plants grew: consensus has not been reached.

2.3.2.2.8 Production of cement from clinker. CTSH was proposed by the EC that on the grounds that cement and clinker are two different articles of trade with different characters and properties, uses and names. Clinker is obtained from firing limestone that contains a suitable proportion of clay. Clinker consists mainly of calcium silicates in pebble form. The clinker cannot be used as a building material unless transformed into cement. It does not have the same bonding effect as cement when mixed with fine and coarse aggregates to produce concrete for use in construction. Cement, on the other hand, has to meet certain specifications such as a minimum fineness of 225 m^2/kg and a minimum compressive strength in order to be used in concrete work. Various types of cement can be produced from the same clinker. To obtain cement from clinker, the clinker has to be ground to a more finely and inter-ground ingredients and additives are introduced during the grinding process. It is considered that it is the existence of a new product and not the process that determines whether a substantial transformation has occurred.

On the other hand, countries like Australia, Chile, India, the USA, etc. felt that production of cement from clinker is a "simple" process. It is merely a case of grinding the clinker to produce cement. Grinding alone is not considered a substantial transformation. It was noted that the HS subheading explanatory note defines "Portland cement" as "cement obtained by grinding Portland clinker with the possible addition of a small quantity of calcium sulphate" and that it might be necessary to define supplementary criteria to qualify the rule in order to separate "simple" grinding and thus proposed for CTH.

At present the proposal of CTH is pending a decision from the CRO for this product.

2.3.2.2.9 Dyeing or printing of yarn and fabrics. The textile sector has seen varied and different proposals for determining origin. The issue of what would constitute substantial transformation for dyeing or printing of yarn and fabrics has been under debate for some time without any resolution.

Countries like Australia, China, the EC, Egypt, Kenya, Norway, Philippine, India have stated that permanent dyeing or printing from unbleached or pre-bleached yarn with at least two preparatory or finishing operations is a substantial transformation. Permanent dyeing or printing substantially transforms uncoloured into coloured yarn. Dyeing not only adds great value to the yarn but also transforms it into a distinct and different commercial product with different uses. The resulting product has new characteristics and qualities. This process permanently changes the grey yarn by imparting new characteristics and permanently giving colour or pattern to the yarns, which gives them their final appearance. Turkey has felt that a value addition of 50 per cent is necessary for granting origin. On the other hand, Argentina, Brazil, Canada, Japan, Mexico, Thailand and the USA felt that neither dyeing alone nor dyeing and printing together results in a substantial transformation. A yarn of one country that is dyed and/or printed in another country should not be considered to originate in the latter country.

In the case of fabrics, Singapore has been of the view that permanent dyeing or printing alone can be considered as substantial transformation because the dyed or printed good is often used as a finished product without being subjected to any other processes. Australia, China, the EC, Egypt, Japan, Kenya, Norway, Philippines, Pakistan, India, Turkey, etc. have taken more or less a similar position as with yarn. They have stated that dyeing or printing substantially transforms an uncoloured or dyed fabric (textile article) into an attractive, beautifully designed fabric (textile article). The resultant product becomes commercially distinct and is put to different and specific uses. The resulting product has new characteristics and qualities. The said operations actually transform a raw material, such as a raw fabric (textile article), unusable as it stands, into a fabric that can undergo subsequent transformations such as making up. These processes permanently change the grey fabric (textile article) by imparting new characteristics and permanently giving colour or pattern to the fabrics (textile article). Permanent printing from unbleached or pre-bleached fabrics with at least two preparatory or finishing operations is a substantial transformation. In the case of thermo –printing, which consists of applying motifs using thermal processes, printing should be accompanied by impregnation of the transfer paper to be considered a substantial transformation.

Hong Kong felt that dyeing or printing, accompanied by at least one preparatory or finishing operation, is considered substantial transformation for finished fabrics. The USA opined that neither dyeing nor printing alone nor dyeing and printing together results in a substantial transformation. A fabric of one country that is dyed and/or printed in another country should not be considered to originate in the latter country.

Both these issues are yet to be resolved by the CRO.

2.3.2.2.10 Assembly of watches from movements.   This is another product where a consensus has yet to be reached. Canada, Korea, the USA, Venezuala have proposed for the criteria of "CTH, except HS 91.08 or 91.09" on the basis of the logic that the essence of a watch, or clock, is a device that indicates the time or measures the intervals of time. A movement is defined in the HS chapter notes as a device capable of determining intervals of time. There is no difference in the essential character between a watch and a movement and it is the movement that imparts the essential character of a watch. In the manufacture of a watch or clock, the assembly of the movement is considered the last substantial transformation because at the stage of completion of the movement the essential character of the watch – time – telling – is already fixed. The final assembly from movement to watch does not substantially change the essential character of time – telling and cannot amount to substantial transformation. As the essential character and quality of a watch or a clock is determined by the movement, the origin of the movement is most important from a commercial point of view.

China, the EC, India, Japan, Mexico, New Zealand, etc. have preferred to use only CTH as criteria. They felt that the structure of the HS reflects that movements and watches are essentially different commercial goods. Various finished goods can be obtained from the same movement by final assembly. While the movement is important, timekeeping is a minimum requirement. The movement does not represent time and is invisible after assembly. It is the change from components to a watch that is the last substantial transformation in watch manufacture. The accuracy, durability and life span of a watch are determined and guaranteed by the final assembly. Testing and adjustment, which constitute an essential part of assembly, are also of particular importance because they determine the above – mentioned quality of a watch.

At the moment, the option of CTH is before the CRO. In view of the above, it is important to look at the proposals relating to the WTO ROO Harmonization Work Programme for select sectors like textiles and clothing, machinery and equipments, electrical and electronics products, automobiles, etc. This has been presented in the Appendix to this chapter.

The primary rules relating to textiles including minor processing operations that will not affect the origin, value-added rule and chapter residual rules as under the negotiation in the CRO are given in the Appendix to this chapter. Similarly, for the non-textile industrial goods (items belonging to chapters 84–90, HS), the present text, which is being negotiated in the CRO including *inter alia* provisions relating to assembly and disassembly, collection of parts, parts and accessories produced from blanks, application of value added rules primary and residual rules, are given in the Appendix to this chapter.

2.3.3 WTO members' status of ROO implementation

The ARO allows the countries to prescribe their own NPROO till such time as an agreement on harmonization is achieved. Different countries have taken different positions on this issue. Article 5 of the ARO prescribes that each member shall provide to the Secretariat, within 90 days after the date of entry into force of the WTO Agreement for it, its rules of origin, judicial decisions and administrative rulings of general application relating to rules of origin in effect on that date. If, inadvertently, a ROO has not been provided, the member concerned shall provide it immediately after this fact becomes known. Lists of information received and available with the Secretariat shall be circulated to the members by the Secretariat. The Committee on ROO had discussed on several occasions the issue of notification to the WTO about members' NPROO and PROO with regard to its work programme. It can be observed that 80 members have made notifications of NPROO and 114 members have made notifications of PROO. A summary of these notifications is given in Table 2.4.

Table 2.4   Status of notification of non-preferential ROO

I. Members with Non-Preferential Rules of Origin

Albania (G/RO/N/47)	Hong Kong, China (G/RO/N/1,	Peru (G/RO/N/4 & 5, 49, 50 & 52)
Argentina (G/RO/N/2, 10 & 16)	10, 24, 30, 37, 46 & 59)	Qatar (G/RO/N/25)
Armenia (G/RO/N/ 41 & 53)	Japan (G/RO/N/1)	Senegal (G/RO/N/10)
Australia (G/RO/N/1)	Jordan (G/RO/N/30)	South Africa (G/RO/N/3)
Burkina Faso (G/RO/N/19)	Korea (G/RO/N/1 & 63)	Suriname (G/RO/N/24 & 43)
Canada (G/RO/N/1)	Lesotho (G/RO/N/56)	Switzerland (G/RO/N/ 4 & 60/Rev.1)
China (G/RO/N/37/ Rev.1)	Liechtenstein (G/RO/ N/60/Rev.1)	Chinese Taipei (G/RO/ N/37)
Colombia (G/RO/N/1)	Madagascar (G/RO/ N/11)	Tunisia (G/RO/N/7 & 61)
Croatia /G/RO/N/36)	Mexico (G/RO/N/12)	Turkey (G/RO/N/8 & 28)
Cuba (G/RO/N/3)	Moldova (G/RON/36)	Ukraine (G/RO/N/57)
EC (G/RO/N/1)	Morocco (G/RO/N/2)	US (G/RO/N/1 & 6)
Former Yugoslav Rep. of	New Zealand (G/RO/ N/1)	Venezuela (G/RO/N/1 & 10)
Macedonia /G/RO/N/45)	Niger (G/RO/N/19)	
Georgia (G/RO/N/37)	Norway (G/RO/N/ 8 & 62)	

II. Members with Non-Preferential Rules of Origin

Bolivia (G/RO/N/9)	Haiti (G/RO/N/20)	Nicaragua (G/RO/N/10)
Brazil (G/RO/N/14)	Honduras (G/RO/N/3)	Oman (G/RO/N/32)
Brunei Darussalam (G/RO/N/5)	Iceland (G/RO/N/5)	Pakistan (G/RO/N/16)
Burundi (G/RO/N/33)	India (G/RO/N/1)	Panama (G/RO/N/23)
Chad (G/RO/N22)	Indonesia (G/RO/ N/16)	Papua New Guinea (G/RO/ N/32)
Chile (G/RO/N/6)	Israel (G/RO/N/13)	Paraguay (G/RO/N/21)
Costa Rica (G/RO/N/1)	Jamaica (G/RO/N/4)	Philippines (G/RO/N/6)
Dominica (G/RO/N/24)	Kenya (G/RO/N/9)	Saudi Arabia (G/RO/N/48)
Dominican Rep. (G/RO/N/9)	Macao, China (G/RO/ N/21)	Singapore (G/RO/N/3)
El Salvador (G/RO/N/10)	Malaysia (G/RO/N/6)	Thailand (G/RO/N/1)
Fiji (G/RO/N/17)	Maldives (G/RO/N/22)	Trinidad & Tobago (G/RO/ N/7)
Ghana (G/RO/N/44)	Mauritius (G/RO/N/1)	Uganda (G/RO/N/12)

(*Continued*)

Table 2.4 Continued

Guatemala (G/RO/N/21)	Mongolia (G/RO/N/20)	United Arab Emirates (G/RO/N/17)
Guyana (G/RO/N/42)	Namibia (G/RO/N/26)	Uruguay (G/RO/N/12)

III. Members that have not notified Non-Preferential Rules of Origin

Angola	Ecuador	Rwanda
Antigua & Barbuda	Egypt	Saint Kitts & Nevis
Bahrain	Gabon	Saint Lucia
Bangladesh	Gambia	Saint Vincent & Grenadines
Barbados	Grenada	Sierra Leone
Belize	Guinea Bissau	Solomon Islands
Benin	Guinea, Rep. of	Sri Lanka
Botswana	Kuwait	Swaziland
Cambodia	Kyrgyz Rep.	Tanzania
Cameroon	Malawi	Togo
Cape Verde	Mali	Tonga
Central African Rep	Mauritania	Viet Nam
Congo	Mozambique	Zambia
Côte d'Ivoire	Myanmar	Zimbabwe
D.R. of Congo	Nepal	
Djibouti	Nigeria	

Source: WTO G/RO/W/129.

2.4 Country of Origin Labeling (COOL) requirements of the USA

The US COOL requirement was introduced in 1992 but it did not receive any appreciable attention and was reintroduced in 1997. The legislation inched along until 2002 when it was included in the 2002 Farm Bill and finally found itself in the 2008 Farm Bill. The measure has been criticized as being too expensive and not necessary.

The COOL measure includes: the *Agricultural Marketing Act of 1946*, as amended by *The Farm, Security and Rural Investment Act of 2002* and the *Food, Conservation, and Energy Act, 2008*; the Interim Final Rule on *Mandatory Country of Origin Labeling of Beef, Pork, Lamb, Chicken, Goat Meat, Perishable Agricultural Commodities, Peanuts, Pecans, Ginseng, and Macadamia Nuts*; on *Mandatory Country of Origin Labeling of Muscle Cuts of Beef (including Veal), Lamb, Chicken, Goat and Pork, Ground Beef, Ground Lamb, Ground Chicken, Ground Goat, and Ground Pork* and the Final Rule on *Mandatory Country of Origin Labeling of Beef, Pork, Lamb, Chicken, Goat Meat, Perishable Agricultural Commodities, Peanuts, Pecans, Ginseng, and Macadamia Nuts* ("Final Rule").

This scheme has been severely criticized by the principal exporters of these products to the US, especially Canada and Mexico, and this has been taken up at the Dispute Settlement Mechanism of the WTO. Canada has argued that COOL measure appears to be inconsistent with the US' obligations under the WTO Agreement, including: Articles III: 4, IX: 2, IX: 4, and X: 3 of GATT 1994; Articles 2 of the TBT Agreement, or, in the alternative, Articles 2, 5 and 7 of the SPS Agreement; and Article 2 of the Agreement on Rules of Origin. These violations appear to nullify or impair the benefits accruing to Canada under those Agreements. Moreover, this measure appears to nullify or impair the benefits accruing to Canada in the sense of Article XXIII: l(b) of GATT 1994.

On the other hand, according to the US, this measure is due to the food supplies that have come under intense scrutiny in recent years in the US where items like tomatoes, beef, tamales have all been subject to recalls. The US has further argued that the labelling ensures quality that consumers may be made aware of as labelling empowers the consumer to make better choices. Country of origin labelling will, therefore, provide the consumers with more information but, ultimately, consumers will decide what they prefer.

The above arguments on labelling requirements on food products through origin certification can serve an important human cause, provided their stipulations and implementation are not such so as to make this provision act as a barrier to trade. It would also be worth exploring if the same objectives could also be met through other instruments.

2.5 Preferential Rules of Origin

ROO are the criteria needed to determine the national origin of a product. By definition, each product can only originate in one country. If a product is produced wholly in one country, determining the origin is not a difficult task. However, in a world where more and more goods are produced through the amalgamation of inputs from different sources (countries), conferring origin to a product is not always an easy task. ROO are complex if one is to determine the country of origin of a product when its production or manufacturing takes place in more than one country or several inputs are used from several sources. These rules are necessary to ensure that the provisions applying selectively on the basis of origin are not avoided by minimal processing, trade deflection and similar circumvention methods.

Countries that are participating as members in Regional Trade Agreements, i.e. FTAs or PTAs, offer zero or reduced duty access (tariff preferences) on imports from the trade partners (the Participating Countries) and, therefore, often apply a different set of rules to determine the origin of products to grant preferential tariff treatment. These rules are known as PROO. The justification for PROO is to prevent trade deflection, or simple trans-shipment, whereby products from non-participating countries (non-RTA members) are redirected through a RTA partner to avoid the payment of customs duties. Hence the role of PROO is to ensure that only goods originating in participating countries enjoy tariff or other preferences. Additionally, the purpose is also to ensure that the countries that have high MFN duties or higher restrictions for imports can protect their revenue erosion. Therefore, they are invariably an integral part of preferential trade agreements such as bilateral and regional free trade agreements and the non-reciprocal tariff preferences that developed countries offer to developing countries under the GSP (Generalized System of Preferences) Scheme.

The PROO can also be manipulated to achieve other objectives, such as protecting domestic producers. Restrictive ROO raise the costs of supplying the markets of preferential partners by requiring changes in production that lead to the use of higher cost inputs and through the expenses that are incurred in proving conformity with the rules. These costs mean that only a proportion of products that are eligible for preferential treatment will actually be granted preferential access and will constrain market access relative to that which is promised on paper in the trade agreement. The impact of PTAs on market access and hence trade flows is a function of both the extent of preferential tariff liberalization and the ROO. The ROO are, therefore, a key element in determining the magnitude of the economic benefits that accrue from trade agreements and who receives them. The costs of administering the systems of ROO and the expenses incurred by firms to prove conformity to these rules are equally important. Such costs will be greater if there is a degree of uncertainty or unpredictability in the application of the systems of ROO and in particular with regard to the acceptance of certificates of origin by customs officials in the foreign market. These costs act to reduce the value of the tariff preferences that are made available through free trade and preferential trade arrangements.

ROO may also be an important factor determining the investment decisions of the multinational firms. Additionally, for such firms, not only the issue of complying with the rules on sufficient processing is important, but the cost of proving compliance with those ROO is also equally important. Therefore, ROO that vary across products and agreements add considerably to the complexity and costs of participating in and administering trade agreement. The burden of such costs falls particularly heavily upon small and medium-sized firms. Therefore, a clearer understanding of PROO and their proper application is of utmost importance for the implementation and success of any agreement. The survey conducted by the WTO (2002) on rules of origin in RTAs makes useful observations. It highlights that ROO are a necessary part of regional trade agreements and there is no single method for origin determination that is applied within all agreements and to all products. Thus, various criteria for determining the origin exist. Only in a few cases are ROO based on a single criterion; normally two or more criteria are combined. In addition, exceptions to and derogations from the general criteria – for example, differing tolerance or absorption rules in sensitive products – are manifold. While this survey analyses two models of ROO, viz. the "pan-European" (PANEURO)-model and the NAFTA-model, it lacks in fully comprehending the Asian model of ROO, which is focused upon in this book (Box 2.2).

Box 2.2 Highlights of the survey

1. Rules of origin are a necessary part of regional trade agreements. But no single method for origin determination is applied within all agreements and to all products.

2. Various criteria for determining origin exist. Only in a few cases are rules of origin based on a single criterion; normally two or more criteria are combined. In addition, exceptions to and derogations from the general criteria – for example, differing tolerance or absorption rules in sensitive products – are manifold. In some cases these significantly modify what appears at first sight to be simple origin regimes.

3. Some rules of origin with a development-oriented focus are simple and liberal (e.g. COMESA). Other regimes containing multiple exceptions and tailor-made product provisions appear in themselves to act as potential barriers to trade.

4. Two major models of rules of origin currently exist: the "pan-European" (PANEURO)-model and the NAFTA-model of rules of origin, which differ significantly from each other. While variations within the PANEURO-model are very limited, significant differences apply in relation to the NAFTA-model of rules of origin (e.g. on the percentage of regional-content requirements and of tolerance rules, sector-specific exceptions).

Source: WTO (2002).

2.6 Literature survey

Over the years there has been a growing interest related to the theoretical analysis of FTAs especially with regard to ROO. The traditional literature has viewed market access negotiations solely in terms of tariff and non-tariff negotiations. At this stage it may be mentioned that the perceptions about the ROO have changed and evolved over time, becoming reflected in different formulations. This is evident from the literature on the subject, which will be presented below.

Arguments that restrictive ROO could undermine the utility of FTA, due to cumbersome conditions of ROO, were put forth by Grossman (1981). It was argued that the exporters may choose to export the goods under MFN tariff rather than seeking preferential tariff treatment.

The implications of alternative ROOs in the long and short run have been dealt with by Krishna and Krueger (1995). They explain these with the help of two forces at work on the use of domestic inputs. First, the content rule tends to distort inputs use towards FTA inputs. Secondly, as output changes, so does domestic input use in the same direction. In case of imperfect competition, there is even more reason to be concerned with the form of ROOs. Even forms that are equivalent under perfect competition can have quite different effects in the presence of market imperfections. ROO tend to lead to FDI in the lower cost country in the FTA, as this provides access to the FTA market at a lower cost to the investor. It has also been argued that ROO are themselves hidden protection (Ju *et al.*, 1998) as they create what looks like tariffs on imported intermediate inputs and affect the price of domestically made inputs.

From an analytical point of view, the role of ROO, that is the rules that are designed to determine the origin of products in international trade, has usually been restricted to a "secondary" or "supportive" function (Estevadeordal, 2000). That restrictive ROO lead to the diversion of production to the FTA's intermediate good producer at the expense of the other FTA final goods producer, and the raw material producing non-member was argued by Rodriguez (2001), as Krishna and Krueger (1995) also pointed out that restrictive ROO will lead to increased investment in the FTA due to which production is reallocated among FTA members, and trade is diverted from non-members.

Within any (PTA) origin rules exist in order to prevent third countries from taking advantage of the PTA concessions. The rules thus are there to preserve the existing external protection of countries within the PTA. However, depending on their formulation, they can also increase that level of external protection, resulting in trade suppression and trade diversion as observed in the context of the European context (Augier *et al.*, 2003). However, on a more positive note their results suggest that ROO do indeed restrict trade, that the cumulation of such rules could increase trade in the order of 50 per cent, and that the impact is greater on intermediate than manufacturing trade.

The fact that ROO raise production costs and create administrative costs has been found by Anson *et al.* (2003). They argue that in the case of the recent wave of North–South PTAs, the presence of ROO virtually limits the market access that these PTAs confer to the Southern partners. In the case of NAFTA, they have estimated that up to 40 per cent of Mexico's preferential access to the US market in 2000 (estimated at 5 per cent) was absorbed by ROO-related administrative costs with non-administrative costs for Mexican firms of about 3 per cent US of import value.

It is generally believed that PROO matter only as long as there are MFN tariffs. Thus, the key to undercutting PROO's negative trade effects lies ultimately in the success of multilateral liberalization. Should the multilateral trade rounds result in deep MFN tariff lowerings and the proliferation of PTAs engender a dynamic of competitive liberalization worldwide, the importance of PROO as gatekeepers of commerce would automatically begin to fade (Estevadeordal and Suominen, 2003).

It is also suggested that the form of the ROO, the intensity of the sector it is applied to, and the extent of input substitutability have important roles to play in determining the effects of such restrictions. It is asserted that the literature on ROO can be encapsulated in four laws. First, ROO can insulate an industry from the consequences of an FTA and it can provide hidden protection for intermediate inputs used by it. Secondly, the precise form of the ROO matters. Thirdly, the time period matters. Responses to ROO take time. Short-run partial equilibrium effects can differ greatly from long run, general equilibrium ones. Fourthly, having more restrictive ROO may result in higher not lower imports. It was emphasized that this point is quite subtle and provides a warning to policy-makers and potential users that ROO may well backfire (Krishna, 2005).

On the other hand, there are studies that focus on the positive effects of rules of origin as well. According to Krishna (2005) too, there are some positive trade effects of ROO. Incorporating intermediate inputs into a small-union general-equilibrium model, Duttagupta and Panagariya (2003) develop the welfare economics of preferential trading under the ROO demonstrating that a welfare-reducing FTA that was rejected in the absence of the ROO becomes feasible in the presence of these rules. Secondly, a welfare-improving FTA that was rejected in the absence of the ROO is endorsed in their presence, but upon endorsement it becomes welfare inferior relative to the status quo. This could happen because 'the ROO increases the price of the regionally produced intermediate input and hence effectively provides protection to it. The FTA that was unattractive to the input exporter in the absence of a ROOcan now become attractive. Therefore, the ROO could make a previously infeasible FTA feasible' (ibid.) One may argue that a combination of different origin-rules contributes to such an effect. Using a three country, partial equilibrium structure, Falvey and Reed (2008) demonstrate the conditions under which the imposition of a binding Rule will be welfare- improving for an importer facing competitive export suppliers.

Evolving an appropriate system of ROO is necessary in regional trading arrangements.. So far there has not been any standard framework that could be used as a reference-point by the policy-makers in devising origin criteria in a regional grouping. It is noticed that there has been very little work done at the analytical or empirical levels in terms of assessing the economic effects of ROO systems despite the fact that such an assessment would form the very basis of evolving the origin system. This is partly because the economic theory has so far not provided a "standard" against which the efficacy, benefits and costs of ROO could be determined (Falvey and Reed, 1997). Methodological difficulties as well as lack of relevant statistical information have also constrained empirical analysis (Hoekman, 1993).

The foregoing survey of literature suffers from several limitations. There is growing interest related to the theoretical analysis of RTAs and rules of origin, however, very little analytical research, especially with regard to the economic effects of ROO has been carried out. In the following discussion we have attempted to provide fresh insights into the economics of rules of origin under RTAs.

At this stage, an attempt has been made to put together some of the major economic effects of ROO under a regional preferential trading arrangement. In so doing, the developmental role of the origin rules has been kept at the centre of our analysis whereby it is understood that it is in the overall long run interest of member countries of a regional grouping to abide by ROO requirements. However, this is not to deny that too stringent origin rules could also restrict trade flows. What follows is a profile of some of these effects. The positive and negative implications are dealt with separately.

2.7 Developmental role of ROO

There could be several positive effects that the ROO can cast in a preferential trading arrangement. These effects will vary from country-to-country and the provisions built under different agreements. Some of these effects are discussed below.

2.7.1 Precluding imports from non-members

In any preferential trading arrangement members set their own external tariffs but give preferential tariff treatment to each other. The divergence between external tariffs of the members and the regional preferential tariffs is a potential source of trade deflection (Shibata, 1967; James, 1997). In the absence of any ROO within the regional grouping the country with lowest external tariffs is likely to serve as an entry point into the regional market for the goods of the non-member countries. In this sense, ROO are important tools for checking trade deflection from one member country to another member country of third country goods.

This is an objective worth pursuing, as these types of trade flows do not forge adequate backward and forward linkages in the member country that imports these goods first. It is clear that in the absence of ROO, the preferential trading arrangement becomes a customs union with the lowest external tariff of a particular member serving as a common external tariff for all the members. Therefore, compliance to rules of origin should form an integral part of any preferential trading arrangement at the regional level in order to prevent trade deflection.

2.7.2 Building supply capabilities through value addition

The three modalities of determining origin of a product aim at substantial transformation in inputs. Thus, ROO together, facilitate value-addition in the country of manufacturing. Whether it is in the form of meeting a local-content requirement as a proportion of value-added or changes in tariff heading or a particular processing requirement, all have a developmental role to play. Such requirements, checking the import content of value addition, have the potential for generating backward and forward linkages in a country adhering to the rules.

Thus, a member country is prevented from becoming a mere trading country as these requirements act as a deterrent to assembly kind of production activities. The ROO thus, have important implications for the development of the manufacturing sector as a whole, which in turn, contributes towards enhancing the export supply capabilities of the member country. Realizing this, there has been a tendency to give protection to producers of intermediate goods by several countries with the help of ROO implementation as opposed to protection offered to producers of final manufactured goods. Hence, while devising the rules in any regional grouping the developmental effects of them must not be overlooked.

2.7.3 Augmenting intra-regional trade

A regional preferential trading arrangement having the provision of cumulative ROO is more liberal than the one not having it. This is because under regional cumulation facility imports by a member country of the regional grouping from other member countries of the same grouping are considered as originating in the importing country and not as imports. It has the potential to engender intra-regional trade flows of different categories of goods among the member countries.

It also has a favourable trade balance effect for the country using the cumulation provision. Moreover, there is a possibility that the first round of trade diversion effects is converted into trade creation effects in the long run. Each of these effects of cumulation facility is briefly discussed. According to the cumulation rule products and inputs sourced from within the regional grouping are considered as originating from the country where the last manufacturing takes place. In other words, sourcing from within the regional grouping is exempted from the value addition norms, as it is not considered as imports into the country in which the manufacturing process takes place.

This facility could play a catalytic role in intra-regional trade expansion in raw, semi-finished and intermediate products. Since cumulative provision is used with a view to export to the regional market, trade in finished goods also expands. Therefore, this provision has a favourable effect on trade in different categories of goods within a region.

2.7.4 Trade balance effect

Member countries of a regional grouping could use the origin rules for expanding their exports. By focusing on export expansion, member countries could try to improve their trade balance with other member countries of the regional grouping. For instance, a member country could import inputs from regional market, undertake processing and abide by ROO requirements with greater ease by resorting to cumulation mechanism and finally export back to the regional market by taking advantage of the preferential tariffs. This is yet another positive effect of the cumulation provision, which is quite relevant to those regional groupings in which trade imbalance between members acts as a constraint to intra-regional trade flows.

2.8 Trade creation and trade diversion

At this stage, it is important to trace the evolution of literature on trade creation and diversion. Viner (1950) in his famous book on study of trade agreements emphasized the static effects of regional integration. Viner coined the terms *trade creation* and *trade diversion*. Trade creation results from replacement of expensive domestic production by cheaper imports from the regional trading partner. Trade diversion is effect of the replacement of initial cheaper imports from outside world by expensive imports from the partner country.

This needs to be explained further that the trade creation occurs when parties to any regional trade agreement import cheaper goods produced by members of the same bloc. It causes an increase in welfare. However, trade diversion happens mainly when imports from countries outside the bloc area are reduced after the agreement takes place. More competitive suppliers are then substituted for suppliers less competitive which are located in member countries. This phenomenon is related with a loss in welfare and efficiency.

Since 1950, commercial integration between countries has been taking place mainly in two ways. The first one refers to the multilateral system, which involves organizations like GATT and WTO. According to the theories of international trade, this way always comes with improvements in welfare and efficiency. The second one refers to regional agreements about which, otherwise, economic theory does not say if they are good or bad. Thus, empirical works can help us to know if the effects of these agreements are positive or not.

The empirical literature of international integration also has been using extensively two criteria of welfare and efficiency, to gauge welfare implications of any trading agreement by taking recourse to the Vinerian concepts of trade creation and trade diversion. In a novel attempt of our linking the concepts of trade creation and diversion to the framework of rules of origin, it is important to understand fully the mechanisms of their occurrences.

To understand how trade creation or trade diversion can happen one would need to make certain theoretical assumptions. Let us assume that that there are three trading entities in the world, countries India (I), Sri Lanka (SL) and Rest of the World (ROW). Each country has supply and demand for a particular product X. All the three countries in question are trading among themselves on an MFN-basis (i.e. the same tariff will apply to imports of X irrespective of the source of import).

Now let us assume that I and SL form an FTA and the bilateral import tariff on product X is liberalized to zero per cent. While countries I and SL will trade between themselves duty-free on X, if imported from ROW the MFN tariff will apply (which will by definition be higher than the FTA treatment to X). Let us analyse the welfare or efficiency effects of trade creation and diversion separately.

2.8.1 Trade creation

As discussed earlier, trade creation means that due to an FTA trade occurs from a more efficient producer of the product X. Theoretically, in all cases trade creation would be welfare-improving. Let us understand it with the help of the following:

The supply and demand lines for country I are represented by D and S, respectively. The free trade supply prices of X from countries SL and ROW are given as P^{SL} and P^{ROW}. We assume that ROW is the most efficient supplier of the product X and thus exports X to the market of I at a lower price than country SL. Further, it is assumed for simplicity that before FTA between I and SL, I imposes MFN tariff on X whereby $t^{SL} = t^{ROW}$ set on imports from both SL and ROW. The tariff raises the landed prices of X to P_T^{SL} and P_T^{ROW}, in the market of I for the imports from SL and ROW, respectively. The size of the tariff is denoted in Figure 2.3, which shows that MFN Tariff of I = $P_T^{SL} - P^{SL} = P_T^{ROW} - P^{ROW}$.

As evident from Figure 2.3, considering that the domestic selling price in country I of product X, displayed as P^I is less than the tariff-inclusive prices of P_T^{SL} and P_T^{ROW}, the product will not be imported into the market of I. In that case, I would meet its own domestic demand at $S^1 = D^1$. Subsequently, in the post-FTA stage between I and SL when I imposes zero tariff on product X on the imports from country SL, $t^{SL} = 0$ but t^{ROW} remains at MFN level – which is by definition higher than liberalized tariff under the bilateral FTA (i.e. $t^{ROW} > t^{SL}$).

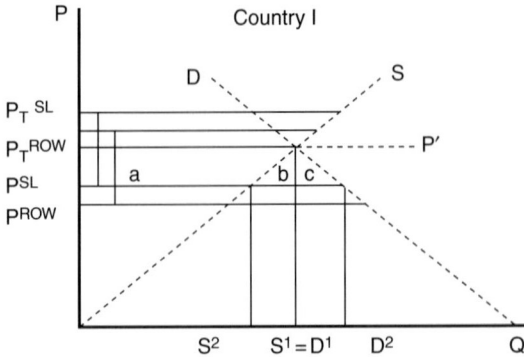

Figure 2.3 Trade creation.

Clearly, the landed prices of X in I when imported from SL and ROW would be P^{SL} and P_T^{ROW}, respectively. Since $P^{SL} < P^I$, it is only natural that I would now import X from country SL post – FTA. Under the I-SL FTA, imports from SL into the market of I would rise to $D^2 - S^2$ due to the lower landed price P^{SL}. This is the trade creation effect of the bilateral I-SL FTA with a switch in trade from an inefficient domestic supplier of I to an efficient supplier in SL.

2.8.2 Trade diversion

The trade diversion effect is opposite from the trade creation effect as explained earlier. Let us understand it with the help of the following:

The supply and demand lines for country I are represented by D and S, respectively. The free trade supply prices of X from countries SL and ROW are given as PSL and PROW. We assume that ROW is the most efficient supplier of the product X at a lower price than country SL into the market of I. Further, it is assumed for simplicity that before FTA between I and SL, I imposes MFN tariff on X whereby tSL = tROW set on imports from both SL and ROW. The tariff raises the landed prices of X to PTSL and PTROW, in the market of I for the imports from SL and ROW, respectively. The size of the tariff is denoted in the diagram which shows that MFN Tariff of I = PTSL – PSL = PTROW – PROW.

Now, in the pre-FTA scenario due to the tariff, X will be imported by I from ROW because it is cheaper to do so than importing from SL. In other words, PTROW < PTSL (see Figure 2.4).

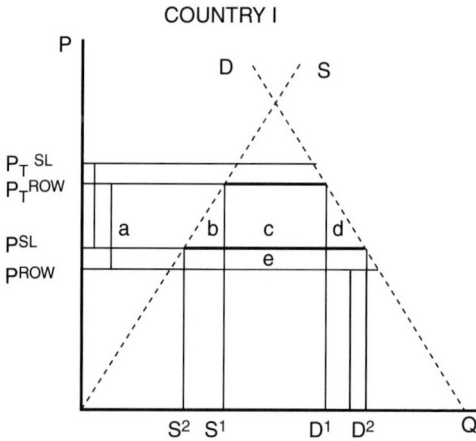

COUNTRY I

Figure 2.4 Trade diversion.

Let us introduce a bilateral FTA between I and SL whereby the import tariff imposed by I on X when imported from SL is eliminated to zero per cent, i.e. tSL = 0 but tROW remains at MFN-level.

The landed prices of X imported by I from SL and ROW are now PSL and PTROW, respectively. Under the I-SL FTA, now the PSL < PTROW therefore I would import all of X from country SL and theoretically would import nothing from ROW. With this, import of X by I would rise to D2 – S2 as displayed in the above diagram. Under this scenario, the SL will replace ROW from the market of I despite being lesser efficient producer of X than ROW. In this situation trade is considered to be diverted from a more efficient supplier (ROW) to a less efficient supplier (SL).

The existing research has largely discussed the consequences of FTAs in terms of trade creation and diversion. There is hardly any research on how consequences of FTAs in terms of trade creation and diversion could change when ROO are brought into the analytical framework.

It is important to emphasize that there could be trade diversion in favour of regional sources of products and away from extra-regional ones due to regional-content requirements or the cumulative ROO. Nevertheless, there could be trade-creation as well due to the expansion of production activities, product diversification and growth of the economies, induced by the initial spurts of trade diversion. In this sense, a favourable effect on intra-regional trade is expected in the long run. Hence, origin rules not only prevent trade deflection in a regional grouping but also contribute to the development process of member countries through different trade and value addition effects. This issue has been deliberated upon in Chapter 3 while evaluating the merits and demerits of ROO-criteria.

2.9 Stimulating intra-regional trade and investment linkages

Cumulation is an instrument that allows the manufacturers of goods to import raw materials or inputs from a country that is party to the same regional trade agreement without undermining the origin of a product. In effect, such imported materials from RTA partner countries are treated as being of domestic origin of the exporting country. A regional preferential trading arrangement having the provision of cumulative ROO is more liberal and better as it enhances the intra-regional trade prospects.

It has the potential to stimulate intra-regional trade flows of different categories of goods among the participants. It also has a favourable trade balance effect for the country using the cumulation provision. The provision of 'cumulation' enhances the possibility of sourcing of inputs from the region and thereby facilitates the backward–forward linkages of industries in the RTA partners. This ultimately leads to intra-regional investment flows as well as transfer of technology. It may be highlighted that the restrictive effects of ROO on intra-regional trade arising out of countries' high import dependence could somewhat be reduced if countries take greater advantage of the regional cumulation facility.

Whether it is in the form of meeting a local-content requirement as a proportion of value-added or change in tariff heading or a particular processing requirement, all have a developmental role to play as they create greater economic activities in the exporting participant. The ROO thus have important implications for the development of the manufacturing sector as a whole, which in turn, contributes towards enhancing the export supply capabilities of the member country and thereby leading to greater economic activity and growth in the region.

In a nutshell, origin rules not only prevent trade deflection in a regional grouping but also contribute to the development process of participants through different trade and value addition effects. However, they should be designed in a manner that is not trade restricting and that they should not become trade barriers due to their complex methods of implementation.

2.10   Developmental perspective of ROO

The above discussion provides a new perspective on the economic effects of ROO in terms of them playing a developmental role through two channels. First, be it any modality, e.g. change in tariff classification or percentage stipulation or a specific process test, all of them emphasize manufacturing, an also manufacturing with value-addition, This is the essence of the expression as 'substantial transformation'. Given that value-addition is a sum of factor payments, and the labour-intensities in products specialized in by the developing world, they can contribute to employment generation and income generation. This could be termed as the 'preferential-trade-led developmental effects of ROO'. Secondly, ROO in a regional trade zone necessitate attracting extra-regional FDI into the region. These again have potential developmental effects of the kind highlighted above. This could be termed as 'preferential-trade-led-FDI-led developmental effects of ROO'.

2.10.1   Developmental loss due to elimination of Rules of Origin

The same can be argued from a different angle, in terms of the developmental loss if PROO are eliminated. Alan *et al.* (2008) have analyzed the effect of textile and clothing import barriers and regulations on US welfare and sectoral activity. They found that the effects of quantitative restraints have declined after the ATC, although remaining quantitative measures in 2005 still imposed about 20 per cent of the welfare cost estimated in pre-2005 studies of these barriers. Tariffs in these sectors remain high and continue to reduce welfare. This book includes a new and careful examination of PROO-based foreign demand in these sectors, and finds that the effect of foreign demand is substantial for textile and clothing output, trade, and employment.

Elimination of quantitative restraints, tariffs and PROO differ markedly from one another in their effect on welfare and other macroeconomic variables. Eliminating only ROO would reduce GDP by $169 million and welfare by $696 million, as US textile and clothing manufactures lose significant sources of export demand. Adding elimination of quantitative restraints leads to improvement in both GDP ($117 million) and welfare ($1170 million), while worsening textile and apparel output decline only slightly (0.0 per cent). Removal of all textile and apparel barriers and ROO is estimated to increase net US welfare by $2.04 billion while decreasing US textile and clothing output by an additional 1.4 per cent. Elimination of quantitative restraints provides more than twice the welfare gain from the elimination of tariffs, while ROO-driven demand reduction reduce welfare and account for 82 per cent of the output loss from complete liberalization of textile and clothing trade.

2.11 Downbeat effects

Apart from the positive implications of ROO, as highlighted above, there are certain adverse implications that also need to be taken into consideration. It is often argued that the rules of origin might (i) inhibit intra-regional trade, and (ii) favour high cost and inefficient production. Some suggestions to tackle these problems are also made.

2.11.1 Limiting regional trade linkages

In a regional grouping, where several countries lack natural resources and have underdeveloped industrial base, their dependence on imported inputs might pose problems for their adherence to originating-status norms. This in turn might hinder their intra-regional exports.

In such a situation there appears to be a trade-off between the objectives of preventing trade deflection on one hand and intra-regional trade expansion, on the other. Hence, ROO need to be evolved by taking this aspect into account.

2.11.2 Favouring inefficiency

ROO may also enforce inefficiencies within the regional groupings as the rise in production costs could adversely influence the competitiveness of products. Increase in costs might well offset the margin-of-preferences-effect of tariffs under a PTA or a FTA. This could ultimately obstruct intra-regional trade. In specific production lines the local-content requirements could enforce substitution of the imported inputs with often-costlier domestic as well as regional inputs.

The percentage criterion needs to be carefully devised and judiciously implemented along with other tests of origin, as substitution in favour of high cost inputs makes it easier to meet the origin requirements. This kind of test would favour enterprises that are inefficient and production bases that are marked with high wage-cost.

2.12 Balancing development and downbeat effects

ROO influence both import patterns and export prospects. If they are too stringent they may provide import protection but also scuttle export prospects and if they are too liberal the converse may be true.

Thus, a combination of different modalities can give the policy space to balance the objectives of export promotion and efficient imports actually originating from the member countries. This issue is very important in cases of FTAs especially in the context of rules of origin which are being devised. There cannot be just one ideal ROO formulation that can induce only the developmental effects as it would inherently bring in its downbeat effects as well. Therefore, a balance between the two effects would be dependent upon the stage of economic development of member countries and this makes the formulation of ROO much more complex and a major negotiating challenge. The challenges relating to finding the overall balance by maximizing the development effects and minimizing the downbeat effects by the countries negotiating rules of origin, especially the developing countries, are reflected in the subsequent chapters. In this regard, we have attempted to address the issue of finding the balance by making some policy-prescriptions in Chapter 7.

2.13 Restrictiveness index

An index approach is one way to assess the degree of restrictiveness of government interventions where price and quantity measures of the impact of those interventions, such as ROO, are not readily available. An index quantifies prevailing restrictions into a summary measure to facilitate comparisons on a common basis across PTAs.

Different ROO restrict trade differently. The index focuses on the extent to which identified ROO-related regulatory barriers may restrict trade between members and non-members. In doing so, it also recognizes that ROO have effects that reduce or modify the value of tariff concessions in trade agreements – for example, by affecting the degree of certainty of tariff concessions or through compliance or administration costs. In calculating the index, allowance has been made for factors influencing certainty of market access, compliance costs and other considerations.

Index methodologies have previously been applied to analyze origin rules in NAFTA and EU-related agreements (Estevadeoral 2000, Brenton and Manchin 2002, Augier *et al.*, Gasiorek and Lai-Tong 2003, Estevadeordal and Suominen 2003). Indexes developed in those studies have focused on particular provisions of ROO – for example, whether a change in tariff classification (CTC) is at the tariff item (HS 8-digit), sub-heading (6-digit), heading (4-digit) or the chapter (2-digit) level. They have also taken into account other factors affecting the restrictiveness of origin rules, including: tariff phase-out schedules;

cumulation; duty drawback; tolerance; and outward processing provisions in a PTA.

This study by the Australian Productivity Commission (2004) and Gretton and Gali (2005) expands on the range of ROO factors examined in earlier studies and includes, for example, details of regional value content requirements and factors influencing market access in the index (Box 2.3).

Box 2.3 Restrictive index methodology

The index methodology involves specifying a *regimen* of provisions or criteria used to determine origin in a PTA, a *weight* for each criterion reflecting its relative importance in the index and a *score* reflecting the restrictiveness of the variant implemented in the ROO regime. Because economic theory and existing studies do not provide a readily available 'standard' against which any particular method or provision for determining origin can be judged, the weights and scores were assigned subjectively by reference to other studies and the nature of the provision. The methodology allows ROO to be analysed in terms of their characteristics, with the index value of a particular regime reflecting *ex ante* the restrictiveness of the origin rules faced by firms. However, the index alone does not provide a measure of the ex post effects of an implementation of ROO such as the adverse impacts on firms choice of production technology and ways of working, and national welfare.

For a particular ROO regime, the index value reflects the number of restrictions applied, the relative importance of each of those restrictions (the weight) and the restrictiveness of each variant (the score). Overall, a higher index value indicates a more restrictive trading environment on account of ROO. Nevertheless, in interpreting index values, it should be borne in mind that, while an index provides a measure to quantify all relevant restrictions related to preferential ROO that can be identified by available information sources, a higher score may simply reflect a greater availability of information rather than a more restrictive regime. This study attempts to overcome this limitation by using the best known, reviewed and compiled sources of information on preferential ROO. In addition, it should be noted that the provisions in the PTAs are assessed in the index according to the actual provision in agreements, rather than the extent to which the

Box 2.3 Continued

provision may have been implemented. Where the degree to which PTA members implement ROO provisions differs, the index values reported may also differ from their 'true' or underlying values.

The index is a measure of the restrictiveness of a ROO regime, at the margin. That is, it assumes that the provisions are relevant to firms' decision-making and activities. For example, ROO provisions would typically not be relevant for items with MFN tariffs of zero (ie where the margin of preference afforded to a PTA member is zero), since compliance with an origin rule would not confer a financial benefit to the PTA exporter. It would also not be relevant when ROO have no effect on firms' production and trade decisions.

The determination of weights for restriction categories is designed to reflect the economic significance of restrictions in a PTA on firms' productive efficiency. However, their expected impact on merchandise trade flows of member and non-member countries also depends on the external tariff environment of a PTA.

Source: Gretton and Gali (2005).

2.14 ROO Development Index (RDI)

As has been discussed earlier very little work has been done to examine the developmental dimension of rules of origin as the entire focus was to look at the rules of origin as an impediment to trade. The fact that in any RTA the economic activities take place only because of ROO has so far been neglected. RTA without any ROO has no meaning and thereby while at one point of time it eliminates the circumvention of trade taking place through non-members, it enforces certain degree of linkages among RTA members thereby facilitating the intra-regional trade and investment. The developmental dimensions of ROO therefore cannot be neglected. In the above background based on the commonly followed practices of some of the important ROO, an attempt has been made to quantify the development index of ROO (based on Das and Ratna, forthcoming). Additionally, the quantification of ROO development index is also imperative, given the fact that the restrictiveness index fails to capture the realities associated with RTAs in the developing world, especially in the Asia-pacific region.

In constructing the RDI, we have looked at the parameters that have been discussed in the earlier section. The RDI has been constructed by taking into account the following criteria: (i) *general criteria* and (ii) *additional criteria*.

The structure of the index is presented in Table 2.5.

We have constructed the RDI by further classifying the general criteria into *four* sub-classes. A relatively high index value has been assigned to general criteria because of predominance of the experiences of the rules of origin formulations in the context of developing Asia, especially India. The weight assigned to the general criteria, on the whole, is 0.80 out of a total RDI value of unitary. The RDI value of the general criteria is further disaggregated into sub-classes on the basis of frequency of use and their likely importance in ROO regimes in this region's specific contexts.

Of the four sub-classes under the general criteria, the cumulation has been accorded the highest RDI value on account of the conceptual logic built in the preceding section and the region-specific RTAs in vogue.

The change in tariff classification, value added content both the local and the regional value added and the additional criteria have been given an RDI value of 0.2 which also contribute to the developmental dimension, however, in a relatively lesser proportion than cumulation. Given the fact that minimal operations are merely to prevent trade in goods that are produced by simple operations, this sub-class is given a lesser RDI value of 0.1.

Coming to the sub-classes under the additional criteria, the RDI value has been developed again on the basis of this region's experiences. In this regard, it was found that the product-specific rules (PSRs) are devised

Table 2.5 ROO Development Index value

	Development Index value	Index distribution
ROO Development Index	1	
I. General Criteria	0.8	
I.1 Change in tariff classification		0.2
I.2 Local/regional value added content		0.2
I.3 Minimal or non-qualifying criteria		0.1
I.4 Cumulation		0.3
II. Additional criteria	0.2	
II.1 PSR		0
II.2 Duty drawback allowed		0.1
II.3 Outward processing not allowed		0.1

Source: Authors' estimates.

as either more stringent provisions to protect the domestic industry or formulated as more liberal than the general rule, without looking into the actual economic reality. The outcome of negotiations has been on the basis of preferences indicated by the RTA members. In both the situations the PSRs are not prone to contributing to the developmental objectives since they are in either situation not amenable for generation of additional economic activities.

The sub-class of duty drawback allowed has been given the RDI value of 0.1 as it does contribute to some economic activity, though they are much less in their intensity.

It is very important to highlight the treatment of outward processing in the construction of the RDI. Since such a provision does not contribute at all to the manufacturing process in the RTA members, we have assigned an RDI value of 0.1 to this sub-class. Having such a provision usually negates the developmental objective of the RTA member as the investment inflow and technology transfer which would have been otherwise attracted and have entailed additional economic activity remains in those countries from where these outward processing are allowed.

2.14.1 Explaining the factorization of development index criteria

In addition to the above criteria, there are several other factors of the ROO that influence the origin of the product and the economic activity of the RTA member country, thereby influencing the trade flows. These factors relate to the level of CTC at which the substantial transformation should take place (HS 2-, 4- 6-, 8-digit), local/regional value added content, minimal operations, cumulation provisions, tolerance or *de minimis* thresholds, provisions relating to drawback allowed and outward processing not allowed.

As has been explained earlier, the factorization value is indicative of the developmental roles which the above factors can play. If the above factors relating to rules of origin provisions are either too stringent or too liberal, the developmental outcomes would be nearly negligible. This being the case the maximum developmental objectives can only be met if an overall balance is envisaged between the two extremes. It is with this reason that our development-oriented ROO index is completely distinct from all the previous works on the subject.

In view of the above, to attain the maximum developmental objectives, based on the existing ROO provisions in this region, we have identified the factor values as presented in the Table 2.6.

Table 2.6   Factorisation of development index criteria

		Specification	Multiplying factor
General Criteria	*Change in tariff classification*	Tariff item (HS 8-digit)	(–) 1
		Sub-heading (HS 6-digit)	0.5
		Heading (HS 4-digit)	1
		Chapter (HS 2-digit)	(–) 1
	Local/regional value added content	0–29%	0
		30–50%	0.5
		51%	1
		52–70%	0.75
		Above 70%	1
	Minimal or non-qualifying criteria	*Type of specified manufacturing process test applied*	
		No test	0
		Test prescribed	1
	Cumulation	*Type of cumulation*	
		Full	1
		Diagonal	0.8
		Bilateral	0.4
		No cumulation	0
Additional criteria		*Provisions that go beyond cumulation*	
		Tolerance or *de minimis* allowed	1
		Absorption principle	0.6
		Tracing test	0.4
		Absorption principle, tracing and tolerance tests not used	0
		Duty drawback	
		Drawback allowed	1
		Drawback not allowed	0
		Outward processing	
		Outward processing included	(–) 1
		Outward processing excluded	1

Source: Authors' estimates.

The above factors have been considered on the basis of conceptual framework developed below on the basis of some of the important existing ROO formulations in RTAs.

2.14.1.1   *General criteria*

2.14.1.1.1 Change in tariff classification.   The change in tariff classification at the HS 2-digit level provides the highest order of processing and at the HS 8-digit level the processing requirements are too liberal. In either case, the developmental effect of ROO is negated. Therefore, we have given both a multiplying factor value of (–) 1. The change in tariff classification at the HS 4-digit level entails the maximum degree of 'substantial transformation' as also recognized by the WTO ROO Agreement in the case of even non-preferential trade flows. Thus, the highest developmental effect would be achieved under this ROO provision and hence, the multiplying factor value of 1 is assigned. The change in tariff classification at the HS 6-digit level entails relatively lesser degree of 'substantial transformation' and hence, the multiplying factor value of 0.5 is assigned.

2.14.1.1.2 Local / regional value added content. We have given the highest multiplying factor value of 1 if the value added content is either 51 per cent or above 70 per cent. In case of value added being greater than 70 per cent the developmental objectives would be higher as the exporting RTA member will achieve the highest order of economic activity. This however, is not realistic in the present age of global production chains and networks. Therefore, we have also assigned the multiplying factor value of 1 in case of 51 per cent value added as the product should at least have the contribution from the exporting RTA member of more than half, even if it is just one percentage point higher. Under this scenario, the product would at least have the majority equity in terms of raw material and intermediate, processing and factor costs; profits; transportation costs etc. emanating from the RTA member where it is manufactured. This conceptual consideration is akin to the concept of 'ownership' of a company where the majority equity of 51 per cent decides the owner. On the similar lines, with a value added of 51 per cent the ownership of the product to be exported would lie with the exporting RTA partner while at the same time it also allows considerable degree of flexibility to source other materials from non-members of RTA and thereby making it logically *'made in the particular RTA member'.*

The logic of different percentages of value addition from the developmental angle prompts us to assign the multiplying factor value of 0.75 for 52–70 per cent; 0.5 for 30–50 per cent; and nil for 0–29 per cent.

2.14.1.1.3 Minimal or non-qualifying criteria. Considering that the stipulations of minimal criteria sift out those processes that cannot be considered as those contributing to 'substantial transformation' and development, their presence in a ROO formulation is assigned a multiplying factor value of 1 and because their absence does not entail any development in the exporting RTA member, the multiplying factor value assigned is nil.

2.14.1.1.4 Cumulation. Cumulation allows the RTA members to count materials purchased from other members as originating within that RTA for the purpose of determining origin. In Full Cumulation any processing in any RTA member can be counted as originating, regardless whether processing is sufficient or not to confer originating status to the materials involved. In this case, the extent of value added contribution made in another RTA member is taken even if the material as a whole does not originate. Therefore we have given the highest multiplying factor value as in this case the maximum development in the region can take place.

In case of Diagonal Cumulation, the value added content of other RTA member can only be cumulated if the material sourced is originating. If the RTA member's material is not originating, even though there is some value added generated in that member due to some processes, the entire value added is discarded. This is often called "whole or nothing approach". Thus a factor value of 0.8 is assigned in this case.

In case of Bilateral Cumulation, the degree of flexibility decreases as the choice of partner is limited and hence a factor of 0.4 is assigned.

Finally, No Cumulation is assigned a value of zero or nil.

2.14.1.2 Additional criteria

2.14.1.2.1 Provisions that go beyond cumulation. The Tolerance or *de minimis* rules allow certain percentage of non-originating materials that could be used in manufacturing a product which is otherwise not accepted ROO. A maximum ceiling (*de minimis*) prescribed for treating the product as originating. We have given this the highest multiplying factor of 1 as it takes into account the developmental needs of an RTA member. This is so because this provision provides for flexibility in terms of preventing a substantial manufacturing process from being excluded from getting preferential tariff treatment due to the use of a very small fraction of non-originating input in an RTA member.

In the case of the Absorption Principle and Tracing provisions a non-originating input acquires originating status by satisfying a specified stipulation. The non-originating material is considered to be 100 per cent originating once incorporated into a final product under this provision. Just as in the case of the Tolerance Principle, these cases also, however to a lesser extent, provide flexibility in terms of preventing a substantial manufacturing process from being excluded from getting preferential tariff treatment. Therefore, Absorption Principle and Tracing provisions have been assigned the multiplying factor values of 0.6 and 0.4, respectively. Of the alternatives, tracing tests are treated as the least liberalizing because they restrict valuations to include only originating materials. By contrast, under tolerance rules or the absorption principle, the full value of the material input is given originating status if an initial test is satisfied. Tolerance tests are treated as the most liberal of the options because they are regarded as providing the greatest scope for raising the level of 'originating' content' (Australian Productivity Commission, 2005; see also Gretton and Gali, 2005).

2.14.1.2.2 Duty drawback. A presence of duty drawback provisions in the ROO framework has a developmental effect whereas their absence would have no development effect on account of duty drawback. Under the duty drawback provisions the tariffs due on imported materials used in the production of export items are refunded. The effect could be reduced cost of inputs used to produce an exportable, thus facilitating manufacturing in the exporting RTA member. What is more it has a second round of developmental impact in the exporting RTA member due to the demand-pull factor in the importing RTA member as duty drawback provisions make the exportable more price-attractive. It is with this reasoning that we have assigned the multiplying factor value of 1 to the duty drawback provisions and zero in the case of an absence of duty drawback provisions. Origin rules that disallow or derogate drawback arrangements for exporters are treated as more restrictive than rules that do not (Australian Productivity Commission, 2005).

2.14.1.2.3 Outward processing. For the reasons explained in the preceding section the inclusion of outward processing provision has been assigned the multiplying factor value of (–) 1 as it does not contribute to the economic activity of the exporting RTA member. If the same is excluded it is given the multiplying factor value of 1.

Based on above, the empirical results of the RDI value are presented in Chapter 5.

2.15 Gravity model

An attempt would be made to estimate the effects of ROO on trade econometrically. The analysis will take recourse to the standard gravity model in which the imports into country *i* from country *j*, can be expressed as:

$$Ln\ (Mij) = \alpha_0 + \beta_1\ Ln\ (GDP_i) + \beta_2\ Ln\ (PoP_i) + \beta_3\ Ln\ (GDP_j)$$
$$+ \beta_6\ Ln\ (PoP_j) + \beta_5\ (Dist_{ij}) + \beta_4 Z_i + \mu$$

Where:

Mij: Imports by country i to country j (Mn. dollars)
GDPk: GDP of country k, (k = i,j)
Popk: Population of country k (k = i,j)
Distij: Distance between the respective countries.
Z: the set of dummy variable (ROO RDI for different trading partners)

2.16 Measuring trade deflection

The possibilities of trade deflection of goods from one member country to another in any regional preferential trading arrangement could be evaluated by taking cognizance of customs tariff regimes of the member countries, the stages of development of member countries and the realities of the regional market. In so doing, the following two indices have been considered: trade deflection ratio, and the comparative advantage/disadvantage of a country in a particular product group measured by revealed comparative advantage index.

2.16.1 Trade deflection ratio

At HS 4-digit level an index of trade deflection can be calculated, on an illustrative basis, say between India and Sri Lanka by considering the difference in their respective customs regimes (see Panchamukhi and Das, 2001). The trade deflection ratio is defined as the following:

$$TR = (1 + t_I)/(1 + t_{SL})$$

where t_I is India's external tariff and t_{SL} is Sri Lanka's external tariff. Higher the TR greater is the possibility of trade deflection.

The trade deflection ratio has been derived as below:

Any product of a third country would be prone to trade deflection say, for instance, from Sri Lanka into India if the cost of importing from Sri Lanka is less than the cost of importing the same product directly from the third country source into India.

If the FoB price of the product X is P_X and CIF factor between a third country and Sri Lanka is R1 and it is subjected to Sri Lanka's tariff rate

t_{sl} the price would become $P_xR1(1 + t_{sl})$. If the product faces another factor R2 of CIF while reaching the point of entry into India and it is further subjected to the South Asian Free Trade Area (SAFTA) preferential tariff rate; its price would become $P_xR1(1 + t_{sl}) R2(1 + t_{SAFTAI})$, where India's tariff rate under SAFTA to non-LDCs is given as t_{SAFTAI}. Similarly, the price of the same product imported directly into India would be subjected to a CIF factor R3 and the Indian tariff rate t_I. The price would then be $P_xR3(1 + t_I)$.

Therefore, the price of a product being imported into Sri Lanka from a third country source and further imported into India under SAFTA from Sri Lanka is $P1 = P_xR1(1 + t_{sl})R2(1 + t_{SAFTAI})$, and the price of the same product imported directly into India from the same third country source is $P2 = P_xR3(1 + t_I)$.

Under the scenario of no trade deflection $P1 = P2$.

or, $$P2/P1 = P_xR3(1 + t_I)/P_xR1(1 + t_{sl})R2(1 + t_{SAFTAI}) = 1$$

or, $$\frac{R3}{R1R2}\ \frac{(1+t_I)}{(1+t_{sl})(1+t_{SAFTAI})} = 1$$

Assuming that the CIF factors R1, R2 and R3 are constant at a given point of time since they are structural variables and tariff rates under SAFTA would tend to be zero or near-zero in the immediate future, the trade deflection ratio (TR) would be:

$$TR = (1 + t_I)/(1 + t_{sl}) = 1$$

If TR is greater than one it would suggest possibilities of trade deflection and vice versa.

The methodology discussed above which combines the computation of trade deflection ratio, revealed comparative advantage index and trade share analysis is capable of providing clues towards formulating any changes in a rules of origin system.

2.16.1.1 *TDR: an extended approach*

For a more accurate and realistic estimate of trade deflection, the conceptual basis needs to be extended further (Das, 2010). To begin with, consider trade deflection possibilities from Nepal into India, as captured above as TDR_{NI}. In the same vein, trade deflection possibilities from India into Nepal would be denoted as TDR_{IN}.

It needs to be highlighted that TDR_{IN} is not only a function of the tariff-differentials between the two countries, as traditionally perceived by the existing literature. Instead, TDR_{IN} would also depend upon the possibilities of trade deflection between India and her other RTA partners. In which case,

$$TDR_{IN} = f (TDR_{SLI,} TDR_{SI,} TDR_{THI...} TDR_{nI)}$$

where, SL stands for Sri Lanka, S for Singapore, TH for Thailand and n for n number of India's RTAs. These countries have been chosen to be denoted since these are all India's existing RTA partners.

The trade deflection possibilities would be uniform between one RTA pair and another if the tariff differentials and rules of origin formulations are uniform between them for a specific product. Quite often tariff differentials may not be uniform for a product; hence there is a strong case for ROO harmonization across RTAs in order to have the minimum possibilities of trade deflection – which has been the basic objective of ROO.

2.17   Rules of Origin and geographical indications (GI)

As has been discussed earlier, the basic objective of ROO is to determine the origin of a product and the products are classified into different categories depending on use of inputs. Issue of what will entail 'substantial transformation' is also discussed. In this regard, a new dimension that can be explored for determining the ROO relate to the provisions of Geographical Indications (GI). Here we have tried to discuss if there is any necessity to have any criteria on any product that has been registered in one of the RTA members as a GI product. In general, in RTAs such provisions are silent, thereby making it imperative for the GI products to go through the test of criteria for determining the origin. GI products are not only 'wholly obtained' instead they are a step ahead as they are not only country-specific but location-specific in a particular country. Since GI status is accorded to products after necessary examination and registration formalities they need to be exempt from ROO Tests for determining origin. This would make the implementation of ROO on GI products time- and cost-saving and simple. This would further facilitate meeting the developmental objectives of ROO. Given above, one would need to explore if GI products in different countries such as the French Champagne, Indonesian Batik printed Garments and made-ups, Indian Darjeeling Tea, Banarsi Sarees, Kashmiri Pashmina Shawls, Bangladeshi

Silk, Swiss watch and chocolates, etc. can be treated as originating in respective countries on the basis of their GI certification.

In summary, the chapter initially deals with a whole gamut of NPROO and PROO issues and takes into cognizance various disputes and legal interpretational issues relating to the ARO of the WTO to assess if the rules of origin can be used as a trade policy instrument and if so in what manner.

This chapter has presented a brief overview of different elements of rules of origin and documented the existing literature relating to them. Further, the chapter presents a novel approach towards ROO, as distinct from the existing knowledge on the subject, in a variety of ways. The most important contribution of this chapter is to bring the development focus to the whole issue apart from ROO being treated as a commercial policy instrument. In so doing, the chapter constructs a *development index* as opposed to restrictiveness index of rules of origin as prevalent in the literature. This breaks a new ground in the trade policy-making process as a whole. Moreover, the chapter also offers new insights into ROO in terms of trade deflection, trade creation / diversion, geographical indications in a manner that is entirely new.

Appendix: Proposals Relating to WTO ROO Harmonization Work Programme: Select Sectors

CHAPTER 50–57

Primary Rule: Minor processing operations not affecting origin.

For the purposes of determining the country of origin for goods falling within Chapter 50 that are not wholly obtained in one country, the following individual processes, considered singly, shall not affect the origin of the goods concerned, whether or not such processes result in changes of classification:

(a) Working or finishing one or more edges by hemming, rolling, whipping or similar means or by knotting fringe;
(b) Cutting fabrics, yarns or other textile materials; or separating goods produced in the finished state by cutting along dividing threads;
(c) Assembling or joining goods by sewing or stitching for convenience of shipment or other temporary purposes;
(d) Putting up goods for retail sale or in sets or ensembles.]

CHAPTER 58

Definition: Embroidery

For the purposes of heading 58.10 embroidery in strips or in motifs means:

(a) embroidered fabric not exceeding 30 cm in width (strips);
(b) embroidery in a motif, whether or not rectangular in shape, which is capable of being enclosed in a square or rectangular frame the area of which is no more than 1 square meter.

Chapter Note: Application of the value added rule:

(a) The term "**50% value added rule**" shall mean manufacture where the increase in value acquired as a result of working and processing, and if applicable, the incorporation of parts originating in the country of manufacture represents at least 50% of the ex-works price of the product.
(b) The term "**ex-works price**" shall mean the price to be paid for the product obtained to the manufacturer in whose undertaking the last working or processing is carried out (this price shall not include internal taxes which are, or may be, repaid when such product is exported);
(c) The term "**value acquired as a result of working and processing and incorporation of parts originating in the country of manufacture**" shall mean the increase in value resulting from the assembly itself, together with any preparatory, finishing and checking operations, and from the incorporation

of any parts originating in the country where the operations in question were carried out, including profit and the general costs borne in that country as a result of the operations;

Primary Rule: Minor processing operations not affecting origin

For the purposes of determining the country of origin for goods falling within Chapter 58 that are not wholly obtained in one country, the following individual processes, considered singly, shall not affect the origin of the goods concerned, whether or not such processes result in changes of classification:

(a) Working or finishing one or more edges by hemming, rolling, whipping or similar means or by knotting fringe;
(b) Cutting fabrics, yarns or other textile materials; or separating goods produced in the finished state by cutting along dividing threads;
(c) Assembling or joining goods by sewing or stitching for convenience of shipment or other temporary purposes;
(d) Putting up goods for retail sale or in sets or ensembles.]

Chapter Residual Rule

[When application of the primary rules of this chapter (including the product specific rules provided in the matrix) does not result in a determination of a country of origin, the country of origin shall be determined as follows:

The country of origin of quilted fabrics of heading 58.11 of this Chapter shall be the country in which the exterior textile fabric was formed, or in the case of a good containing textile fabrics of more than one country, the origin of the good is the country in which the exterior textile fabric that predominates by weight was formed.]

CHAPTER 59

Primary Rules: Minor processing operations not affecting origin

For the purposes of determining the country of origin for goods falling within Chapter 59 that are not wholly obtained in one country, the following individual processes, considered singly, shall not affect the origin of the goods concerned, whether or not such processes result in changes of classification:

(a) Working or finishing one or more edges by hemming, rolling, whipping or similar means or by knotting fringe;
(b) Cutting fabrics, yarns or other textile materials; or separating goods produced in the finished state by cutting along dividing threads;
(c) Assembling or joining goods by sewing or stitching for convenience of shipment or other temporary purposes;
(d) Putting up goods for retail sale or in sets or ensembles.]

Chapter Residual Rule

[When application of the primary rules of this chapter (including the product specific rules provided in the matrix) does not result in a determination of a country of origin, the country of origin shall be determined as follows:

> The country of origin of fabrics of this Chapter, except textile wall coverings of heading 59.05, shall be the country where the textile fabric was formed, or in the case of a good containing textile fabrics of more than one country, the origin of the good is the country in which the textile fabric that predominates by weight was formed.]

CHAPTER 61

Definition: Assembly in a Single Country

[(a) For the purposes of this chapter, and subject to paragraph (b), the term "assembled in a single country" means that all of the assembly operations following the cutting of the fabric to parts, or the knitting or crocheting to shape of the parts, have been performed in that country.

(b) For the purposes of paragraph (a) performing or not performing operations such as the following shall not affect the determination of whether the good has been assembled in a single country:
  - attaching to garments or accessories items such as accessories, buttons and other fasteners, pockets, trimmings, cuffs, plackets, labels, foot straps, ornaments, belt loops, epaulettes collars;
  - making button holes, hemming, pressing, stone or acid washing.]

Chapter Note: Application of the value added rule

(a) The term "**50% value added rule**" shall mean manufacture where the increase in value acquired as a result of working and processing, and if applicable, the incorporation of parts originating in the country of manufacture represents at least 50% of the ex-works price of the product.

(b) The term "**ex-works price**" shall mean the price to be paid for the product obtained to the manufacturer in whose undertaking the last working or processing is carried out (this price shall not include internal taxes which are, or may be, repaid when such product is exported);

(c) The term "**value acquired as a result of working and processing and incorporation of parts originating in the country of manufacture**" shall mean the increase in value resulting from the assembly itself, together with any preparatory, finishing and checking operations, and from the incorporation of any parts originating in the country where the operations in question were carried out, including profit and the general costs borne in that country as a result of the operations;

Primary Rule: Minor processing operations not affecting origin

For the purposes of determining the country of origin for goods falling within Chapter 61 that are not wholly obtained in one country, the following individual processes, considered singly, shall not affect the origin of the goods concerned, whether or not such processes result in changes of classification:

(a) Working or finishing one or more edges by hemming, rolling, whipping or similar means or by knotting fringe;
(b) Cutting fabrics, yarns or other textile materials; or separating goods produced in the finished state by cutting along dividing threads;
(c) Assembling or joining goods by sewing or stitching for convenience of shipment or other temporary purposes;
(d) Putting up goods for retail sale or in sets or ensembles.

Chapter Residual Rule

When application of the primary rules of this Chapter (including the product specific rules provided in the matrix) does not result in a determination of a country of origin, the country of origin shall be determined as follows:

(1) Where the primary rule for a good assembled from parts requires that the good be wholly assembled in a single country, the country of origin of such a good that was not wholly assembled in a single country, is the country in which the most significant assembly operations were performed in the making-up of the good, without regard to the addition of buttons and other fasteners, belt and hanger loops, belts, patch pockets, labels, foot straps, epaulettes, ornaments and other minor components.
(2) The country of origin of other goods of this Chapter shall be the country where the textile fabric or knit-to-shape components was formed, or in the case of a good containing textile fabrics or knit-to-shape component of more than one country, the origin of the good is the country in which the textile fabric or knit-to-shape component that predominates by weight was formed.]

CHAPTER 62

Definition: Assembly in a Single Country

(a) For the purposes of this chapter, and subject to paragraph (b), the term "assembled in a single country" means that all of the assembly operations following the cutting of the fabric to parts have been performed in that country.
(b) For the purposes of paragraph (a) performing or not performing operations such as the following shall not affect the determination of whether the good has been assembled in a single country:
  – attaching to garments or accessories items such as accessories, buttons and other fasteners, pockets, trimmings, cuffs, plackets, labels, foot straps, ornaments, belt loops, epaulettes, collars;
  – making button holes, hemming, pressing, stone or acid washing.]

Chapter Note: Application of the value added rule

(a) The term "**50% value added rule**" shall mean manufacture where the increase in value acquired as a result of working and processing, and if applicable, the incorporation of parts originating in the country of manufacture represents at least 50% of the ex-works price of the product.

(b) The term **"ex-works price"** shall mean the price to be paid for the product obtained to the manufacturer in whose undertaking the last working or processing is carried out (this price shall not include internal taxes which are, or may be, repaid when such product is exported);

(c) The term **"value acquired as a result of working and processing and incorporation of parts originating in the country of manufacture"** shall mean the increase in value resulting from the assembly itself, together with any preparatory, finishing and checking operations, and from the incorporation of any parts originating in the country where the operations in question were carried out, including profit and the general costs borne in that country as a result of the operations;

Primary Rule 1: Minor processing operations not affecting origin

For the purposes of determining the country of origin for goods falling within Chapter 62 that are not wholly obtained in one country, the following individual processes, considered singly, shall not affect the origin of the goods concerned, whether or not such processes result in changes of classification:

(a) Working or finishing one or more edges by hemming, rolling, whipping or similar means or by knotting fringe;
(b) Cutting fabrics, yarns or other textile materials; or separating goods produced in the finished state by cutting along dividing threads;
(c) Assembling or joining goods by sewing or stitching for convenience of shipment or other temporary purposes;
(d) Putting up goods for retail sale or in sets or ensembles.

Chapter Residual Rule

[When application of the primary rules of this Chapter (including the product specific rules provided in the matrix) does not result in a determination of a country of origin, the country of origin shall be determined as follows:

(1) Where the primary rule for a good assembled from parts requires that the good be wholly assembled in a single country, the country of origin of such a good that was not wholly assembled in a single country, is the country in which the most significant assembly operations were performed in the making-up of the good, without regard to the addition of buttons and other fasteners, belt and hanger loops, belts, patch pockets, labels, foot straps, epaulettes, ornaments and other minor components.
(2) The country of origin of other goods of this Chapter shall be the country where the textile fabric or knit-to-shape components was formed, or in the case of a good containing textile fabrics or knit-to-shape component of more than one country, the origin of the good is the country in which the textile fabric or knit-to-shape component that predominates by weight was formed.]

CHAPTER 63

Primary Rule 1: Minor processing operations not affecting origin

For the purposes of determining the country of origin for goods falling within Chapter 63 that are not wholly obtained in one country, the following individual processes, considered singly, shall not affect the origin of the goods concerned, whether or not such processes result in changes of classification:

(a) Working or finishing one or more edges by hemming, rolling, whipping or similar means or by knotting fringe;
(b) Cutting fabrics, yarns or other textile materials; or separating goods produced in the finished state by cutting along dividing threads;
(c) Assembling or joining goods by sewing or stitching for convenience of shipment or other temporary purposes;
(d) Putting up goods for retail sale or in sets or ensembles.

Chapter Residual Rule

[When application of the primary rules of this chapter (including the product specific rules provided in the matrix) does not result in a determination of a country of origin, the country of origin shall be determined as follows:

The country of origin of goods of this Chapter shall be the country where the textile fabric was formed, or in the case of a good containing textile fabrics of more than one country, the origin of the good is the country in which the textile fabric that predominates by weight was formed.]

A. Primary Rule/Note for Chapters 84–90

Goods obtained by disassembly

A change of classification which results from the disassembly of goods shall not be considered as the change required by the rule set forth in the matrix. The country of origin of the parts recovered from the goods shall be the country where the parts are recovered, unless the importer, exporter or any person with a justifiable cause to determine the origin of parts demonstrates another country of origin on the basis of verifiable evidence such as origin marks on the part itself or documents.

Collection of parts

Where a change in classification results from the application of HS General Interpretative Rule 2(a) with respect to collections of parts that are presented as unassembled articles of another heading or subheading the individual parts shall retain their origin prior to such collection.

Recertification or retesting

A change of classification which results from the recertification or retesting of the good shall not be considered as the change required by the rule set out in the matrix.

Assembly of the collection of parts

Goods assembled from a collection of parts classified as the assembled good by application of General Interpretative Rule 2 shall have origin in the country of assembly, provided the assembly would have satisfied the primary rule for the good had each of the parts been presented separately and not as a collection.

(e) *Parts and accessories produced from blanks*
  (1) The country of origin of goods that are produced from blanks which, by application of the HS General Interpretative Rule 2(a), are classified in the same heading or subheading as the complete or finished goods, shall be the country in which the blank was finished provided finishing included configuring to final shape by the removal of material (other than merely by honing or polishing or both), or by forming processes such as bending, hammering, pressing or stamping.
  (2) Paragraph 1 above applies to goods classifiable in provisions for parts or parts and accessories, including goods specifically named under such provisions, and to goods classifiable in headings 84.80 and 84.83.

B. Notes for Chapters 84–90 applicable to primary rules contained in Column (4)

Application of the value added rule

The term **"50% value added rule"** shall mean manufacture where the increase in value acquired as a result of working and processing, and if applicable, the incorporation of parts originating in the country of manufacture represents at least 50% of the ex-works price of the product.

The term **"ex-works price"** shall mean the price to be paid for the product obtained to the manufacturer in whose undertaking the last working or processing is carried out (this price shall not include internal taxes which are, or may be, repaid when such product is exported);

The term **"value acquired as a result of working and processing and incorporation of parts originating in the country of manufacture"** shall mean the increase in value resulting from the assembly itself, together with any preparatory, finishing and checking operations, and from the incorporation of any parts originating in the country where the operations in question were carried out, including profit and the general costs borne in that country as a result of the operations;

C. Primary Rules/Notes with regard to Column (3)

When Primary Rule/Note A above does not apply and the other primary rules contained in column (3) are not met in the last country of production, the following shall be applied in sequence:

(a) When the good is produced from materials or components that changed classification but did not satisfy the primary rule applicable to the good, the country of origin of the good is the country that furnished all or the major portion of that material or component.
(b) The following rules apply only to goods classifiable under provisions for "parts" or "parts and accessories" and which are not described by name in the Harmonized System, applied in sequence.
  (1) Goods produced by assembly of 5 or more parts(whether or not originating), other than parts provided for in rule A2(c)(3) shall have origin in the country of assembly.

(2) Goods produced as a result of processing nonoriginating components other than parts provided for in rule A2(c)(3) into a device or apparatus capable of performing one or more new mechanical or electrical functions shall have origin in the country of such processing.

(3) The following parts shall not be counted for purposes of rule A2(c)(1) nor shall the operations described be deemed to result in a new mechanical or electrical function for purposes of rule A2(c)(2):

   (i) the attachment of machinery to a base;

   (ii) the installation of machinery or apparatus into cabinets or similar encasements;

   (iii) the attachment of parts of general use as defined in Note 2 to Section XVI of the Harmonized System or similar parts of plastic (Chapter 39);

   (iv) the attachment of handles, dials, knobs, hand cranks, and other consumeroperated controls;

   (v) the attachment of a power cord or change of mains voltage/ frequency by adding transformer, adapter or converter;

   (vi) the installation of batteries, accumulators, sensors, thermostats or other articles not designed to become a permanent part of the good;

   (vii) the attachment of accessories or parts (including printed circuits with components assembled thereon), which serve only to enhance the operation of the machine or device;

   (viii) the addition of manuals, warranty cards, certificates of conformance to standards (with or without testing), or labels;

   (ix) washing, cleaning; removal of dust, oxide, oil, paint or other coverings;

   (x) simple painting and polishing operations;

   (xi) affixing or printing marks, labels, logos and other distinguishing signs on products or their packaging; or

   (xii) the installation of software.

D. Primary Rule applicable to Subheadings 8471.50, 8471.60, 8471.70 and 8471.80

For the purposes of subheadings 8471.50, 8471.60, 8471.70 and 8471.80, the assembly of goods of those subheadings in the same housing with units of other subheadings within that group shall be origin conferring.

E. Residual Rules/Notes for Chapters 84–90 applicable to rules contained in Column (3)

For purposes of Rule 1(e) of Appendix 2 the following residual rules shall be applied in sequence:

1. For goods classifiable under provisions for "parts" or "parts and accessories" and which are not described by name, the country of origin shall be the country of assembly provided the goods are produced by the assembly of two or more parts (other than parts of general use, as defined in Note 2 to

Section XV or similar parts of plastic (Chapter 39)), and one or more of the parts (other than parts of general use, as defined in Note 2 to Section XV or similar parts of plastic (Chapter 39)) satisfies the requirements for origin in the country of assembly. For purposes of this rule, the following parts shall not be counted nor shall the operations described be deemed to be origin conferring operations:

the attachment of machinery to a base;

the installation of machinery or apparatus into cabinets or similar encasements;

the attachment of parts of general use as defined in Note 2 to Section XV of the Harmonized System or similar parts of plastic (Chapter 39);

the attachment of handles, dials, knobs, hand cranks, and other consumer-operated controls;

the attachment of a power cord or change of mains voltage/frequency by adding transformer, adapter or converter;

the installation of batteries, accumulators, sensors, thermostats or other articles not designed to become a permanent part of the good;

the attachment of accessories or parts (including printed circuits with components assembled thereon), which serve only to enhance the operation of the machine or device;

the addition of manuals, warranty cards, certificates of conformance to standards (with or without testing), or labels;

washing, cleaning; removal of dust, oxide, oil, paint or other coverings;

simple painting and polishing operations;

affixing or printing marks, labels, logos and other distinguishing signs on products or their packaging; or

the installation of software.

2. When the good is produced from materials originating in a single country that did not undergo the change in classification or did not otherwise satisfy the primary rule applicable to the good, the country of origin is the country in which those materials originated;

3. The country of origin shall be the country of origin of that material (or functional element) that gives the good its essential character, to the extent to which the principle of essential character can be applied. Otherwise, the country of origin shall be the country in which the major portion of those materials originated, as determined on the basis of weight.]

Source: WTO (2009) G/RO/W/111/Rev.4

3
Merits and Demerits of Rules of Origin

ROO are used to determine the origin of goods that may enter a country under preferential treatment, i.e. they are used to establish whether the goods are eligible for special treatment under a regional trading arrangement between two or more participants. The main purpose is to ensure that the benefits of preferential tariff treatment are confined to only those products which have been harvested, grown, produced or manufactured in the exporting RTA member. Products that originate in third countries, i.e. the non-RTA members, and merely passing through, or undergo only a minor or superficial process in the signatory exporting country, are not entitled to any preferential benefit. Evolving an appropriate system of ROO is necessary in regional trading arrangements to fulfil various objectives. Unfortunately, there has not been any standard framework that could be used as a reference-point by the policy-makers in devising origin criteria in a regional grouping (Ratna & Ramanan 2005).

Having highlighted some of the conceptual issues in the preceding chapter, different modalities of ROO are critically evaluated in this chapter. These include a detailed examination of issues relating to wholly obtained and not wholly obtained products; merits and demerits of change in tariff classification test, percentage test and specific process test; cumulation; duty drawback rule; absorption test, tolerance test, neutral elements, interchangeable materials and minimal operations or the non-qualifying operations.

3.1 Different product classification under Rules of Origin

Depending upon the nature of inputs used in manufacture of a finished product that a country wants to export, the classification of export product is determined. A product is wholly obtained or manufactured in one country only when all the inputs have been used that were produced or originated in the exporting country, and thus according originating status is straight and simple. Problems arise if the product is produced in a country with the help of sourcing inputs not only domestically but also from other countries. In which case originating-status is conferred on the last country where "substantial transformation" took place. These issues concerning how a product would be classified according to either of these two categories mentioned above are discussed in detail below.

3.1.1   Wholly obtained or produced category

The primary products that are grown, explored or obtained locally or, in the case of manufactured product if it is produced from the inputs that are originating locally, they are classified as *"wholly obtained or produced"* in the exporting partner country. Under such a situation it is easier to establish the origin of the product. In such cases, the proof that the product was produced in the preferential trade partner is normally sufficient. If and when a product for export is wholly obtained or produced in a single country, no one can deny that this country is the country of origin. The criterion for classification of product is interpreted strictly. Even a minimal content of the imported materials, parts or components, or those inputs the origin of which cannot be determined, makes the finished products concerned lose their description of "wholly produced or obtained". Therefore, in all the FTAs/PTAs a list of *"wholly obtained or produced"* items is prescribed. Though there are slight variations in defining what constitutes wholly obtained or produced the broad principles remain the same in all agreements. A list of such products is given in Table 3.1.

From Table 3.1 it may be inferred that defining what constitutes "wholly obtained or produced" is easy and in many a cases there is lot of commonality. The major difference relates to the origin of fish caught in the EEZs. In some cases it is the registration and/or flagship that determines the origin, while in others it is either the EEZ territory of the RTA partner or the ownership of the ship or vessel in terms of equity holding. There is no uniformity on this issue and a similar position has even existed in the WTO where this issue is still being debated under the Harmonization Work Programme, as discussed in the previous chapter. There was an agreement among all Members that the origin of fish and other products taken from the territorial sea (not exceeding 12 nautical miles) of a country should be the coastal state. The outstanding

Table 3.1 Provisions relating to wholly obtained or produced category in different RTAs

Asia Pacific Trade Agreement	SAFTA	NAFTA: Article 415: definitions	EC GSP ROO: Article 68	ASEAN FTA	ASEAN – Republic of Korea FTA	ASEAN China FTA
(a) raw or mineral products extracted from its soil, its water or its seabeds; (b) agricultural products harvested there; (c) animals born and raised there; (d) products obtained from animals referred to in paragraph (c) above;	*Rule 5: Wholly produced or obtained* Within the meaning of Rule 4(a), the following shall be considered as wholly produced or obtained in the territory of the exporting Contracting State (a) raw or mineral products extracted from its soil, its water extending upto its	(a) mineral goods extracted in the territory of one or more of the Parties; (b) vegetable goods, as such goods are defined in the Harmonized System, harvested in the territory of one or more of the Parties; (c) live animals born and raised in the territory of one or more of the Parties; (d) goods obtained from hunting, trapping or fishing in the territory of one or more of the Parties;	(a) mineral products extracted from its soil or from its seabed; (b) vegetable products harvested there; (c) live animals born and raised there; (d) products from live animals raised there; (e) products obtained by hunting or fishing conducted there;	(a) Plant and plant products grown and harvested, picked or gathered there; (b) Live animals born and raised there; (c) Goods obtained from animals referred to in sub-paragraph (b) above; (d) Goods obtained from hunting,	(a) plants and plant products harvested, picked or gathered after being grown there; (b) live animals born and raised there; (c) goods obtained from live animals referred to in sub-paragraph (b); (d) goods obtained from hunting, trapping, fishing, aquaculture, gathering or capturing conducted there;	(a) Plant and plant products harvested, picked or gathered there; (b) Live animals born and raised there; (c) Product obtained from live animals referred to in paragraph (b) above; (d) Products obtained from hunting, trapping, fishing, aquaculture, gathering or capturing conducted there;

(*Continued*)

Table 3.1 Continued

Asia Pacific Trade Agreement	SAFTA	NAFTA: Article 415: definitions	EC GSP ROO: Article 68	ASEAN FTA	ASEAN – Republic of Korea FTA	ASEAN China FTA
(e) products obtained by hunting or fishing conducted there; (f) products of sea fishing and other marine products taken from the high seas by its vessels; (g) products processed and/or made on board its factory ships exclusively from products referred to in paragraph (f) above⁻	Exclusive EEZ or its sea bed extending up to its seabed or continental shelf; (b) Agriculture, vegetable and forestry products harvested there; (c) animals born and raised there; (d) products obtained from animals referred	(e) goods (fish, shellfish and other marine life) taken from the sea by vessels registered or recorded with a Party and flying its flag; (f) goods produced on board factory ships from the goods referred to in subparagraph (e) provided such factory ships are registered or recorded with that Party and fly its flag; (g) goods taken by a Party or a person of a Party from the seabed or beneath the seabed outside territorial waters, provided	(f) products of sea fishing and other products taken from the sea outside its territorial waters by its vessels; (g) products made on board its factory ships exclusively from the products referred to in (f); (h) used articles collected	trapping, fishing, aquaculture, gathering or capturing conducted there (e) Minerals and other naturally occurring substances, not included in subparagraphs (a) to (d), extracted or taken from its soil, waters, seabed or beneath its seabed;	(e) minerals and other naturally occurring substances, not included in subparagraphs (a) through (d), extracted or taken from its soil, waters, seabed or beneath its seabed; (f) products of sea-fishing taken by vessels registered with the Party and entitled to fly its flag, and other products taken by the Party or a person of that Party, from the waters, seabed	(e) Minerals and other naturally occurring substances, not included in paragraphs (a) to (d), extracted or taken from its soil, waters, seabed or beneath their seabed; (f) Products taken from the waters, seabed or beneath the seabed outside the territorial waters of that Party, provided that Party has the

(h) parts or raw materials recovered there from used articles which can no longer perform their original purpose nor are capable;

(i) used articles collected there which can no longer perform their original purpose there nor are capable of being restored or repaired and which are fit only for disposal or for the

to in clause (c) above;

(e) products obtained by hunting or fishing conducted there,

(f) products of sea fishing and other marine products from the high seas by its Vessels;

(g) products processed and/or made on board its factory ships exclusively from

that a Party has rights to exploit such seabed;

(h) goods taken from outer space, provided they are obtained by a Party or a person of a Party and not processed in a non-Party;

i. waste and scrap derived from

ii. production in the territory of one or more of the Parties, or

iii. used goods collected in the territory of one or more of the Parties, provided such goods are fit only for the recovery of raw materials; and

(i) (i) goods produced in the territory

there fit only for the recovery of raw materials;

(i) waste and scrap resulting from manufacturing operations conducted there;

(j) products extracted from the seabed or below the seabed which is situated outside its territorial waters but where it has exclusive exploitation rights;

(f) Products of sea-fishing taken by vessels registered with a Member State and entitled to fly its flag and other products1 taken from the waters, the seabed or waters, seabed and beneath the seabed in accordance with international law3;

(g) Products of sea-fishing and other marine products taken from

or beneath the seabed outside the territorial waters of exploit1 the natural resources of such waters, seabed and beneath the seabed under international law2;

(g) products of sea-fishing and other marine products taken from the high seas by vessels registered with a Party or entitled to fly the flag of that Party;

(h) goods produced and/or made on board factory ships

rights to exploit such waters, seabed and beneath the seabed in accordance with international law;

(g) Products of sea fishing and other marine products taken from the high seas by vessels registered with a Party or entitled to fly the flag of that Party;

(h) Products processed and/or made on board factory ships registered with a Party or entitled

(Continued)

Table 3.1 Continued

Asia Pacific Trade Agreement	SAFTA	NAFTA: Article 415: definitions	EC GSP ROO: Article 68	ASEAN FTA	ASEAN – Republic of Korea FTA	ASEAN China FTA
recovery of parts or raw materials; (j) waste and scrap resulting from manu-facturing operations conducted there; (k) goods produced there exclusively from the products referred to in paragraph(a) to (j) above.	products referred to in clause (f) above; (h) raw materials recovered from used articles collected there; (i) waste and scrap resulting from manu-facturing operations conducted there; (j) products taken from the seabed, ocean	of one or more of the Parties exclusively from goods referred to in subparagraphs (a) through (i), or from their derivatives, at any stage of production;	there exclusively from products specified in (a) to (j). 2. The terms 'its vessels' and 'its factory ships' in paragraph 1(f) and (g) shall apply only to vessels and factory ships: – which are registered or recorded in the beneficiary country or in a Member State,	the high seas2 by vessels registered with a Member State and entitled to fly the flag of that Member State; (h) Products processed and/or made on board factory ships registered with a Member State and entitled to fly the flag	registered with a Party and entitled to fly its flag, exclusively from products referred to in subparagraph (g); (i) goods taken from outer space provided that they are obtained by the Party or a person of that Party; (j) articles collected from there which can no longer perform their original purpose nor are capable of being restored	to fly the flag of that Party, exclusively from products referred to in paragraph (g) above; (i) Articles collected there which can no longer perform their original purpose nor are capable of being restored or repaired and are fit only for disposal or recovery of parts of raw materials, or for recycling

floor or subsoil thereof beyond the limits of national jurisdiction, provided it has the exclusive rights to exploit that sea bed, ocean floor or subsoil thereof;

(k) goods produced there exclusively from the products referred to in clauses (a) to (j) above.

– which sail under the flag of a beneficiary country or of a Member State,

– which are at least 50% owned by nationals of the beneficiary country or of Member States or by a company having its head office in that country or in one of those Member States, of which the manager or managers, Chairman of

of that Member State, exclusively from products referred to in sub-paragraph (g) above;

(i) Articles collected there which can no longer perform their original purpose nor are capable of being restored or repaired and are fit only for disposal or recovery of parts of raw

or repaired and are fit only for the disposal or recovery of parts of raw materials, or for recycling purposes;

(k) waste and scrap derived from:
(i) production there; or
(ii) used goods collected there, provided that such goods are fit only for the recovery of raw materials; and

purposes[4]; and

(j) Goods obtained or produced in a Party solely from products referred to in paragraphs (a) to (i) above.

(Continued)

Table 3.1 (Continued)

Asia Pacific Trade Agreement	SAFTA	NAFTA: Article 415: definitions	EC GSP ROO: Article 68	ASEAN FTA	ASEAN – Republic of Korea FTA	ASEAN China FTA
			the Board of Directors or of the Supervisory Board, and the majority of the members of such boards are nationals of that beneficiary country or of the Member States and of which, in addition, in the case of companies, at least half the capital belongs to that beneficiary country or to the	materials, or forrecy- cling purposes; (j) Waste and scrap derived from: (i) produc- tion there; or (ii) used goods col- lected there, pro- vided that such goods are fit only for the recovery	(l) goods obtained or produced in the territory of the Party solely from goods referred to in sub-paragraphs (a) through (k).	1 Plant here refers to all plant life, including fruit, flowers, vegetables, trees, seaweed, fungi and live plants 2 Animals referred to in paragraph (b) and (c) covers all animal life, including mammals, birds, fish, crustaceans, molluscs, reptiles, bacteria and viruses. 3 Products refer to those obtained from live animals without further processing,

1 Includes mineral fuels, lubricants and related materials as well as mineral or metal ores.

2 "Vessels" shall refer to fishing vessels engaged in commercial fishing, registered in the country of the Contracting State and operated by a citizen or citizens of the Contracting State or partnership, corporation or association, duly registered in such country, at least 60 per cent of equity of which is owned by a citizen or citizens and/or Government of such Contracting State or 75% by citizens and/or Governments of the Contracting States. However, the products taken from vessels, engaged in commercial fishing under Bilateral Agreements which provide for chartering/leasing of such vessels Member States or to public bodies or nationals of that beneficiary country or of the Member States,

– of which the master and officers are nationals of the beneficiary country or of the Member States, and

– of which at least 75% of the crew are nationals of the beneficiary country or of the Member States.

3. The terms «beneficiary country» and «Community» shall also cover the territorial waters of that country or of the Member States 1 "other products" refers to minerals and other naturally occurring substances extracted from the waters, seabed

4. Vessels operating on the high seas, including factory ships on which the fish caught is worked or processed, shall be considered as part of the territory of the beneficiary country or of the Member State to which they belong, provided that they satisfy

of raw materials; and

(k) Goods obtained or produced in a Member State from products referred to in sub-paragraphs (a) to (j).

1 The Parties understand that for the purposes of determining the origin of products of sea-fishing and other products, "rights" in sub-paragraph (f) of Rule 3 include those rights of access to the fisheries resources of a coastal state, as accruing from agreements or other arrangements concluded between a Party and the coastal state at the level of governments or duly authorised private entities.

including milk, eggs, natural honey, hair, wool, semen and dung.

4 This would cover all scrap and waste including scrap and waste resulting from manufacturing or processing operations or consumption in the same country, scrap machinery, discarded packaging and all products that can no longer perform the purpose for which they were produced and are fit only for discarding or for the recovery of raw

(Continued)

Table 3.1 Continued

Asia Pacific Trade Agreement	SAFTA	NAFTA: Article 415: definitions	EC GSP ROO: Article 68	ASEAN FTA	ASEAN – Republic of Korea FTA	ASEAN China FTA
	and/or sharing of catch between Contracting State will also be eligible for preferential treatment. 3 In respect of vessels or factory ships operated by Government agencies, the requirements of flying the flag of the Contracting State do not apply. 4 For the purpose of this Agreement, the term "factory ship" means any vessel, as defined used for processing and/or making on board products exclusively from those products referred to in clause (f) of Rule 6.		the conditions set out in paragraph 2or beneath the seabed outside the territorial waters. 2 For products of sea-fishing obtained from outside the territorial waters (e.g. Exclusive Economic Zone), originating status would be conferred to that Member State with whom the vessels used to obtain such products are registered with and whose flag is flown in the said vessel, and provided that Member State has the rights to exploit it under inter-national law. 3 in accor-dance with international law, registration of ves-sels could only be made in one Member State.		2 "International law" in sub-paragraph (f) of Rule 3 refers to generally accepted international law such as the United Nations Convention on the Law of the Sea	materials. Such manufacturing or processing operations shall include all types of processing, not only industrial or chemical but also mining, agriculture, construction, refining, incineration and sewage treatment operations.

Source: Authors' compilation from different RTAs.

question concerns the origin of fish and other products taken from the EEZ (not exceeding 200 nautical miles). The WTO Members are divided on this issue as highlighted in the context of PROO in the previous chapter. One view relates to conferring origin to the country whose flag the vessel is flying. The other view is to confer origin to products of sea-fishing and other products taken within the territorial sea and/or EEZ of a coastal state, to be considered as wholly obtained in that coastal state. There is no consensus on this issue and even in RTAs there are different formulations that exist depending on which countries are partners there.

3.1.2 Not wholly obtained or produced category

It has been discussed earlier in this chapter that determining the origin of "wholly obtained or produced" category of product is easy and simple, however, determining the country of origin of a products is difficult due to globalization of economic activities, the trend of outsourcing, and the use of a mix of inputs supplied by many foreign countries and of domestic origin. Therefore, for such cases a general term of *"not wholly produced or obtained"* is used. In these cases, the ROO define the methods by which it can be ascertained that the particular product has undergone *sufficient working* or process or has been subject to a *substantial transformation* (in general these terms can be used interchangeably) in the territory of another member of the FTA or PTA and that it has not simply been trans-shipped from a non-qualifying country or been subject to only minimal processing. Unfortunately, there are no simple and standard ROO that can be identified as performing the role of preventing trade deflection. A number of different rules are available, each of which can have different implications for a producer of a given product. Three main methods used for *"not wholly obtained or produced"* to establish if sufficient processing or substantial transformation has been undertaken are:

  (i) change of tariff classification;
 (ii) value addition;
(iii) specific manufacturing process.

3.1.2.1 Change of tariff classification

Under this criterion, origin is granted if the exported product falls into a tariff classification that is different from the tariff classification of any imported inputs that are used in its production.

This approach is used in a majority of current preferential trade agreements and features in both EU agreements and the NAFTA. Application of this approach has been facilitated by the widespread adoption of the HS. There is, however, the issue of the level of the classification at which change is required. Most agreements specify that the change should take place at the tariff heading level (that is at the 4-digit level known as CTH).

3.1.2.1.1 Change-in-tariff-heading (CTH) test. The CTH test is applied to determine if there is a change at the first 4-digit HS numbers between the non-originating inputs (includes imported as well as undermined origin inputs) and the finished export product. If the change takes place then it qualifies for being considered as originating. The CTH test is a straightforward method, which is easy to implement. As Vermulst (1992) puts it, "The advantages of the CTH test are its conceptual simplicity, its ease of application and its lack of discretion. Furthermore, the adoption by most countries of the HS means that a similarly applied CTH test will normally lead to uniform determination of origin in such countries." This test is widely used in various preferential schemes, precisely because it can overcome many of the problems associated with the percentage criterion such as bias in favour of high cost production and its susceptibility to changing world prices.

However, this rule alone might not be sufficient for conferring originating status as the HS codes were devised primarily for the purposes of commodity classification and collection of statistical data and not for origin determination purposes. It is generally realised that in the following two circumstances this rule might not serve its purpose. First, when change in tariff heading is not sufficient to confer origin. In such cases application of certain specified processes or domestic/import content requirements becomes necessary. Secondly, when certain processing operations are by themselves sufficient enough to confer origin even if the tariff heading of the final product does not change as compared to the tariff headings of its constituents.

Another problem associated with this rule is in terms of the level of commodity classification/aggregation at which this rule should be applied such that any change in commodity code is treated as substantial transformation. The EC considers HS classification at 4-digit level whereas US-Canada FTA allows determination to be made at all levels of disaggregation (Stephenson and James, 1995). The level of aggregation has a bearing on the restrictiveness of this rule. The following observation made by Palmeter as cited in Hoekman (1993) illustrates this point: "The Canada–US Free Trade Agreement requires change at the chapter level of the Harmonized System to confer origin. All dairy products are included within a single chapter. Consequently, the origin of manufactured dairy products such as cheese will always be the country in which the milk was produced, regardless of where the cheese was made."

In fact, many products at HS 4-digit level would not receive originating status if the CTH rule alone is applied. For instance, sweetened cocoa powder is classified as HS 1806.10 but all sweetened cocoa based-products are classified as HS 1806.2 to 1806.9. Therefore, in this case no change in tariff heading would occur at HS 4-digit level despite the fact that value addition takes place. Similarly, manufacturing coffee substitutes, fruit juices and transforming imported sodium nitrate into fertilizer cannot receive originating status under the CTH rule if applied at HS 4-digit level.

3.1.2.1.2 Change-in-tariff-subheading (CTSH) test. The CTSH test is applied to determine if there is a change at the first 6-digit HS numbers between the non-originating inputs (includes imported as well as undermined origin inputs) and the finished, i.e. export product change to this split heading from any other split of this heading or from any other heading. If the change takes place then it qualifies for being considered as originating. CTSH test is much liberal and less onerous than the CTH test.

3.1.2.1.3 CTH and CTSH: substitutes or complements? Under the tariff-shift approach, origin is granted if the exported product falls into a different part of the tariff classification to any imported inputs that are used in its production. This approach is used in the vast majority of current preferential trade agreements and features in both EU agreements and the NAFTA. The WTO (2002) shows that of 87 FTAs and other preferential trade agreements investigated, 83 used change of tariff classification in the determination of origin. This "tariff-shift" method is also the basis of the efforts by the WCO to harmonize non-preferential rules of origin and as such brings a degree of consistency to the world trading system. Application of this approach has been facilitated by the widespread adoption of the HS. There is, however, the issue of the level of the classification at which change is required. Most agreements specify that the change should take place at the heading level (that is at the 4-digit level).

However, the HS was not designed as a vehicle for conferring origin, its purpose being to provide a unified commodity classification for defining tariff schedules and for the collection of statistics. Thus, in particular cases it can be argued that change of tariff heading will not identify sufficient processing whilst in other cases it can be that substantial transformation can occur without change of tariff heading. As a result, in many agreements there is a different rule for different products. For example, in the NAFTA whilst around 40 per cent of tariff lines require change of tariff heading for most tariff lines (54 per cent) it is change of chapter (2-digit level) that is required Estevadeordal *et al.* (2003). The requirement of change of chapter is more restrictive than change of heading. For a small number of products in the NAFTA it is only change of sub-heading that is required.

Thus, whilst in principle the change of tariff classification could provide for a simple uniform method of determining origin in practice instead of a general rule there are many individual rules and as such the determination of the ROO can be influenced by domestic industries in a way that reduces the impact on competition of preferential trade agreements. Nevertheless, the change of tariff classification rule, once defined, is clear, unambiguous and easy for traders and manufacturers to learn. It is *relatively* straightforward to implement. In terms of documentary requirements it requires that traders keep records that show the tariff classification of the final product and all the imported inputs.

Thus, the change of tariff classification is best applied as a general rule, for example by requiring change of tariff heading for all products, and a positive determination of origin. This is generally not the case and further whilst change of tariff heading is used in the majority of preferential trading agreements it is seldom the only method applied. In many agreements, including those involving the EU and the US, change of tariff classification is applied to some products whilst the other methods described below will be applied to other products. This typically leads to considerable complication in the determination of origin in preferential agreements. Further, for certain products rules will be stipulated that require satisfaction of more than one method to confer origin. In some agreements for some products two or more methods will be stipulated and satisfaction of any one of the methods will be sufficient to confer origin.

3.1.2.1.4 Economic rationale for CTH vis-à-vis CTSH. The CTH rule enforces bilateral cumulation within a bilateral FTA and enhances bilateral trade. To illustrate, if a partner country fulfils the maximum of its raw material requirements through imports and technically the final product qualifies for a CTSH rules, by stipulating a CTH rule would imply that the partner country necessarily imports its material from its other RTA partner so as to qualify for preference under the bilateral cumulation provision. However, in the case of CTSH rule such possibilities would be limited.

The CTH rule also ensures in the partner country the usage of a particular kind of technology whereby the raw materials have to be necessarily sourced from other HS 4-digit level classifications. In such a situation CTH safeguards national economic interests given the state of technology in different sectors of our country.

The application of the CTH rule also ensures certain minimum amount of local value addition in that country. Not all manufacturers in other countries produced the final product from basic raw material as different manufacturers are at different stages of production. Thus, CTH can ensure local value addition for granting originating status to products and extending tariff preferences. In the case of CTSH such value addition possibilities might be compromised. It may be mentioned, that in the case where only the percentage test is applied the accuracy of value addition is not guaranteed because of the likelihood of accounting manipulations.

ROO influence both import patterns and export prospects. If they are too stringent they may provide import protection but also damage export prospects and if they are too liberal the converse may be true. Both the identification of products for the CTSH rule as well as treating them as derogations, become extremely relevant dimensions for the trade dynamics of a country.

3.1.2.2 Value added

As a general rule, under the percentage criterion, imported inputs (i.e. materials, parts, and components) are considered to have undergone substantial transformation if a given percentage of value is added to the imported inputs used for manufacture of the finished product.

This requirement can be defined in two ways either:

(a) by providing the minimum percentage of the value of the product (on free on board [FOB] value or ex-factory price/cost) that must be added in the exporting country (*direct method of calculation*), or
(b) by providing the maximum percentage of non-originating inputs to be used in manufacturing the exported product (*indirect method of calculation*).

In practice, it is the latter that is more commonly used in several agreements. However, this method also has certain limitations as the value added content would change depending on several factors like exchange rate fluctuations, inefficient manufacturing processes, etc.

For the calculation of value added, different agreements use different methods of treating the "profit" of local trader. While in some agreements this is taken into account, in cases of others it is not. This issue has always been a bone of contention of various negotiations for RTAs.

3.1.2.2.1 Percentage test. The percentage criterion is applied in three forms. First, through an *'import-content stipulation'*, which sets a maximum allowable limit of imports expressed in terms of percentage of imported parts and materials *vis-à-vis* total requirements of parts and materials. Secondly, through a *'domestic-content-requirement'* whereby a minimum percentage of total value-added should be necessarily achieved with the help of domestically obtained inputs. And thirdly, through a *'value-of-parts test'*, which examines whether the originating parts reach a certain percentage of the total value of parts. As has been stated earlier the percentage criteria are not foolproof methods for conferring origin.

Each of these forms stipulates that a certain percentage of value-added in the country of last manufacturing, obtained with the help of local inputs, is necessary for getting originating status to a product. It is quite obvious that either we calculate import content or the domestic content we arrive at the same result. However, in practice this might not always be the case. This is due to the fact that in order to arrive at a percentage, different definitions of both the denominator and numerator are used under different preferential schemes.

I Calculation of value added
Import content requirement equals to:

$$\frac{\text{Value of imported non-RTA partner materials, parts or produce} + \text{Value of undetermined, origin materials parts or produce}}{\text{FOB Price}} \times 100\% \leq X\%$$

II Calculation of value added
Domestic content requirement equals to:

$$\frac{\text{RTA partner material cost} + \text{Direct labour cost} + \text{Direct overhead cost} + \text{Other cost} + \text{Profit}}{\text{FOB Price}} \times 100\% \geq X\%$$

The domestic content requirement is calculated with varying methods in different RTAs. To illustrate, the formula of calculation in India's RTAs is given above and the details are in Box 3.1.

It has been pointed out by Vermulst (1992) for the purposes of calculations, if total cost plus profits give the sales price and import content is obtained by adding the FOB or cost, insurance and freight (CIF) cost of all non-originating materials, the ratio of the import-content to sales price would be the reference value for the percentage test. Similarly, the domestic content could be obtained by deducting the cost of non-originating materials from sales price or by adding up all the domestic cost components. This could be used to calculate the percentage of domestic content in sales price. Theoretically, the two calculations of import content and domestic content should yield the same results. Yet, in practice it might not be so. If the import-content rule is applied the two calculations give the same results as in the case

Box 3.1 Method of calculation of domestic content

1. FOB price:
   a. **FOB price** = ex-factory price + other costs
   b. **Other costs** in the calculation of the FOB price shall refer to the costs incurred in placing the products in the ship for export, including but not limited to, domestic transport costs, storage and warehousing, port handling, brokerage fees, service charges, etc.

2. Formula for ex-factory price:
   a. **Ex-factory price** = production cost + profit
   b. Formula for production cost,
      i. **Production cost** = **cost of raw materials** + labour cost + overhead cost
      ii. **Raw materials** shall consist of:
         • Cost of raw materials
         • Freight and insurance
      iii. **Labour cost** shall include:
         • Wages
         • Remuneration
         • Other employee benefits associated with the manufacturing process

(*Continued*)

Box 3.1 Continued

iv. **Overhead costs**, (non-exhaustive list) shall include, but not limited to:
  - real property items associated with the production process (insurance, factory rent and leasing, depreciation on buildings, repair and maintenance, taxes, interests on mortgage)
  - leasing of and interest payments for plant and equipment
  - factory security
  - insurance (plant, equipment and materials used in the manufacture of the goods)
  - utilities (energy, electricity, water and other utilities directly attributable to the production of the good)
  - research, development, design and engineering
  - dies, moulds, tooling and the depreciation, maintenance and repair of plant and equipment
  - royalties or licenses (in connection with patented machines or processes used in the manufacture of the good or the right to manufacture the good)
  - inspection and testing of materials and the goods
  - storage and handling in the factory
  - disposal of recyclable wastes
  - cost elements in computing the value of raw materials, i.e. port and clearance charges and import duties paid for dutiable component

Source: Authors' summary based on India's RTAs.

of Canadian and Japanese GSP rules and the EC's preferential rules. For instance, a 30 per cent import content rule implies 70 per cent domestic content and the two calculations match. However, in the case of US preferential and Australian GSP rule and EC, Australian and Canadian non-preferential rules the domestic-content rule is adhered to and in the case of US and Australian GSP schemes and Australian and Canadian non-preferential rules, "... not all domestic content is considered relevant ...". For instance, the US domestic content excludes selling, general and administrative (SGA) expenses and profit. The US preferential domestic content (numerator) calculations concentrate mainly on the value of originating materials and direct costs of processing rather than basing the calculations on the point at which products leave the factory.

Again with regard to import content (the numerator), it has been pointed out, "... the question arises as to at what level imported, non-originating parts ought to be valued, that is in ascending order: ex-works, free on board (FOB), cost, insurance and freight (CIF) or into-factory (delivered). The answer to this question is consequential because each subsequent level leads to a higher price and thereby makes satisfaction of the import/domestic-content test more difficult". It needs to be highlighted that the US considers the FOB level; the EC, Australia, Canada and Japan consider the CIF value and in the case of value-of-parts test the EC has valued non-originating (and originating) parts on an into-factory basis. Therefore, due to different definitions of numerator (that is domestic content and import content), the two results differ.

With regard to the denominator, the sales price is not used in a uniform manner across preferential schemes. Different preferential schemes use it with certain adjustments made, depending on the terms and conditions of sale. For instance, the EC uses ex-works price whereas the Japanese GSP uses FOB export price that is ex-works price plus the cost of inland freight and handling costs.

In the case of the US, the denominator is a kind of price at exportation. The price at exportation is defined as either the appraised value at importation or the FOB value. The price at exportation in US is determined by including local selling, general and administrative expenses and profits (although these are not counted in domestic content calculations). The CIF costs are not included. It is important to highlight that the appraised value is determined by the US Customs Service, which only implies that it is not always possible for foreign exporters to assess *a priori* whether they would be able to meet the requirements of the domestic-content rule.

Another major lacuna in the percentage criterion has been in the nature of bias that exists against low cost and efficient production systems in a particular country. It is easier for a particular exporter in a country to satisfy the percentage criterion if its domestic costs of operation are high due to certain inefficiencies, say, inefficiency in resource use. Similarly, a bias against a production base, which is marked with low labour costs, is also intrinsic to the percentage test.

Moreover, a producer's ability to conform to percentage criterion depends on the nature of fluctuations in world prices of materials. Therefore, given the percentage criterion in one year producers might be able to export but in a subsequent year they might fail in exporting the same product (Vermulst, 1992).

3.1.2.3 Specific manufacturing process

This rule defines certain manufacturing or processing operations that a product must undergo in the exporting country to confer origin (positive test) or manufacturing or processing procedures that do not confer origin (negative test).

The formulation of these rules can require the use of certain originating inputs or prohibit the use of certain non-originating inputs. Rules based upon specific manufacturing processes are widely used often in conjunction with change of tariff classification and/or the value added criterion, and are a particular feature of the rules applied to the textiles and clothing sectors.

This test is widely used in the United States in its non-preferential and preferential trading as well as by the EC. Although the merit of this test lies in its capacity to deal with the specifics of a particular production process yet laying down separate tests for all products is costly and burdensome.

For instance, in the EU NPROO for T-shirts (HS 6109), the origin is supposed to be in the country where the *complete making-up* was done. It poses problems for monitoring as well.

3.1.2.4 Product specific rules

This rule defines the origin criteria for a product at 6- or 8-digit HS level by using any one or a combination of different criteria.

The PSR serve a dual purpose: they can either be more liberal than the general rule to allow imports at a more relaxed criteria or they can be stringent so as to make it impossible to allow any preferential imports, thereby bringing that product in the *de facto* exclusion list.

The obvious question that follows is why ROO are so important as to have such a strong bearing on the outcome of international trade negotiations. The answer perhaps lies in the conceptual ambiguity that envelopes this policy instrument in developing countries. Whether or not a product has originated in a particular country is decided if the product has undergone substantial transformation. There are three major ways of determining this: first, the change in tariff-heading test, implying that the tariff heading of the final product is different from the tariff-headings of its inputs. Secondly, a percentage test is applied, according to which a minimum percentage of total value addition should be achieved with the help of domestic inputs. Finally, specified process tests require a product to undergo certain stipulated processes. In addition, these rules are applied in conjunction with non-qualifying operations whereby certain processes do not confer origin to a product.

However, agreement on implementing these tests is often difficult. For instance, the extent of 'substantial transformation' for different products would depend on the level of disaggregation (i.e. HS 4- or 6-digit level) on which tariff-shift is envisaged. Similarly, fixing of percentages of minimum value addition varies between products, depending on the prevailing labour costs and the product-specific import dependence of the country in terms of intermediates (Das, 2004b).

3.2 Trade-off between trade creation and trade deflection: assessment of different tests

An assessment can be made to correlate the three tests that have been discussed earlier *vis-à-vis* trade creation and trade deflection. In this context the analysis of Stephenson and James (1995) as displayed in Figure 3.1 is relevant. According to which, there is a trade-off between the objectives of trade creation and preventing trade deflection through different tests of ROO. This trade-off is the least in the case of CTH and followed by process test and percentage test. This has its own implications for the developmental role of different ROO tests and vindicates the analysis presented in the previous chapter. In other words, this conclusion is in consonance with our new approach towards the ROO Development Index (RDI).

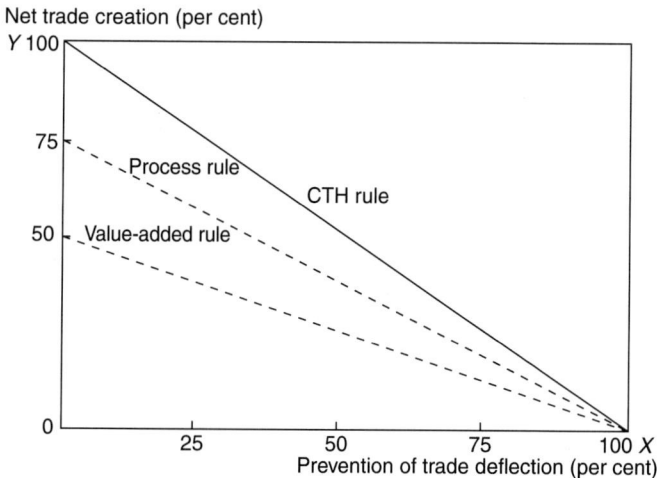

Source: Stephenson and James (1995).
Figure 3.1 Trade-off between net trade creation and prevention of trade deflection in an RTA with differing ROO.

The upshot of the foregoing discussion is that ROO are implemented rigorously in different preferential trading schemes. But they differ quite significantly in terms of their modalities. It has been also noticed that each modality has its own merits and demerits but the change in tariff heading test is the most transparent and objective one as compared to the other tests. However, in several instances it needs to be supplemented with the percentage test and specific process test.

3.3   Other dimensions of Rules of Origin

There are several other typical features of the ROO of preferential trade schemes, which can influence whether or not origin is conferred on a product and hence determine the impact of the scheme on trade flows. These are cumulation, tolerance rules and absorption. The treatment of duty drawback and of outward processing outside of the free trade or preferential trade partners can also be important. Some of these are dealt explained below.

3.3.1   Cumulation

Cumulation is an instrument allowing producers to import materials from a specific country or regional group of countries without undermining the origin of the product. In effect the imported materials from the identified countries are treated as being of domestic origin of the country requesting preferential access. There are three types of cumulation, bilateral, diagonal and full (Box 3.2).

The most basic form is bilateral cumulation, which applies to materials provided by either of two partners of a preferential trade agreement. Secondly, there can be *diagonal cumulation* on a regional basis whereby parts and materials from anywhere in the specified region that qualify as originating can be used in the manufacture of a final product, which can then be exported with preferences to the partner country market. Finally, there can be *full cumulation* whereby any processing activities carried out in any participating country in a regional group can be counted as qualifying content regardless of whether the processing is sufficient to confer originating status to the materials themselves.

To increase the intra-regional trade and facilitate the sourcing patterns within the region, in the context of a PTA, the concept of cumulation plays a crucial part in ROO schemes. It extends the possibility to use low cost sources of inputs without compromising the originating status of a final product by allowing to include intermediate products and operations to count originating for the final product even when they

Box 3.2 Cumulation: an illustration

In case of *Partial or Diagonal Cumulation*, only those parts and materials from any member country of PTA/FTA which qualify as originating, if used in the manufacture of a final product in member country would be accounted for calculation of value addition under regional cumulation. Such materials which are non-originating would be discarded for calculation of regional cumulation. If the finished product is then exported to other partner country market the final product will enjoy preferential market access based on these calculations. (*The bottom line being that only such materials would be taken into account for calculating value addition under cumulation which are "originating" as per the RoO. Materials which are "non- originating" will not be accounted for*). (*Case I of Scenario II*).

In case of *Full Cumulation*, any processing activities carried out in any participating country in a regional grouping can be counted as qualifying content regardless of whether the processing is sufficient to confer originating status to the materials themselves or not. (*Therefore any value addition ranging from 1–49% done in RTA partner country would be accounted under full cumulation.*) (*Case II of Scenario I*).

Source: ibid.

are not produced in the own country. The possible extent of cumulation depends on the applied rules:

3.3.1.1 Bilateral cumulation

Bilateral cumulation operates between two countries and allows producers in either partner country to use materials and components *originating* in the other's country as if they originated in their own country.

3.3.1.2 Diagonal cumulation

Diagonal cumulation operates between more than two countries and allows producers to use materials and components *originating* in either country that is part of the agreement. In one form this is an extension of bilateral cumulation by extending it to the regional level.

Diagonal / partial cumulation by requiring more stages of production and/or higher value added to be undertaken in the lower cost country may make it more difficult for the products produced by outsourcing to qualify for preferential access.

3.3.1.3   Full cumulation

Full cumulation takes into account all of the operations conducted within the countries who are members to an agreement – even if they are carried out on non-originating material. Thus, there is no more restriction to only use originating materials and components for the final good. Full cumulation allows for more fragmentation of production processes among the members of the regional group and so stimulates increased economic linkages and trade within the region. Under full cumulation it may be easier for more developed higher labour cost countries to outsource labour intensive low-tech production stages to less developed lower wage partners whilst maintaining the preferential status of the good produced in low-cost locations.

There are generally three ways of determining the cost of a product for calculating the regional value content.

- The Ex-Factory Cost includes overheads costs, labour costs and raw materials cost.
- The Ex-Factory Price includes overheads costs, labour costs, raw materials cost and *profit*.
- The FOB price includes overheads costs, labour costs, raw materials cost, *profit and costs of inland transportation*.

Figures 3.2 and 3.3 illustrate the Global System of Trade Preferences (GSTP) Participating States A, B and C engaging in such an activity. Country B (GSTP-B) sources the raw materials from GSTP-A for manufacturing a finished product and then exports it to GSTP-C. Whether preferential access would be available in GSTP-C or not would depend on the nature of cumulation, i.e. whether partial or full.

Scenario I : Material meets ROO criteria (partial or full cumulation - same treatment)

GSTP-A	GSTP-B	GSTP-C
$12	$8	$25
(Input A = 50% VA)	(Design, printing and coating) (100%)	(Final product)

If the qualifying value addition criteria is 50% (current GSTP norm)
Figure 3.2   All or nothing approach (I).

Scenario II: Material does not meet ROO criteria

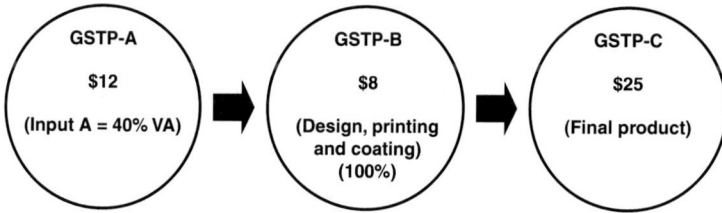

Figure 3.3 All or nothing approach (II).

GSTP Regional Content = $12 (since product is originating in GSTP A)
+ $8 / $25 = 80%

Product qualifies for preference (originating) as the value addition due to cumulation is 80% against prescribed value addition of 50%

Case I – **If Partial Cumulation is applied:**

GSTP Regional Content = $0(since material is non-originating in GSTP A as the value addition is 40% only) + $8 / $25 = 32%

PRODUCT DOES NOT QUALIFY FOR PREFERENCE (NON-ORIGINATING)

Case II – **If Full Cumulation is applied:**

GSTP Regional content = 40% of 12 ($4.8 in country GSTP A) + $8 (value addition in country GSTP B) = 4.8 + 8/25 = 12.8/25 = 51.2% and therefore the good would qualify for preference.

Source: ibid.

One important issue that has been noticed in the case of determining origin of a product under the cumulation provision, especially regarding Asia, relates to the minimal value added criteria in the exporting country. In the SAARC preferential Trading Agreement (SAPTA) or SAFTA it can be seen that the overall regional value added under the cumulation provision is 10 percentage points higher than the single country obligation. In the case of regional cumulation the agreement prescribes that the aggregate regional content from all the members should be at least 50 per cent with a minimum of 20 per cent value added coming from the final exporting country. A similar provision exists in India Sri Lanka FTA where under the regional cumulation an overall value added of 35 per cent is prescribed with a minimum of 25 per cent coming from the exporting country. This means that the other country is allowed to have a value addition of only 10 per cent under the regional cumulation. In the case of ASEAN FTA, there is no such obligation on the final exporting country to have a minimal valued added. In the case of ASEAN a total of 40 per cent value added is required. Having such a provision of cumulation like ASEAN is better able to facilitate a better intra-regional trade and integration of industries (without being dislocated to other RTA partner) than the one in SAFTA. The individual country obligation of 20 per cent sometimes may be very difficult to achieve and even if a product has a regional content of more than 50 per cent it may not qualify for preferences.

There are other related issues that are also addressed in the ROO. They relate to their definition and treatment, some of which are discussed below.

3.3.2   Duty drawback

The term drawback means refunding duties paid on imported goods when they are further exported to third countries. The "no drawback" provision was provided to prohibit this, e.g. in the case when intermediate non-preferential goods are imported to undergo further processing and then are exported as final goods under preferential access to third countries. This rule ensures that duties applicable to third country materials are paid to protect certain industries within a free trade area.

This rule makes it mandatory for the exporting countries to allow repayment of duties on non-originating inputs that are used in the production of a final product as drawback refund if the final product is exported to a free trade or preferential trade partner. Some agreements contain explicit no-drawback rules that will affect decisions relating to the sourcing of inputs by firms exporting within the trade area and will reduce the previous incentives towards the use of imported inputs from non-participating countries towards the use of originating inputs from participating countries. In almost all the bilateral agreements the EC has with its trade partners, this provision is invoked.

3.3.3   Tolerance or de *minimis*

Such rules allow a certain percentage of non-originating materials to be used without affecting the origin of the final product. It should be noted that this rule applies to the CTH and the specific manufacturing rules but does not affect the value added rules. Thus, the tolerance rule can act to make it easier for products with non-originating inputs to qualify for preferences under the CTH and specific manufacturing process rules.

3.3.4   Absorption principle

This provides that parts or materials that have acquired originating status by satisfying the relevant ROO for that product can be treated as being of domestic origin in any further processing and transformation. In other words, any non-originating materials are no longer taken into account when assessing the nature of further operations. This is of particular relevance to the value-added test. For example, in the production of a particular part origin is conferred if imported materials constitute 20 per cent of the final price of the part and are less than the maximum 30 per cent import content ROO. This part will then be treated as 100 per cent originating when incorporated into a final product. The 20 per cent import content of the part is not taken into account when assessing the import content of the final product. The converse of this is that if the part does not satisfy the relevant ROO then it is deemed to be 100 per cent non-originating.

3.3.5 Neutral elements

'Neutral elements' refer to such factors of production as plant and equipment, fuel, machinery and other elements whose origin is not to be taken into account in determining the origin of the product. While in some ROO it is explicitly mentioned, in others a definition or how to treat them is silent. However, in both the cases the net result is the same. Irrespective of their origin, they are accounted for the local value addition.

3.3.6 Interchangeable materials

The ROO also provide for how to treat the interchangeable materials as in some cases it is not commercially practical to keep separate stocks of interchangeable materials originating in different countries. It is provided that the country of origin of each of the commingled materials may be allocated on the basis of an inventory management method recognized in the country in which the materials or goods were commingled.

3.3.7 Minimal or non-qualifying operations

Since the basic objective of ROO is to prevent trade deflection or trans-shipment of goods from non-RTA partners, the ROO identify certain operations or process through which the origin of a product cannot be conferred even if other conditions of the ROO are met. They are designed with the objectives that such operations have nothing to do with the actual manufacturing process of that product nor do they alter the basic nature of a product. Such operations relate to packaging and repackaging, disassembly and assembly products, marketing labelling, etc. An illustrative list of such operations is given in (Boxes 3.3–3.7):

Box 3.3 Minimal or non-qualifying operations: Asia Pacific Trade Agreement (APTA)

(i) Operations to ensure the preservation of products in good condition either for transportation or storage (ventilation, spreading out, drying, chilling, placing in salt, sulphur dioxide or other aqueous solutions, removal of damaged parts, and like operations);
(ii) Simple operations consisting of removal of dust, sifting or screening, sorting, classifying, matching (including the making-up of sets of articles), washing, painting, cutting up;
(iii) Changes of packaging and breaking up and assembly of consignments;
(iv) Simple slicing, cutting or repacking or placing in bottles, flasks, bags, boxes, fixing on cards or boards, etc.
(v) The affixing of marks, labels or other like distinguishing signs on products or their packaging;
(vi) Simple mixing;
(vii) Simple assembly of parts of products to constitute a complete product;
(viii) Slaughter of animals;
(ix) Peeling, unflaking, grain removing and removal of bones; and
(x) A combination of two or more operations specified above.

Source: (APTA).

Box 3.4 Minimal or non-qualifying operations: Japan GSP

The following minimal processes are not accepted as obtaining origin status:

1. Operations to ensure the preservation of products in good condition during transport and storage (drying, freezing, placing in salt water and other similar operations);
2. Simple cutting or screening;
3. Simple placing in bottles, boxes and other similar packing cases;
4. Repacking, sorting or classifying;
5. Marking or affixing of marks, labels or other distinguishing signs on products or their packaging;
6. Simple mixing of non-originating products;
7. Simple assembly of parts of non-originating products;
8. Simple making-up of sets of articles of non-originating products;
9. A combination of two or more operations specified in 1–8.

Box 3.5 Minimal or non-qualifying operations: EC GSP

Article 70

1. Without prejudice to paragraph 2, the following operations shall be considered as insufficient working or processing to confer the status of originating products, whether or not the requirements of Article 69 are satisfied:

   (a) preserving operations to ensure that the products remain in good condition during transport and storage;

   (b) breaking-up and assembly of packages;

   (c) washing, cleaning; removal of dust, oxide, oil, paint or other coverings;

   (d) ironing or pressing of textiles;

   (e) simple painting and polishing operations;

   (f) husking, partial or total milling, polishing and glazing of cereals and rice;

   (G) operations to colour sugar or form sugar lumps; partial or total milling of sugar;

   (h) peeling, stoning and shelling, of fruits, nuts and vegetables;

   (i) sharpening, simple grinding or simple cutting;

   (j) sifting, screening, sorting, classifying, grading, matching; (including the making-up of sets of articles);

   (k) simple placing in bottles, cans, flasks, bags, cases, boxes, fixing on cards or boards and all other simple packaging operations;

   (l) affixing or printing marks, labels, logos and other like distinguishing signs on products or their packaging;

   (m) simple mixing of products, whether or not of different kinds, where one or more components of the mixtures do not meet the conditions laid down in this section to enable them to be considered as originating in a beneficiary country or in the Community;

   (n) simple assembly of parts of articles to constitute a complete article or disassembly of products into parts;

   (o) a combination of two or more of the operations specified in points (a) to (n);

   (p) slaughter of animals.

2. All the operations carried out in either a beneficiary country or the Community on a given product shall be considered together when determining whether the working or processing undergone by that product is to be regarded as insufficient within the meaning of paragraph 1.

Box 3.6 Minimal or non-qualifying operations: ASEAN CEPT

Article 6: Minimal operations and processes

1. Operations or processes undertaken, by themselves or in combination with each other for the purposes listed below, are considered to be minimal and shall not be taken into account in determining whether a good has been originating in one Member State:
   (a) ensuring preservation of goods in good condition for the purposes of transport or storage;
   (b) facilitating shipment or transportation;
   (c) packaging or presenting goods for sale.

2. A good originating in the territory of a Member State shall retain its initial originating status, when exported from another Member State, where operations undertaken have not gone beyond those referred to in paragraph 1.

Box 3.7 Minimal or non-qualifying operations: SAFTA

Rule 7: Non-qualifying Operations

The following shall in any event be considered as insufficient working or processing to confer the status of originating products, whether or not there is a change of heading:

1. operations to ensure the preservation of products in good condition during transport and storage (ventilation, spreading out, drying, chilling, placing in salt, Sulphur dioxide or other aqueous solutions, removal of damaged parts, and like operations).

2. simple operations consisting of removal of dust, sifting or screening, sorting, classifying, matching (including the making-up of sets of articles), washing, painting, cutting up;

3. (i) changes of packing and breaking up and assembly of consignments,
   (ii) simple slicing, cutting and repacking or placing in bottles, flasks, bags, boxes, fixing on cards or boards, etc., and all other simple packing operations.

4. the affixing of marks, labels or other like distinguishing signs on products of their packaging;

(*Continued*)

Box 3.7 Continued

5. simple mixing of products, whether or not of different kinds, where one or more components of the mixture do not meet the conditions laid down in these rules to enable them to be considered as originating products; and mere dilution with water or another substance that does not materially alter the characteristics of the product;

6. simple assembly of parts of products to constitute a complete product;

7. a combination of two or more operations specified in (1) to (6);

(*Source*: ibid.)

It can be seen from the above descriptions that in each RTA the intentions of the members are not to forgo any tariff on the transhipment of products or a minimal processing so as to transform the size, shape or packing, etc. of the product that is imported. While issues like transportation, packaging or repackaging, prevention of products, etc. have been prescribed in almost all the agreements there are differences on the other operations. Again, on all such issues, there is no common minimal processes across the agreements and the processes have been prescribed by looking into the export interest of the member countries in any RTA. Most of the agreements prescribe that even if these operations are performed together (more than two operations) the origin will not be conferred. In certain cases, if two or more operations are performed together they may lead to substantial transformation, however, in certain agreements despite having achieved the CTC or value added test the product will not be treated as originating if they have been achieved through these minimal operations. In the agreements there is nothing that explicitly mentions about how the value added contribution from these operations will be treated. However, the fact remains that even these operations would entail some value added in the country where these operations have been performed. Given the nature of the calculation to determine the total value added in the exporting country, the component of value added relating to these minimal operations are taken into account. Therefore, though these operations do not confer origin, the value added generated during such operations are taken into account for determining the origin of the product. This is one of the lacunae in those agreements. A general summary of

Table 3.2 Merits and demerits of different ROO

Rule	Merits	Demerits	Policy dilemmas
CTC*	• Promotes value addition, checks trade deflection and enhances mutual trade. • Simple, clear and transparent. • Easy to implement. • Entails less administrative cost	• It fails to confer origin in several cases as the HS was not designed for granting originating status • On occasions, change in tariff classification does not ensure substantial transformation • Sometimes substantial transformation can occur without CTC • Over a medium or long term due to change in technology, the processing methods change and hence the CTC also undergoes change	• Level of classification at which change required: higher the level the more restrictive is the rule • How to combine other rules when CTC fails • Ambiguity in several processes that cannot be captured by this rule
Percentage test	• Promotes value addition, checks trade deflection and enhances mutual trade. • If defined in terms of maximum import content, it can also be implemented easily. • Good complement for cases where CTC fails.	• Complex in application – requires firms to have sophisticated accounting systems. • Difficult to monitor at customs entry points • Sensitive to changes in exchange rates, labour costs, input prices, etc. • High administrative costs of implementation • Prone to accounting manipulations	• The level of value added required to confer origin • The valuation method for imported materials – methods which assign a higher value (e.g. CIF) than ex-factory price will be more restrictive on the use of imported inputs • Calculation of value addition subject to malpractices
Specific process test	• Promotes value addition, checks trade deflection and enhances mutual trade. • Straightforward. • Provides for certainty if rules can be complied with	• Implementation problems due to documentary requirements • Difficult to comply with. • Leads to product specific rules. • Depends on technology, which differs from sector to sector.	• Difficulty in pinning down formulation of the specific processes: the more procedures required the more restrictive. • Should test be negative (processes or inputs which cannot be used) or a positive test (what can be used) – negative test more restrictive.

Notes: *CTC means change in tariff classification at different levels disaggregation of HS nomenclature for instance CTH (change in tariff classification at HS 4-digit level), CTSH (change in tariff sub-heading is at HS 6-digit level) and CC (change in tariff heading at HS chapter level).
Source: Authors' compilation (see also Brenton, 2003a and Vermulst, 1994).

the merits and demerits of rules of origin is given as an Appendix to this chapter.

3.4 Harmonisation of Preferential Rules of Origin

As is evident from the earlier discussions, each RTA has devised its own ROO though presumably for meeting the same objectives. So far there has not been any standard framework that could be used as a reference-point by the policy-makers in devising origin criteria in a regional grouping. The issue of ROO assumes special importance in the context of assessing their merits and demerits as it would be expected that through harmonization of ROO their efficacy would only improve.

Given the above background, one would have serious thoughts if harmonization of PROO were possible? To answer this question, the common elements of PROO would need to be considered. At the same time the differences need to be examined. While it may not be a difficult to attempt harmonization of the common elements, it may be difficult, if not impossible, to harmonize such elements where differences exist. Overcoming these differences may be difficult as each member of RTA would have different objectives for framing such rules and in some cases there could be conflicting interests.

On the one hand, it is not uncommon for a single country to apply several sets of rules, depending on to which RTA the country belongs. For instance, certain types of goods produced in Mexico, both a NAFTA member and a partner in the EU–Mexico agreement, may be subject to two rather different origin determination mechanisms depending on whether they are shipped to North America or Europe, although the Mexican Authorities have made sure that similar principles are applied in the context of both RTAs (see also the next point). For RTA members a question arises is whether expected benefits from preferential access in other partners' markets will outweigh the inconvenience. Related production and sourcing decisions by companies already established or considering to invest in participating countries may vary accordingly. Viewed from the perspective of RTA participants the proliferation and overlap of differing systems of ROO is perhaps less a problem of systemic incompatibility than of increased transaction costs for involved traders.

On the other hand, it appears that the same basic mechanisms or criteria are used by all RTAs, although in varying combinations. As RTAs proliferate, a small number of models, initially formulated by major trading partners such as the US or the EU, are replicated in the new agreements concluded between them and third countries. Cumulation initiatives further expand the coverage of these models and promote harmonisation among participants. Most of Europe now benefits from the effects of the European cumulation area and similar benefits with respect to preferential access should probably be expected in the Americas once the FTAA process is concluded.

From the perspective of non-participating countries the stakes are obviously different than for participating countries. Although the increased transaction costs arising from the proliferation of ROO affect third country traders too, for them there is the added question of the more or less restrictive character of the rules in discouraging external sourcing. Most RTA members make sure that RTA provisions, including ROO, are appropriately published and publicly disseminated. If, however, such rules are not sufficiently transparent or predictable they can represent a trade barrier in their own right. This may also be the case if their discretionary character is subject to protectionist capture. Moreover, where the ROO allow minimal or no third country inputs (as is often the case with respect to sensitive sectors), producers in RTA members have a strong incentive to avoid such inputs so as to preserve the preferential status of their own products. In this case third country supplies are not simply denied the preferential access provided for by the RTA, in practice they often lose access altogether. In addition to the resulting diversion of trade flows, this situation may provide a considerable incentive for potential investors to establish within the RTA region, rather than at its periphery. Third country inputs may be widely allowed in several sectors among those covered by RTAs. For instance, in the context of NAFTA, printed circuits assemblies for magnetic tape recorders and other sound recording apparatus have to be produced in the NAFTA region but third country inputs can be used without limitation for their production. It is mainly with respect to sensitive sectors, like textiles and clothing, agricultural or automotive products where the comparison of RTA schemes with the situation that would have prevailed without them leads to concerns about protectionist capture. Often these sectors have been left out of the agreements altogether. In other cases, although detailed product-specific rules have been introduced in order to bring transparency and predictability and reduce the capture potential of more discretionary methods of determination, protectionist interests may have found their way into the texts at the drafting stage and thus been consolidated and "institutionalised" through this incorporation. The stringency of special sectoral rules ensures that third country inputs have very restricted access to the market, especially inputs of a higher value or level of processing. Sometimes the complexity of these rules is such that it may be difficult even for products from the beneficiary countries to qualify.

Although it appears that RTA preferential systems contain more restrictive rules than non-preferential systems adopted domestically by the Parties to an RTA, it is not clear that domestic preferential schemes, such as the GSP schemes, are less restrictive than comparable RTA schemes. Indeed, it has been argued that the potential advantage of such domestic preferential schemes is seriously curtailed by the complication of applicable rules of origin and the difficulty in qualifying under those rules. There seems therefore to be an increase in complexity when moving from non-preferential to preferential schemes, be they regional or domestic (OECD, 2002).

In this regard, an encouraging example relates to the recent consolidation of bilateral trade agreements among the Southern European countries and a replacement by the common rules as part of an amended Central European Free Trade Agreement (CEFTA) deal. The new CEFTA consolidates 32 bilateral free trade agreements into a single regional trade agreement. The free trade area shall be established in a transitional period ending at the latest on 31 December 2010. New consolidated agreement replaces the complexity of bilateral free trade agreements to improve conditions to promote trade and investment by means of fair, clear, stable and predictable rules.

Before making any attempt for harmonizing the PROO, the following negotiations that are taking place would need to be looked at closely:

(i) ASEAN apart from having its own AFTA now has bilateral FTAs with China and Korea and is negotiating bilateral FTAs with India, Australia and New Zealand. A Working Group is examining possibility of having comprehensive agreement for ASEAN + 6 FTA.

(ii) The APTA has Bangladesh, China, India, Korea, Sri Lanka and Lao PDR as its members and to that effect it is one of the largest RTAs in terms of market size in this region. Attempts are on to enlarge its membership, especially towards Central Asia. It would be worth mentioning that in the APTA (earlier known as Bangkok Agreement) each member was earlier free to maintain its own ROO for grant of tariff preference. An effort was made to harmonize and adopt a common ROO during the Third Round negotiations. The ESCAP Secretariat facilitated the discussions in the Standing Committee and prepared the draft template of common ROO. Negotiations were held on the text. Finally, a consensus was reached on common

ROO that are relatively simple, transparent general and liberal, i.e. a flat rate of a minimum 45 per cent of local value content (35 per cent for least developed countries).

As has been stated earlier, having a closer look at the ROO for these RTAs, it can be easily identified that broader commonality is found on several elements of these ROO and it would be easier to attempt harmonizing these elements (Ratna, 2007). They are:

   (i) General definitions;
  (ii) List of wholly obtained or produced goods;
 (iii) Insufficient or minimal operations or processes that do not confer origin;
 (iv) Neutral elements;
  (v) Consignment criteria;
 (vi) Certificate of origin;
(vii) Denial of preferential tariff treatment;
(viii) Claim for preferential tariff treatment;
 (ix) Administrative arrangements relating to issuance and verification of Certificate of Origin, etc.

It can be noted that there are very little differences regarding the elements listed above and any attempt to harmonize them would yield the desired result. Given the diverse treatments that are specified in different agreements, the following elements would require greater understanding and lengthy discussions relating to harmonization:

  (i) Qualifying criteria for not-wholly obtained or produced goods;
 (ii) Cumulation;
(iii) No drawback rule;
(iv) Treatment of profits by local traders; and
 (v) PSR.

In this entire exercise, the most difficult task would be to relate to harmonization of PSR. On the PSRs one would need to learn lesson from the WTO Harmonization Work Programme. Hence, instead of an overly ambitious harmonization programme, a more realistic approach needs to be taken. In the context of RTAs, it would be desirable to keep the ROO simple, easier to implement and transparent and preferably without any PSRs. Therefore, it would be desirable to follow one single set of general rule as qualifying criteria for the not-wholly obtained or produced goods.

Thanks to the series of multilateral trade negotiations for trade liberalization under the auspices of GATT/WTO, the average tariffs are now much lower. However, the lack of uniformity in ROO would cause unnecessary delay and cost, not only to the customs authorities but also to business and trading communities. This situation must be changed. The establishment of a single set of ROO brings about a number of benefits to public and private sectors. It will certainly reduce the time and costs required thus facilitating trade. It will equally contribute to the international trading system by strengthening certainty, predictability, and consistency of origin determination. It will also reduce number of trade dispute cases by implementing a single set of origin rules.

It would be further important to understand that while harmonization is important, the final result should not be too cumbersome or burdening. Any attempt for Harmonized PROO should not lose sight of the following objectives:

(i) *Trade deflection/circumvention*: The basic objective of the harmonized rules should be to prevent trade deflection. It should also be framed in such a manner that it facilitates and creates trade among the members.

(ii) *Simple*: The harmonized rules should be simple to operate and easy to follow. They should be transparent and predictable.

(iii) *Cost*: For effective and improved market access it is necessary that the rules are made such that the cost of proving the origin of product for procuring the Certificate of Origin is not high. Such burden will have a greater impact on the small and medium enterprises, as a higher cost will nullify their market access margins.

(iv) *Cumulation*: The cumulation rule be made such that it allows greater integration among RTA members and facilitates intraregional trade and investment flows.

(v) *Trade facilitation*: Complex ROO place a greater burden on customs procedures that may compromise progress on trade facilitation. The process of verification be also made simpler as the cost/burden of proof lies with the producer.

(vi) *Sensitivity*: Restrictive ROO targeted at sensitive products are not an effective mechanism for protecting domestic industry. Therefore, ROO should not be devised in a manner that has been formulated for nullifying the tariff concessions.

(vii) *PSR*: The most difficult task will be the harmonization of PSR. Therefore, in the Harmonized Rules the PSRs should be avoided.

(viii) *S&D*: ROO should be devised by taking into account the differential levels of development of the ESCAP members.

3.5 Implementation issues

There are some other crucial dimensions of implementing ROO that would help maximize their merits and minimize their demerits. Some of these are explored below.

3.5.1 Penalties and surveillance

Whenever there is any infringement of any rule or circumvention of ROO, an argument is put forth that the rules need to be modified or dispensed with. It must be highlighted that violation of a particular rule need not necessarily be a poor reflection on the rule per se. Any circumvention of even a well-formulated rule could be a reflection on the enforcement of the particular rule. In this case it is important to note that the roles played by the exporter, importer, and agencies that issue the certificate of origin and the customs are crucial. In most of the cases of circumvention the possible liability vests with these entities. In fact, in NAFTA such cases are dealt with by imposing heavy penalties (Box 3.8). This aspect has so far not received adequate attention, especially in the RTAs of the developing

Box 3.8 Customs steps up NAFTA enforcement

Customs has increased the profile of its enforcement activities under NAFTA. In a notice posted to its web site, Customs makes clear that it views NAFTA enforcement as a priority.

Under NAFTA, goods that meet stringent rules of origin to qualify as "North American" (i.e., Canadian or Mexican) are entitled to duty-free or reduced duty entry into the United States. These rules may require that raw materials or parts undergo a qualifying change in tariff classification, that there be a specified level of value added in North America or both. In addition, the importer must have a signed Certificate of Origin at the time it claims NAFTA benefits.

Box 3.8 Continued

In its notice, Customs identifies trans-shipment as an illegal means of circumventing the ROO. Trans-shipment occurs when non-North American products are sent to Canada or Mexico and then, on importation to the United States, improperly claimed to be originating. These and other means of making false or invalid NAFTA claims may result in substantial penalties to the importer. Customs notes that a recent investigation led to a civil penalty of more than $500,000.

Importers making NAFTA claims should understand the rules of origin and ensure that the NAFTA procedures suppliers and brokers apply to its entries are consistent with the rules and regulations. Where violations are suspected, the importer should seek expert professional advice to determine whether the circumstances warrant a prior disclosure to customs. Importers should also be aware that Customs is actively looking for confidential informants who may have information relating to NAFTA and other customs violations. Thus, internal compliance controls over NAFTA and other customs processes are increasingly important.

Source: http://www.barnesrichardson.com/news/overview.aspx?NewsID= 320910105

countries. It is recognized, however, that the developing countries are coming to terms with such a situation and in some of the recently concluded RTAs in the Asian region such instruments are being made part of the ROO.

3.5.2 Software

One of the biggest challenges that the developing countries face to tackle the problem of circumvention of the ROO relate to their lack of hardware and software capability as well as poor infrastructure. Therefore, it is imperative that these countries attempt implementing various factes of trade facilitating infrastructure relating to the rules of origin through the capacity-building, information and technology – focussing on the hardware side, and computer-aided issuance, monitoring and surveillance software systems.

However, the abovementioned trade facilitating component of ROO will be determined by the capacity of an exporter to manage, store and properly utilize the key data required for compliant origin determination, including classification, the applicable rules of origin, the bill of material (including costs) as well as the ability of the certificate issuing agencies to handle such needs are critical to maintaining a competent, credible and efficient system.

Furthermore, it is immensely important to enhance the requisite competencies of the customs agencies to successfully intervene in cases of such circumvention. This would only be possible if the customs is equally equipped with the hardware and software requisites and is connected with the certifying agencies. For this to happen, especially in the developing countries the customs officials would need a reorientation from the conventional ways of only looking at customs valuation, seizures and revenue collection to devising adequate means for checking instances of circumvention. They also need to be well-versed with different dimensions of ROO, including its developmental dimension. For this, tailor-made capacity-building programmes need to be organized.

This chapter has made an assessment of different dimensions of ROO by dwelling upon different product classifications under rules of origin in terms of wholly obtained and not-wholly obtained products. Within the broad ambit of not-wholly obtained products, the merits and demerits of different tests are analysed that include the change in tariff classification test, percentage test and specific manufacturing test. This chapter presents a detailed new analysis of a comparison between CTH and sub-heading tests. It also brings out the trade-off that exists between trade creation and trade deflection in applying different tests. Furthermore, various other crucial issues pertaining to rules of origin like the cumulation, duty drawback, *de minimis*, minimal operations, etc. are also analysed. Finally, the chapter explores some of the important implementation issues, including rules of origin harmonisation across RTAs.

4
Rules of Origin as Practised in Different RTAs

Having dealt with the merits and demerits of ROO, in this chapter we document and analyse in a comparative framework, wherever possible, ROO as practised in different RTAs, both reciprocal and unilateral. This chapter also highlights illustratively some sectoral approaches to ROO in various RTAs.

Before analysing some of the major RTAs and ROO provisions in them, it would be important to provide an overview of the ROO criteria applied there under. As the issues are very complex it is imperative to entangle them. Let us first examine how the different tests vary across different RTAs and which tests have been used more frequently to determine the origin criteria of products. This would give an idea as to how different countries have tried to meet the objectives of ROO in their RTAs. This would help in finding whether the criteria applied are coherent across the agreements. Such an exploration would also help us know as to which criterion is relatively seen as more important than the others to achieve the objectives of ROO.

In this regard, it would be important to understand how the different tests like CTH, CTSH, value added, specific process, cumulation provisions, etc. have been used in the RTAs that are in place. This is only possible through empirically counting and tabulating the frequency of use of origin criteria in different RTAs. Such an exercise has been undertaken by WTO (2002), the highlights of which are presented in Box 4.1.

It clearly emerges that out of the three criteria used, it is the CTH method that has been the most commonly used. Additional noteworthy feature relates to fact that generally at least two methods have been used with equal importance. In the European agreements generally all the three methods have been used. In case where the percentage criteria has been used, the import content method is much more frequent than the

115

116

Box 4.1 Overview of ROO Tests in RTAs

As can be seen from Table 1, all the three methods for conferring origin are widely used in RTAs, with the CTH method being the most common one, present in 89 of the 93 RTAs examined. Another salient feature is that normally, at least two methods for conferring origin coexist at similar levels of importance, working as complementary methods. In the case of European agreements, all the three methods coexist. That pragmatic approach seems to be a response to the shortcomings inherent to each particular method, as explained previously. While the CTH and percentage methods are generally spread across all HS Chapters, the technical test (TT) applies more in relation to industrial products, including textiles.

Table 1 Frequency of Various General Criteria and Tolerance Rules

RTAs	CTH	Percentage				TT	Tolerance Rule
		Total	MC	DC	VP		
Customs unions (6)	6	2	2 (40–60%)	2 (35–60%)	–	–	3
FTAs and other preferential RTAs (87)	83	75	68 (60–30%)	7 (60–25%)	67	74	85

A common feature of all RTAs using the CTH method is that the substantial transformation operates at the HS heading level (i.e. 4 digit). However, also common to all the RTAs using that method is that in specific cases the CTH rule allows the use of materials classified under the same heading of the customs nomenclature (a "soft" CTH test); in many instances, that exception is either subject to limitations on the maximum value of those materials or to a change of tariff classification at the level of HS sub-headings. In the case of NAFTA and similar agreements, the change in tariff classification may also specify a change in tariff classification at the level of HS chapters.

With regards to the percentage criteria, the import content method is much more frequent than the domestic content method in the universe of RTAs surveyed here, due to the fact that the PANEURO is based on it. The value of parts test is used only in agreements involving European countries. On average, it could be said that a threshold

Box 4.1 Continued

on domestic content varying from 40–60 per cent tends to be normal, as well as its equivalent of 60-40 per cent on import content. Among these, it is worth noting the more liberal rules of origin requirements found in the Canada-Chile FTA – domestic content of 25–35 per cent depending on the method used for calculation – and in the Common Market for Eastern and Southern Africa (COMESA) – 35 per cent domestic content. As shown in Chart 1, the case of the Canada-Chile FTA stands out as containing particularly low regional content thresholds among the four "NAFTA-like" agreements.

The technical test criterion is used as a general method for conferring origin in a majority of the RTAs surveyed (74 out of 93), in particular in the most recently concluded ones. This method is widely used in sectors such as textiles and chemicals and in all the cases analysed, positive tests are used – with the exception of minimal operations which do not confer origin. In some cases, the substantial transformation requirements are such that, in addition to the fulfilment of other basic criteria, three RTAs also require that the last process of manufacture takes place in one of the RTA parties.

Table 2 presents a synthesis of the different types of *cumulation provisions* which are present in the 93 RTAs considered in this survey. All of them provide for bilateral cumulation. The frequency of diagonal cumulation is relatively high, in particular in RTAs involving European countries (given that the PANEURO uses diagonal cumulation). Full cumulation is a rare feature in RTAs (only in eight cases); again, it appears mainly in RTAs involving European countries (six RTAs).

Apart from the PANEURO, diagonal cumulation also exists in a number of RTAs: those between the EC and the Maghreb countries (cumulation among Tunisia, Morocco and Algeria), the Overseas Countries and Territories (OCTs) and South Africa (in both cases cumulation with ACP countries); between the European Free Trade Association States (EFTA) and Morocco (cumulation with Tunisia once its agreement with EFTA will be concluded); between Estonia and Ukraine (cumulation with Latvia, Lithuania

(*Continued*)

Box 4.1 Continued

and the EC); and between Canada and Israel (cumulation with the United States) – the only RTA providing for diagonal cumulation which does not involve a European country.

Table 2   Frequency of Cumulation Provisions

RTAs	Type of Cumulation			Absorption Principle	Tracing Test
	Bilateral	Diagonal	Full		
Customs unions (6)	6	0	0	2	–
FTAs and other preferential RTAs (87)	87	58	8	81	8

In some of the cases analysed (eight RTAs), cumulation provisions are accompanied by restrictions. In two cases (EC–Algeria and EC–OCTs), the restriction relates to the fact that the diagonal cumulation is non-reciprocal and the inputs from eligible third-parties cannot be cumulated with EC products. Other restrictions identified consist of:

i. setting a maximum value to the cumulation (United States–Israel FTA, in which bilateral cumulation is allowed only up to a maximum of 15 per cent of the value of the final product);

ii. fixing a minimum value for the transformation once cumulation applies (the South Pacific Regional Trade and Economic Cooperation Agreement, SPARTECA, in which products from the South Pacific Islands which cumulate with Australia's inputs and are exported into New Zealand have to have a minimum of 25 per cent of South-Pacific-Island content); or

iii. modifying the general criteria for the rules of origin (in four NAFTA-model RTAs, whereby if bilateral cumulation is used, the calculation of the regional value content of the good can only be made on the basis of the net cost method, and not under the transaction value method).

Source: WTO (2002).

domestic content method as found in the above survey with the general threshold on domestic content varying from 40–60 per cent. In most of the cases the technical test criterion is used as a general method especially for the sectors of textiles and chemicals. As per the survey, bilateral cumulation has been present in these RTAs with the frequency of diagonal cumulation being relatively high.

After having referred to an overview of ROO provisions in different RTAs, we now move on to examine the ROO in cases of some important agreements.

4.1   Generalized System of Preferences (GSP)

The GSP is a unilateral tariff preference scheme offered by developed countries to eligible products originating in designated developing countries. The GSP ROO have played a key role in implementing the GSP schemes for more than 35 years (UNCTAD 1999). As an agreement on Rules of Origin at UNCTAD in 1970 remains as guidelines, the prospective preference-giving countries took appropriate domestic actions to implement their ROO, taking fully into account the agreement. After the 35-year operation of the GSP system, the basic structure of ROO remains the same (UNCTAD 1970) (Box 4.2).

However, GSP ROO in each scheme differ substantially from one scheme to another. For example, the GSP schemes of the EFTA, the EU,

Box 4.2 Main elements in GSP ROO

A. Origin Criteria
    (i) List of wholly produced goods
    (ii) List of minimal processes that do not confer the country of origin
    (iii) Process criterion
    (iii) Percentage criterion

B. Direct Consignment

C. Documentary Evidence
    (i) Combined declaration and certificate of origin
    (ii) Consignment of a small value
    (iii) Verification of Form A
    (iv) Exhibition and fairs

D. Sanctions

E. Mutual Cooperation between Preference-giving and Preference-receiving Countries

F. Special Facilities in Favor of Preference-receiving Countries
    (i) Cumulative Rules of Origin (cumulation)
    (ii) Donor country content rule

Source: UNCTAD.

Box 4.3 Some important GSP ROO

1. European Union
   Goods whose production involved more than one country shall be deemed to originate in the country where they underwent their last, substantial, economically justified processing or working in an undertaking equipped for that purpose, and resulting in the manufacture of a new product or representing an important stage of manufacture. This basic concept is interpreted into process criterion, percentage criterion, or combination of these two criteria in determining the country of origin.

2. Japan
   The country of origin is given to the country where the last substantial process or operation resulting in the manufacture of new characteristics took place. Japan has a shortlist of PSR on selected products.

3. United States
   In the case of GSP Rules of Origin, the US applies the percentage criterion. The cost or value of materials produced in the preference-receiving country and the cost or value of any article incorporated in the eligible article that has resulted from substantial transformation of any imported materials into a new and different article of commerce, plus the direct cost of processing operations performed in the preference-receiving country must not be less than 35% of the appraised value of the merchandise in the US. In short, a minimum 35% local content rule is observed.

Source: Ujiie, Teruo (2006).

and Japan use the process criterion (EU and Japan use a percentage criterion for certain products, such as processed foods, chemicals, and machinery) while those of Australia, Canada, New Zealand, and US use the percentage criterion. Each scheme uses different definitions and requirements, as can be seen in the Box 4.3.

4.2   Asia–Pacific RTAs

In the case of Asia, there are several FTAs in operation and a number of bilateral or regional FTA negotiations are being held. One of the important FTAs in Asia is AFTA among the 10 ASEAN Members. The origin criterion under ASEAN FTA is solely based on the 40 per cent domestic content rule, supported by the regional cumulation among 10 member states of ASEAN. On the other hand, while ASEAN–China FTA prescribes 40 per cent value added as the qualifying criterion, in case of ASEAN–Korea FTA it is CTH or 40 per cent value added criterion. In case of PTAs in the region, while the APTA prescribes for 45 per cent value addition only, the SAPTA prescribes for 40 per cent value addition.

Origin criterion under the Singapore–Australia FTA is based on the 50 per cent domestic content rule. The Singapore–New Zealand follows the 40 per cent domestic content rule. The Singapore–US FTA mainly follows the ROO under NAFTA. While NAFTA origin rules are comprehensive, specific, and detailed, its origin criteria include (i) CTH (either at 4-, 6-, or 8-digit level depending on goods produced) for a number of products; (ii) substantial process (assemble process plus manufacture of major part) for colour televisions and other products (iii) assemble process plus percentage criterion (e.g. 50 per cent domestic content) for watch movements and others; (iv) manufacture of major part plus percentage criterion for footwear and other products; or (v) percentage criterion for automobiles (USTR 2006).

The India–Sri Lanka FTA signed in December, 1998 is considered to be serving as a model for bilateral FTAs, as there is an application of twin criteria, i.e. CTH + 35 per cent value addition to confer origin status. Similarly, in India–Nepal (CTH + 30 per cent), India–Thailand Early Harvest Scheme (CTH + 40 per cent), India–Singapore (CTH + 40 per cent) and SAFTA (CTH + 40 per cent for India, Pakistan, 35 per cent for Sri Lanka and 30 per cent% for LDC members), the twin criteria has been applied.

The heterogeneous nature of such ROOs that are applied in different RTAs could be seen from the Table 4.1.

It can be observed that almost every combination has been used; different qualifying criteria overlap each other and use different cumulation schemes. These cases clearly imply that more, different rules will appear in the near future, creating not only more administrative costs for both public and private sector but also more burden especially for the newcomers entering various markets. This is a major concern among the manufacturing and trading communities.

The complexity of these systems is further increased by the mutual overlapping of trade agreements, making the sourcing process for companies even more complex. For instance, a company that manufactures a product in Singapore has to fulfil different ROO criteria when it wants to export these goods to ASEAN or Japan. Due to different thresholds in

Table 4.1 ROO criteria in different RTAs

RTAs	Type	Qualifying riteria	Cumulation
AFTA	Regional	– Value content needs to be at least 40% – FOB value calculation basis	– Full
ANZCERTA	Regional	– Value content needs to be at least 50% – Factory cost calculation basis	– Bilateral (Full)
APTA	Regional	– Value content needs to be at least 45% (35% for LDCs) – Ex-factory price calculation basis	– Full
China–ASEAN	Regional	– Value content needs to be at least 40% – Elimination of the duty rates for products under the HS Chapter 07 and 08 (vegetables and fruits) which originate in the Party of the Agreement	– Regional
India–Nepal	Bilateral	– Change in Tariff heading (4-digit level) and – Value content needs to be at least 30%	– Bilateral
India–Sri Lanka	Bilateral	– Change in Tariff heading (4-digit level) and – Value content needs to be at least 35% – FOB value calculation basis	– Bilateral
SAFTA	Regional	– CTH – Value content needs to be at least 40% (for India & Pakistan), 35% for Sri Lanka and 30% for LDCs – FOB. value calculation basis	– Diagonal
SAPTA	Regional	– Value content needs to be at least 40% (30% for goods of LDCs) – FOB value calculation basis	– Diagonal
Singapore–Australia	Bilateral	– Value content needs to be at least 50% (Product specific rule: 30%) – Factory cost calculation basis	– Bilateral
Singapore–Japan	Bilateral	– Either CTC (4-digit level) or – Value content needs to be at least 60% – FOB value calculation basis	– Bilateral
Singapore–New Zealand (ANZSCEP)	Bilateral	– Value content needs to be at least 40% – Ex factory cost calculation basis	– Bilateral

123

Table 4.1 Continued

RTAs	Type	Qualifying riteria	Cumulation
Singapore–USA	Bilateral	– Either CTH (2-, 4- or 6-digit level) or/and (for specific products): – Value content needs to be at least 30–60% – *Highly product specific*	– Bilateral
SPARTECA	Regional	– Value content needs to be at least 50% – Factory cost calculation basis – Non-reciprocal	– Bilateral (Full)
Thailand–Australia	Bilateral	– Product specific CTH (4- or 6-digit level) and/or (for specific products): – Value content percentage of 40–55% – FOB calculation basis	– Bilateral
USA–Australia	Bilateral	– CTH (2-,4- or 6-dDigit level) and/or (for specific products): – Value content needs to be at least 35% (Automotive: 50% net cost) – FOB calculation basis	– Bilateral

Source: Ratna (2006).

Table 4.2 South Asian FTA commitments in ROO

FTA / PTA	ROO		
A. Intra-South Asian FTAs	**Bilateral**	**SAFTA (For Non-LDCs Exports)**	**SAFTA (For Partner's Exports)**
India–Afghanistan PTA	CTH + 40%	CTH + 40%	CTH + 30%
India–Bhutan FTA	Manufactures of Bhutan	CTH + 40%	CTH + 30%
India–Nepal FTA	CTH + 30%	CTH + 40%	CTH + 30%
India–Sri Lanka FTA	CTH + 35%	CTH + 40%	CTH + 35%
Pakistan–Sri Lanka FTA	CTSH + 35%	CTH + 40%	CTH + 35%

B. Extra regional South Asian FTAs	
BIMSTEC FTA	CTH + Value Added Undecided
Pakistan–Malaysia FTA	CTH + 40%
India–Thailand FTA (Early Harvest Scheme)	CTH + 40%
India–Singapore FTA	CTH + 40%

Source: Authors' compilation.

value added, its sourcing opportunities and strategic investment decisions could be affected.

4.2.1 South Asia

This section presents an overview of ROO in the current regional economic engagements among SAARC countries. It also compares them with a particular SAARC country's economic cooperation agreement with countries in the extra-SAARC region. It can be observed that the different agreements have differences in terms of ROO formulations, however, broadly they are uniform towards a formulation of CTH plus 40 per cent value addition (Table 4.2).

4.3 EU

The EU ROO are laid down separately for trade in both non-preferential as well as preferential arrangements. Within the PROO specific rules are set for the EU GSP. Under the latter scheme, the change of heading criterion means that a product is considered to be sufficiently worked or processed when the product obtained is classified in a *4-digit* heading of the HS nomenclature, which is different from those in which all the non-originating materials used in its manufacture are classified (European Commission, 2003). An example is the manufacture of a straw basket, classified under heading 4602 of the HS. The list shows for the whole of Chapter 46 the criterion "manufacture in which all the materials used are classified within a heading other than that of the product". As the basket is classified under 4602, while the straw material was imported under 1401, the origin criterion is clearly satisfied.

The value or *ad valorem* criterion is where the value of non-originating materials used may not exceed a given percentage of the ex-works price of a product. (The notions "ex-works price" and "value" are two of the definitions in Article 66.) An example is the manufacture of umbrellas under HS heading 6601, where column 3 in the list reads "manufacture in which the value of all the materials used does not exceed 50% of the ex-works price of the product". Here a comparison has to be made between the ex-works price of the product and the value of all non-originating materials.

The specific process criterion is used when certain operations or stages in a manufacturing process have to be carried out on any non-originating materials. Many examples of this kind of origin criterion can be found in the textile sector, e.g. woven garments of Chapter 62 of the HS, for which column 3 in the list reads "manufacture from yarn". For example the manufacture of a garment starting from non-originating yarn confers origin. This means that weaving and all subsequent manufacturing stages must be carried out in the beneficiary country. A process criterion of this kind implies that starting from an earlier manufacturing stage (e.g. chemical material or natural fibres) also confers originating status, while starting from a later stage (e.g. weaving) does not (European Commission, 2003).

The ROO are very stringent in several cases stipulating that manufacture of a particular product should use all the materials already originating in the country. The range of percentage norms thus goes up to 100 per cent. In the case in which a percentage rule is applied in determining the originating status of a product the value added is taken as ex-works price of the product obtained less the customs value of third-country materials imported into a beneficiary country. The ex-works price is defined as the price paid to the manufacturer in whose undertaking the last working or processing is carried out, provided the price includes the value of all materials used in manufacture, minus any internal taxes which are, or may be, repaid when the product obtained is exported. The customs value is determined in accordance with Article VII of the GATT.

The following illustrations from the ROO system in the existing EU GSP scheme suggest that in many cases these rules are quite stringent. In the case of fruit and nuts classified under HS 0811 – containing added sugar – has the stipulation that all the materials used must already[?] be originating in the preference receiving country. In another case, of aluminium articles, classified under HS 7616, a producer should satisfy the following criteria:

"Manufacture in which:

- all the materials used are classified within a heading other than that of the product, however, gauze, cloth, grill, netting, fencing, reinforcing fabric and similar materials (including endless bands) of aluminium wire, or expanded metal of aluminium may be used, and
- the value of all the materials used does not exceed 50% of the ex-works price of the product"

The above-mentioned EU rules of origin requirements combine the two methods of origin determination, namely the CTH rule and the percentage criterion.

4.4 NAFTA

The NAFTA ROO are a combination of three criteria, namely CTH classification, value addition norms and specified process tests. The changes in

Box 4.4 Example of tariff shift in NAFTA

Products: Breads, pastries, cakes, biscuits (HS 1905.90).

Non-North American input: flour (classified in HS Chapter 11).

Rule of origin: change to heading 1902 through 1905 from any other chapter.

Application: For all products classified in HS headings 1902 through 1905, all non-North American inputs must be classified in an HS chapter other than HS chapter 19 in order for the product to obtain NAFTA tariff preference. These baked goods would qualify for NAFTA tariff preference because the non-originating ingredient (flour) is classified under Chapter 11, not 19.

If, however, these products were produced with non-originating *mixes, then these products would not qualify because mixes are* classified in HS chapter 19, the same chapter as baked goods.

Source: US Department of Commerce (2000).

tariff classification are laid down in terms of change at the *4-digit* level of the tariff classification under the HS system, whereas a CTSH means a change at the *6-digit* level. On several occasions change in tariff classification is combined with regional value content stipulations.

An example of goods containing non-originating inputs but eligible for NAFTA treatment as long as *each* non-NAFTA input undergoes a tariff classification change as specified in NAFTA Annex 401 is provided in the Box 4.4.

It is worth noting that in the case of the NAFTA in sectors like automobiles, the minimum percentage of value-added (under the percentage-test rule) has been graduated upwards from 50 per cent for the first four years up to 1998 and 56 per cent for the next four years up to 2002 and 62.5 per cent thereafter. It is also worth highlighting that even at the starting point the percentage of domestic value added is placed at 50 per cent and not below that.

4.5 Sectoral Rules of Origin as practised in different trade agreements

Having given an overview of ROO across RTAs and a detailed analysis of provisions specific to major RTAs, it is also important to highlight the sectoral divergences or similarities in different RTAs with respect to rules of origin provisions. For this, the two most important sectors, namely automobiles, and textiles and clothing have been chosen. The ROO provisions relating to the automobile sector are presented in Table 4.3 and those relating to the textiles and clothing are documented in Table 4.4. It can be seene that sectoral approaches across RTAs have taken a more stringent approach as far as ROO are concerned.

4.5.1 Automobiles

It has been observed that multiple ROOs are applied increasingly for the same products in different FTAs. Let us take the case of NAFTA ROO for the automobile sector. The restrictiveness in the ROO was constructed by the US in order to limit the utilisation of the agreement by Japan and other automobile manufacturers to export to the US market through Canada and Mexico. At the beginning of negotiations US proposed for 65 per cent value added content which was finally agreed for 62.5 per cent by Canada and Mexico. The impact of these rules was enormous in terms of not only preventing Japanese automobile manufacturers to export to the US from Mexico but it also facilitated investments in North American production of vehicles and parts.

The case of MERCOSUR is yet another example of strong ROO in the case of the automobile sector. At the initial stages of negotiations there was no final regulation on the level of an agreed regional content with respect to automotive products. Subsequently, an ad-hoc Technical Committee was constituted to build consensus on the regional content as well as other modalities.

The ROOs applied to six major automobile and automobile parts products in eleven key concluded FTAs substantiate this point (see Table 4.3). "In the case of ASEAN, for instance, the 40 per cent VC rate applies to all six products under AFTA and the ASEAN–China FTA but more stringent ROOs for three products (for example, 45 per cent VC applied for HS 87.03, 87.04, and 87.08) are found in the ASEAN–Korea FTA. Furthermore, the ROOs for the same products are different in bilateral FTAs involving the same major economy. In the Japan-Thailand EPA, for example, the VC requirement for HS 87.03 and 87.11 is 40 per cent, while in the Japan–Malaysia EPA, it is more restrictive at 60 per cent for the same two products. Similar instances can be found in the case of the Singapore–Australia FTA and the Thailand–Australia FTA" (Kawai and Wignaraja, 2008:127).

It has also been found by Kawai and Wignaraja (2008) that firms are often supportive of alternative ROOs for the same product for several

Table 4.3 Sectoral ROO in different trade agreements: automobiles

		Japan			Korea	China	ASEAN			Singapore		Thailand
FTA		Japan-Malaysia	Japan-Singapore	Japan-Thailand	Korea-Singapore	China-Pakistan	ASEAN Free Trade Area	ASEAN-China	ASEAN-Korea	Singapore-Australia	United States-Singapore	Thailand-Australia
HS code	Product description	EPA (2006)	EPA (2002)	EPA (2007)	FTA (2006)	FTA (2006)	FTA (1993)	FTA (2005)	FTA (2006)	FTA (2003)	FTA (2004)	FTA (2005)
87.01	Tractors (other than works, warehouse equipment)	CTC (6 digit) or RVC of 40%	CTC; last substantial: manufacture*	CTC or RVC of 40%	CTC plus RVC of 55%	RVC of not less; than 40%*	RVC of not less than 40%*	RVC of not less than 40%*	RVC of not less than 40% or a CTC (4 digits)*	VC of not less than 50%*	CTC plus RVC of at least 30% (build up)	CTC plus RVC of 40%
87.03	Motor vehicles for transport of persons (except buses)	CTC or RVC of 60%	CTC; last substantial manufacture*	CTC or RVC of 40%	CTC plus RVC of 55%	RVC of not less than 40%*	RVC of not less than 40%*	RVC of not less: than: 40%*	RVC of 45%	Last process of manufacture within territory of the party	CTC plus RVC of at least 30% (build up)	CTC plus RVC of 40%
87.04	Motor vehicles for the transport of goods	CTC or RVC of 50%	CTC; last substantial manufacture*	CTC or RVC of 40%	CTC plus RVC of 55%	RVC of not less than 40%*	RVC of not less than 40%*	RVC of not less than 40%*	RVC of 45%	VC of not] less than 50%*	CTC plus RVC of at least 30% (build up)	CTC plus RVC of 40%

HS Code	Description										
87.08	Parts and accessories for motor vehicles	CTC or RVC of 40%	CTC; last substantial manu-facture*	CTC or RVC of 40%	CTC plus RVC of 50%/55%	RVC of not less than 40%*	RVC of not less than 40%*	RVC of not: less than 40%*	RVC of 45%	Last process of manufacture within territory of the party	CTC (6 digit) or CTC plus RVC of at least 30% (build up)	CTC (6 digit) plus RVC of 40%
87.11	Motorcycles, bicycles, etc. with auxiliary motor	CTC or RVC of 60%	CTC; last substantial 'manu-facture*	CTC or RVC of 40%	CTC plus RVC of 55%	RVC of; not less than 40%*	RVC of not less than 40%*	RVC of not less than 40%*	RVC of not less than 40%* or a CTC (4 digits)*	VC of not ~ less than 50%*	CTC (4 digit) or CTC plus RVC of at least 30% (build up)	CTC (6 digit) and/or RVC of 40%
87.14	Parts and accessories of bicycles, motorcycles, etc.	CTC or RVC of 40%	CTC; last substantial manu-facture*	CTC or RVC of 40%	CTC (4 digit)	RVC of not less than 40%*	RVC of not less than 40%*	RVC of not less than 40%*	RVC of not less than 40%* or a CTC (4 digits)*	VC of not less than 50%*	CTC (6 digit) or CTC plus RVC of at least 30% (build up)	CTC (6 digit)

Source: Kawai and Wignaraja (2008).

130

Table 4.4 Sectoral ROO in different trade agreements: textile and clothing

Approach or product category	Agreement	
	NAFTA	USVJordan FA
General approach and/or principle(s)	Yarn forward (critical process criterion): Yarn used in each of the successive stages of fabricating textile products (the yarn itself, the fabric, and the sewing thread) must originate in a NAFTA country. Also, each non-originating material used must undergo an applicable change in tariff classification (specified in an Annex), or the good must otherwise satisfy applicable requirements where no tariff classification change is required.	Critical process criterion: Basically, an article must be made of a fibre or fabric manufactured by a Party, or wholly assembled by a Party.
Exception(s)	(a) For many individual product categories, substantial transformation or change in tariff classification must occur. (b) NAFTA-made yarn, fabric, apparel not meeting strict NAFTA content requirements can be eligible for preferential duty treatment up to agreed annual levels.	A textile or clothing product that is knit-to-shape in a Party is considered the growth, product, or manufacture of that Party notwithstanding other rules.
Yarn	Cotton & man-made fibre spun yarn & sewing thread must be of NAFTA origin. Filament yarns must be NAFTA formed; feedstocks not limited. Yarns, sewing thread of other fibres must be spun in a NAFTA country.	If yarn, thread, rope, twine, cordage, etc. the constituent staple fibres must be spun in a Party, or the continuous filament be extruded there.

Fabric	Yarn forward, except: Cotton & man-made fibre knit fabrics and man-made fibre non-woven & specialty fabrics require NAFTA-origin fibre. Coated fabric must have NAFTA-origin fabric, except tire cord & belting, and man-made fibre hose.	Constituent fibres, filaments, yarns must be woven, knitted, tufted, felted, needled, entangled, or substantially transformed by any other fabric-making process in the Party. If a cotton, silk, man-made, or vegetable fabric is dyed, printed, and undergoes 2 or more finishing operations in a Party, it qualifies.
Clothing	Yarn forward, except: Clothing made from fabrics originating in a non-NAFTA country that are in short supply in NAFTA must be cut or knit to shape and assembled in a NAFTA country. Men's dress shirts made from certain cotton and cotton/man-made fiber blend fabrics must under-go substantial transformation. Nightwear and women's underwear of fine count cotton knit fabric must undergo substantial transformation. Bras- sières & all silk & linen clothing must undergo substantial transformation.	Must be wholly assembled in the Party from its component parts.
Other textile items	Yarn forward, except: Fibre in man-made fibre products must be of NAFTA-origin. A fabric forward rule applies to luggage, handbags, flat goods, & curtains of certain yarns. Silk & linen goods must undergo substantial transformation.	Must be wholly assembled in the Party from its component parts.

(Continued)

Table 4.4 Continued

Approach or product category	Agreement	
	ATPDEA	CBTPP
General approach	Critical process criterion: Must be assembled from products of a beneficiary country or the U.S.	Yarn forward (critical process criterion): In most cases, US-made yarn and/or US-made fabric required.
Exception(s)	(a) In some cases, dyeing, printing, & finishing of fabrics must be performed in U.S. (b) If short supply situation in the U.S., President, at request of interested party, may proclaim additional fabrics & yarns eligible for preferential treatment after following certain steps. (c) Articles otherwise ineligible for preferential treatment because constituent fibers or yarns are not wholly ATPDEA- or U.S.-formed can qualify if total weight of such fibers or yarns does not exceed 7% of total weight.	(a) In some cases, dyeing, printing, & finishing of fabrics must be performed in U.S. (b) Short supply situation provisions essentially same as for ATPDEA. (c) Articles otherwise ineligible for preferential treatment because constituent fibers or yarns are not wholly formed in U.S. or CBTPA can qualify if total weight of such fibers or yarns does not exceed 7% of total weight.
Yarn	No provision related to yarn imports per se.	Thread used to assemble a clothing article must have been dyed, printed, or finished in the United States.
Fabric	No provision related to fabric imports per se.	No provision related to fabric imports per se.

133

Clothing	Must be sewn or otherwise assembled in one or more ATPDEA countries or the .S or both from one or more of following components: (a) Fabrics or fabric components wholly formed, or components knit-to-shape, from yarns wholly formed in the US or one or more ATPDEA countries, provided that dyeing, printing, and finishing of the woven and knit fabric components is carried out in US; (b) fabrics or fabric components formed from yarns wholly formed in one or more ATPDEA countries if such fabrics (including certain fabrics not formed from yarns) are in chief value of llama, alpaca, or vicuña; (c) fabrics or yarns, to the extent that apparel articles of such fabrics or yarns are eligible for preferential treatment, without regard to source of the fabrics/yarns, under NAFTA short-supply provisions. Regional fabric provision: an apparel article qualifies if assembled in ATPDEA from fabrics or fabric components formed in an ATPDEA country from yarns wholly US or ATPDEA formed, whether or not article is also made from any of the fabrics or components defined in (a), (b), and (c), unless the article is made exclusively from any of the components defined in (a), (b), or (c).	Fabric forward in most cases, with the following specifics: Must be sewn or otherwise assembled in one or more CBTPA[CBTPP?] countries from fabrics wholly formed and cut, or from components knit-to-shape, in the US from yarns wholly .S formed, and all dyeing, printing, and finishing of the fabrics from which the articles are assembled must be carried out in the US. If cut and sewn, or otherwise assembled, in one or more CBTPA countries from US fabric made from US yarn, US-made thread must be used, with all dyeing, printing, and finishing of the fabrics having been carried out in the US. Knit apparel articles, except socks and certain T-shirts, must be cut and assembled in 1 or more CBTPA countries from US or CBTPA fabric made from US yarn. Non-underwear T-shirts made from CBTPA fabric made of US yarn are subject to quota. The US-made fabric components of brassieres cut and assembled in one or more CBTPA countries and/or the .S must account for at least 75% of customs value.
Other textile items	Luggage: Must be assembled in an ATPDEA country from fabric wholly formed & cut in the US that enters the U.S. on same basis as Mexican production sharing/maquiladora provisions, or assembled from fabric cut in an ATPDEA country from fabric wholly formed in the US from yarns wholly formed in the US.	Luggage: Must be assembled in a CBTPA country from fabric wholly formed and cut in the US from yarns wholly formed in the US if entering under a certain HTS, or assembled from fabric cut in a CBTPA country from fabric wholly formed in US from .S yarn.

(Continued)

Table 4.4 Continued

General approach	Yarn forward (critical process criterion): US-made yarn required in most cases; US-made fabric required in most cases. Must be cut in .S in some cases.	Critical process criterion: (a) Products must be made from Singapore or U.S. yarn. (b) Assembly must be carried out in Singapore.
Exception(s) to rule(s)	(a) Short supply situation provisions essentially same as for ATPDEA and CBTPA (b) Articles otherwise ineligible because constituent fibres or yarns are not wholly formed in the US or a beneficiary country can qualify if the total weight of such items does not exceed 7% of total weight.	(a) CTC required for nearly all individual product categories. (b) A limited yearly amount of textiles & clothing containing non-US or non-Singaporean fibre, yarn, or fabric may qualify for duty-free treatment. (c) Short supply provision for clothing made from fabric or yarn in short supply in US.
Yarn	No provision related to yarn imports per se.	CTC required for all products.
Fabric	No provision related to fabric imports per se.	CTC required for all products.
Clothing	(a) Must be sewn or otherwise assembled in one or more AGOA[in full?] countries from fabric wholly formed and cut, or from components knit-to-shape, in the US from yarns wholly US-formed. If knit-to-shape component is either a US or AGOA country product (made from US yarn) and fabrics are cut in the US or an AGOA country, US sewing thread must be used. (b) If assembled from regional-made fabric (woven or knit-to-shape), that fabric must be made from yarn made in the US or an AGOA country. Imports limited by a cap that increases over time. (c) If assembled in a lesser developed AGOA country, there is no restriction on the source(s) of the fabric or the yarn used to make the fabric.	CTC required for most products, with qualifications in some instances specific to the individual product.
Other	No provision related to non-clothing items per se.	CTC required for all products.

Source: Gelb (2003).

reasons: (i) if they cannot achieve the VC requirement, having another ROO enables them to avail of FTA preference; (ii) as the application for the VC rule may require confidential information on costs, suppliers and many firms are often reluctant to divulge such information; and (iii) some ROOs may be better aligned with the technology and production process of particular industries.

4.5.2 Textiles and clothing

The textiles and clothing is yet another sector that has witnessed diverse, stringent and complex ROO in various RTAs. "An important context of these agreements and programs is that textile and apparel manufacture has been shifting to developing countries, with textiles and apparel accounting for large portions of their exports to developed economies in the last few decades. Because textile and apparel manufacture and trade are important elements of developing country economies, provisions regarding textile and apparel products are prominent in the agreements and programs listed above" (Gelb, 2003:1).

From Table 4.4 it is observed that almost all of the agreements usually require that the value of materials produced in a beneficiary country plus the direct cost of processing in a beneficiary country must equal at least 35% of the total value of the article at its entry into the United States. But up to 15 per cent of the 35 per cent may consist of the value originating in the United States. More specifically in NAFTA textile and clothing products have very broad product coverage and prescribe for the well-known "yarn forward" rule of origin principle.

In nutshell, the agreements have special rules of origin with respect to textiles and clothing, the provisions are extremely detailed, and contain numerous exceptions and qualifications making it quite complex (Gelb, 2003).

A unique feature was noticed in case of the CEPT Scheme. The ASEAN FTA had a general rule of a single criterion of 40 per cent value added. After several years of its implementation members discussed the difficulty their exporters faced in case of exports of items relating to textiles and clothing. A Working Group was constituted to resolve this issue. Finally, the members agreed for an alternative rule for textiles that followed the process-based formulation for determining the origin. Separate and more detailed non-qualifying operations were also devised for this sector so as to take care of trade circumvention from non-AFTA members. The new rules so agreed are given in Table 4.5, signifying the merit of moving from a single rule to a co-equal rule by taking into consideration the actual manufacturing process and availability of technology.

Table 4.5 ASEAN CEPT ROO for textiles and textile products: substantial transformation criterion

Introduction

1. Recognizing that the existing percentage criterion of the CEPT ROO may not be conducive towards the objective of increasing intra-ASEAN trade in textiles and textile products, the 7th AFTA Council at its meeting on 6th September 1995 decided that for the purpose of origin determination of textiles and textile products either the percentage or the substantial transformation criterion can be used by the exporting country. The 7th AFTA Council also decided that an ASEAN Single List identifying the processes for each of the textile and textile products shall be formulated to administer the substantial transformation criterion.
2. When an exporting country chooses to apply the substantial transformation criterion, the following ROO shall apply. The ROO should be read in conjunction with the attached ASEAN Single List.

General rules

Rule 1
A country of origin is that in which the last substantial transformation or process was performed resulting in a new product. Thus, materials which underwent a substantial transformation in a country shall be a product of that country.

Rule 2
A product in the production of which two or more countries are involved shall be regarded as originating in the country in which the last substantial transformation or process was performed, resulting in a new product.

Rule 3
A textile or textile product will be considered to have undergone a substantial transformation or process if it has been transformed by means of substantial manufacturing or processing into a new and different article of commerce.

Rule 4
A new and different article of commerce will usually result from manufacturing or processing operations if there is a change in:
  (i) commercial designation or identity
  (ii) fundamental character, or
  (iii) commercial use.

Rules 5
In determining whether a merchandise has been subjected to substantial manufacturing or processing operations, the following will be considered:
  5.1 The physical change in the material or article as a result of the manufacturing or processing operations;
  5.2 The time involved in the manufacturing or processing operations in the country in which they are performed;
  5.3 The complexity of the manufacturing or processing operations in the country in which they are performed;
  5.4 The level or degree of skill and/or technology required in the manufacturing or processing operations.

Specific rules applicable to textiles and textile products

Rule 6

Textile material or article shall be considered a product of a particular ASEAN country when it has undergone prior to importation into another ASEAN country any of the following:

6.1 Petrochemicals which have undergone the process of polymerization or polycondensation or any chemicals or physical processes to form a polymer;

6.2 Polymer which has undergone the process of melt spinning or extrusion to form a synthetic fiber;

6.3 Spinning fiber into yarn;

6.4 Weaving, knitting or otherwise forming fabric;

6.5 Cutting fabric into parts and the assembly of those parts into a completed article;

6.6 Dyeing of fabric, if it is accompanied by any finishing operation which has the effect of rendering the dyed product directly;

6.7 Printing of fabric, if it is accompanied by any finishing operation which has the effect of rendering the printed product directly usable;

6.8 Impregnation or coating when such treatment leads to the manufacture of a new product falling within certain headings of customs tariffs;

6.9 Embroidery which represents at least five percent of the total area of the embroidered product.

Rule 7

An article or material shall not be considered to be a product of ASEAN origin by virtue of merely having undergone any of the following:

7.1 Simple combining operations, labeling, pressing, cleaning or dry cleaning or packaging operations, or any combination thereof;

7.2 Cutting to length or width and hemming, stitching or overlocking fabrics which are readily identifiable as being intended for a particular commercial use;

7.3 Trimming and/or joining together by sewing, looping, linking, attaching of accessory articles such as straps, bands, beads, cords, rings and eyelets;

7.4 One or more finishing operations on yarns, fabrics or other textile articles, such as bleaching, waterproofing, decating, shrinking, mercerizing, or similar operations; or

7.5 Dyeing or printing of fabrics or yarns.

Rule 8

The following items made of textile materials from outside the ASEAN countries shall be considered as having an ASEAN origin if it has undergone the processes identified in Rule 6 but not merely performing the processes identified in Rule 7.

8.1 Handkerchiefs;

8.2 Shawls, scarves, veils, and the like;

8.3 Travelling rugs and blankets;

8.4 Bed linen, pillow cases, table linen, toilet linen and kitchen linen;

8.5 Sacks and bags, of a kind used for packing of goods.

(Continued)

Table 4.5 Continued

8.6   Tarpaulins, awnings and sunblinds;

8.7   Floor cloths, and dish cloths and other similar articles simply made up.

Certificate of Origin

Rule 9

A Certificate of Origin issued by a competent authority or authorized agency in the exporting ASEAN country shall be required to authenticate the ASEAN origin of the textile product.

Rule 10

In the case two or more countries are involved in the manufacture of a textile product, only the country in which the last substantial transformation or process was performed shall be required to issue the Certificate of Origin.

Rule 11

The Certificate of Origin shall be presented, along with other required documents, to customs authority of the importing ASEAN country.

Rule 12

In case a dispute arises as to authenticity of the ASEAN origin of a textile product, the dispute may be referred to the ASEAN Dispute Settlement Mechanism (DSM) for a decision. In such a case, the customs authority may release the disputed goods after the importer has supplied a guarantee satisfactory to the customs authority.

Source: ASEAN Secretariat website (www.aseansec.org).

The analysis presented in this chapter has tried to give a brief overview of ROO provisions across RTAs; analysed provisions specific to major preferential schemes and RTAs; and highlighted the sectoral approach to ROO formulations, especially in the two major sectors of automobiles, and textiles and clothing.

It is clearly evident that ROO are not only complex within themselves but the diverse treatment that is prescribed under different agreements, especially when some of the countries are parties to more than one agreement, further adds to its complexity and create confusion and difficulty to the businesses and implementing agencies.

5
Rules of Origin in India's RTAs

India has stated that it believes in an open, equitable, predictable, non-discriminatory and rule-based international trading system and has expressed that the Regional Trading Arrangements are viewed as 'building blocks' towards its overall objective of trade liberalization, which complements the multilateral trading system. Initially, India had adopted a very cautious and guarded approach to regionalism and was engaged in only a few bilateral/regional initiatives. In this contexts, we analyse the rules of origin that are being practised in India's RTAs. While so doing we have also tried to examine how Indian business community has looked at this issue. In this chapter we also apply some of the new concepts that were presented in Chapter 2, to examine empirically the Indian experience with ROO under different RTAs.

5.1 RTAs: India's experiences

India was engaged in only a few bilateral/regional initiatives, mainly through PTAs like the Bangkok Agreement (signed in 1975) to exchange tariff concessions in the ESCAP region, the GSTP (signed in 1988) to exchange tariff concessions among G-77 member countries, and SAPTA (signed in 1993) to liberalize trade in South Asia. All these engagements were limited to coverage of goods only and were either driven by political objectives or were signed as solidarity towards South–South Cooperation. These engagements, therefore, achieved limited results in terms of increasing trade volumes with the member countries. With its smaller neighbours like Bhutan and Nepal, the free trade arrangements are on a non-reciprocal basis. India's first true FTA was signed with Sri Lanka in 1998 and is in operation since March 2000. Here also Sri Lanka was given better flexibility in terms of maintaining a larger size of the negative list and the longer period of tariff liberalisation. While India has granted duty-free access to Sri Lanka's goods from 2003, Sri Lanka is required to reciprocate the same by 2008. A PTA with Afghanistan on a very limited number of items is in operation and another PTA has been implemented in 2007 with Chile. India has though signed a PTA with MERCOSUR, the same has not been implemented as MERCOSUR is yet to ratify the agreement.

A recognition that RTAs would continue to feature permanently in world trade was made by India in 2001 when India got engaged with some of its important trading partners/blocs with the intention of expanding its export market and began concluding, in principle agreements for moving in some cases towards a Comprehensive Economic Cooperation Agreement (CECA) that covers FTA in goods (i.e. having a zero customs duty regime within a fixed time frame on items covering substantial trade and a relatively small negative list of sensitive items on which no or limited duty concessions are available), services, investment and identified areas of economic cooperation. Framework Agreements have already been entered into with ASEAN, BIMSTEC, Thailand, etc. with specific road maps to be followed and specified time frames by which the negotiations are to be completed. India has already concluded a CECA with Singapore, which has been implemented since 1 August, 2005. The Agreement on SAFTA was signed by member countries of SAARC in January, 2004. The tariff liberalization programme has been implemented since 1 July 2006, however, this Agreement also covers goods only and not as comprehensive in nature. India has almost concluded its negotiations with ASEAN, Republic of Korea and BIMSTEC. The implementation may start from 2009. India is also negotiating comprehensive agreements with Japan, EC, GCC etc. A summary of India's RTAs is given in the Appendix to this Chapter.

5.2   Evolution of ROO in India's RTAs

India's experience of the ROO dates back to some of its very old PTAs with Nepal, Bhutan, and Tripartite Agreement, where no detailed criterion for determining origin was specified. Most of these agreements prescribed the only condition for a product to enjoy tariff preferences were that such exported goods should be either wholly produced, i.e. grown/produced locally or "manufactured" in the partner country. However, what constitutes "manufacturing" was not defined. It was left to the discretion of exporting country to decide if even packing or simple cutting or slicing would mean manufacturing or not. On a later date this created operational problems at the time of imports in India and the provisions relating to ROO during the review of some of these Agreements were strengthened by providing detailed originating criteria for "not wholly produced or obtained" category of goods. Another important factor which was incorporated in the text of rules of origin was defining detailed 'non-qualifying or minimal operations' that shall not confer origin. With the signing of the Bangkok Agreement (1975) and GSTP (1988) it moved towards linking origin to the local value added criteria. In these agreements 50 per cent local value added was provided.

Since India's initial agreements were PTAs, the simple criterion of value added content was applied. In initial days the origin of the product was linked with at least 50 per cent value added. This principle was almost similar to the equity holding of a company where the majority share of 51 per cent would have meant the majority ownership to a person or legal body. The 50 per cent valued added meant that the exporting country has contributed to half of the value of the export product and therefore a kind of majority holding on that product is there from the exporting country. Therefore if a tariff concession was offered it was meant that the benefit was going to the exporting RTA partner. However, in late 1970s or mid-1980s the developing countries were in a process of seeking investments and technology therefore achieving 50 per cent value addition in a single exporting country was either unachievable on finished products or was next to impossible. This fact was first recognized by the members of SAPTA. Initially in SAPTA, during the initial period 50 per cent value added was provided with 10 per cent lesser value for the LDC Members. Subsequently, in SAPTA, LDC members led by Bangladesh started demanding lowering of value added on the plea that 40 per cent value added for them is too stringent and they cannot export any product under SAPTA. Later on the SAARC Council of Ministers at its Twenty-first Session held in Nuwara Eliya, Sri Lanka, on 18–19 March 1999 agreed to lower the value added content under SAPTA. It prescribed 40 per cent for developing members, i.e. India, Pakistan and Sri Lanka; and 30 per cent for the LDC members, i.e. Bangladesh, Bhutan, Maldives and Nepal.

India had a bilateral agreement with Nepal under which goods produced in Nepal were given a duty free treatment. This facility was first given in 1971 subject to the condition that Nepalese goods contained not less than 90 per cent Nepalese/Indian materials. This value addition requirement was reduced from 90 per cent to 80 per cent in 1978, 55 per cent in 1991 and 50 per cent in 1993. In 1996 when the Treaty of Trade was renewed for five years the value addition requirement was removed. This was done to boost Nepalese exports to India. However, subsequently in late 1990s chances of trade deflection from Nepal was observed. At that time the agreement (which was extended in 1996 for 5 years) only prescribed that the goods should be manufactured in Nepal and neither the criterion of fixed value added was prescribed nor the condition of CTC. The Indian manufacturers of those products were up in arms and made several petitions to Government of India as well as in different Courts. Upon investigation of the cases by the Indian side it was felt that in certain cases the complaints made by Indian industry were proved true. A review of the Treaty was due in 2001 as its validity was ending. The Indian side wanted to introduce the concept of ROO for products that would get tariff preference upon imports to India. Indian side felt that value added criteria would not be sufficient to prevent trade deflection. Meanwhile India had signed FTA with Sri Lanka in 1998 and it was implemented from 2000. The India–Sri Lanka FTA was the first Agreement where the simultaneous application of CTH and local value added was applied. Interestingly, the proposal for the application of twin criteria of CTH and value added was moved by Sri Lanka and was accepted by India. India wanted application of these twin criteria in case of Nepal. Nepal was initially apprehensive, however, later on during the course of review they agreed to a twin criteria of CTH and 35 per cent value added from 6 March 2002. It was also agreed that the value added criteria will automatically be lowered down to 30 per cent with effect from 5 March 2003. At the same time India introduced Tariff Rate Quota on vegetable fats, acrylic yarn, copper products and zinc oxide. These were the items where the deflections were taking place from Nepal to India due to high tariffs in India. Interestingly, in case of vegetable fats and copper products the trade deflection happened from Sri Lanka under the bilateral agreement. While the negotiations on GSTP ROO are being held during the third round negotiations, and India tabling the proposal to lower the threshold; in APTA (earlier known as Bangkok Agreement) the value added criterion has been lowered to 45 per cent from 50 per cent.

Due to instances of trade deflections that were observed in the past India has preferred to have simultaneous applications of three criteria: local content or value added, substantial manufacturing clause (defined as CTH), and detailed non-qualifying operations, in its RTA ROO. In general, in its agreements, India has been seen to follow the following approach towards PROO:

(a) Between FTAs and PTAs India has adopted a more liberal ROO in respect of PTAs.

(b) In the case of FTAs, the simultaneous application of the CTH and value content criterion has generally been applied.

(c) The value content criterion has been variedly applied; the minimum domestic value addition applied is 30 per cent in the case of LDCs and the maximum is generally 40 per cent. India has followed the indirect method by which the non-originating inputs are accounted for calculating the value added content.

(d) India has been slightly cautious towards the PSR and has preferred to have General Rules in its RTAs. Only as an exception India has derogated from the general rules, as would be evident in case of SAFTA and with Singapore.

5.2.1 Substantial transformation through CTSH

One of the biggest challenges that arose from the FTA negotiations for India related to change in India's position from its conventional preference for CTH. As has been explained above, due to apprehensions about trade circumvention the Indian industry, as well as the negotiators, were not inclined to change their position on this issue. In its negotiation with ASEAN this issue became a major bone of contention. ASEAN preferred a value added criterion of 40 per cent (as in the case of ASEAN CEPT Scheme). It was due to their inflexible positions that the Early Harvest Programme as agreed in the bilateral Framework Agreement was dropped. The bilateral negotiations between India and ASEAN were suspended for more than a year due to a lack of consensus on this very issue.

Considering the above, for both India and ASEAN, it was important to identify items at HS 6-digit level wherein 'substantial transformation' takes place through CTSH. Subsequently, a study was launched to explore the issue. The study found that at any given point in time, the state of technology and the production process in any country may be such that it is technically impossible to meet the CTH criterion at HS 4-digit level, hence, on such products derogation from CTH rule becomes imperative. It may be emphasized that such identification is subject to the limitation of the state of technology that exists in any country at a point of time. In this regard, a study was conducted focusing on identification of products at 6-digit HS level of trade classification, which would not qualify for the CTH criterion at the HS 4-digit level (Das, 2004b). The list of identified items is shown in Table 5.1.

It was in mid-2005 that, in a Workshop at the ASEAN Secretariat in Jakarta, the findings of the study were presented to the negotiators of India and ASEAN, and thereafter the negotiations on ROO re-commenced. Finally, both sides agreed to show flexibility in their respective positions

144

Table 5.1   No. of items under CTSH by Chapter

HS Chapter code	Commodity	No. of 6-digit HS lines
02	Meat and edible meat offal.	21
03	Fish and crustaceans, molluscs and other aquatic invertabrates.	12
04	Dairy produce; birds' eggs; natural honey; edible prod. Of animal origin, not elsewhere spec. Or included.	12
05	Products of animal origin, not elsewhere specified or included.	1
06	Live trees and other plants; bulbs; roots and the like; cut flowers and ornamental foliage.	2
07	Edible vegetables and certain roots and tubers.	4
08	Edible fruit and nuts; peel or citrus fruit or melons.	8
09	Coffee, tea, mate and spices.	6
10	Cereals.	1
11	Products of the milling industry; malt; starches; inulin; wheat gluten.	1
12	Oil seeds and olea. Fruits; misc. Grains, seeds and fruit; industrial or medicinal plants; straw and fodder.	2
15	Animal or vegetable fats and oils and their cleavage products; pre. Edible fats; animal or vegetable waxex.	11
16	Preparations of meat, of fish or of crustaceans, molluscs or other aquatic invertebrates.	1
17	Sugars and sugar confectionery.	5
18	Cocoa and cocoa preparations.	1
19	Preparations of cereals, flour, starch or milk; pastrycooks products.	2
20	Preparations of vegetables, fruit, nuts or other parts of plants.	6
21	Miscellaneous edible preparations.	4
22	Beverages, spirits and vinegar.	3
23	Residues and waste from the food industries; prepared animal foder.	1
24	Tobacco and manufactured tobacco substitutes.	2
25	Salt; sulphur; earths and stone; plastering materials, lime and cement.	20
26	Ores, slag and ash.	2
27	Mineral fuels, mineral oils and products of their distillation; bituminous substances; mineral waxes.	9

Table 5.1 Continued

HS Chapter code	Commodity	No. of 6-digit HS lines
28	Inorganic chemicals; organic or inorganic compounds of precious metals, of rare-earth metals, or radi. Elem. or of isotopes.	39
29	Organic chemicals	24
30	Pharmaceutical products	1
32	Tanning or dyeing extracts; tannins and their deri. Dyes, pigments and other colouring matter; paints and ver; putty and other mastics; inks.	1
34	Soap, organic surface-active agents, washing preparations, lubricating preparations, artificial waxes, prepared waxes, polishing or scouring prep.	4
35	Albuminoidal substances; modified starches; glues; enzymes.	1
37	Photographic or cinematographic goods.	1
38	Miscellaneous chemical products.	6
39	Plastic and articles thereof.	1
40	Rubber and articles thereof.	5
41	Raw hides and skins (other than furskins) and leather.	13
43	Furskins and artificial fur, manufactures thereof.	1
44	Wood and articles of wood; wood charcoal.	9
45	Cork and articles of cork.	1
47	Pulp of wood or of other fibrous cellulosic material; waste and scrap of paper or paperboard.	4
48	Paper and paperboard; articles of paper pulp, of paper or of paperboard.	13
51	Wool, fine or coarse animal hair, horsehair yarn and woven fabric.	3
52	Cotton.	30
53	Other vegetable textile fibres; paper yarn and woven fabrics of paper yarn.	1
54	Man-made filaments.	9
55	Man-made staple fibres.	20
58	Special woven fabrics; tufted textile fabrics; lace; tapestries; trimmings; embroidery.	1
60	Knitted or crocheted fabrics.	10
63	Other made up textile articles; sets; worn clothing and worn textile articles; rags	3
68	Articles of stone, plaster, cement, asbestos, mica or similar materials.	2

(*Continued*)

Table 5.1   Continued

HS Chapter code	Commodity	No. of 6-digit HS lines
70	Glass and glassware.	6
71	Natural or cultured pearls,precious or semiprecious stones,pre.Metals,clad with pre.Metal and artcls thereof;imit.Jewlry;coin.	13
72	Iron and steel	34
73	Articles of iron or steel	13
74	Copper and articles thereof.	3
82	Tools implements, cutlery, spoons and forks, of base metal; parts thereof of base metal.	10
83	Miscellaneous articles of base metal.	8
84	Nuclear reactors, boilers, machinery and mechanical appliances; parts thereof.	231
85	Electrical machinery and equipment and parts thereof; sound recorders and reproducers, television image and sound recorders and reproducers, and parts.	139
87	Vehicles other than railway or tramway rolling stock, and parts and accessories thereof.	8
90	Optical, photographic cinematographic measuring, checking precision, medical or surgical inst. And apparatus parts and accessories thereof;	108
91	Clocks and watches and parts thereof.	6
95	Toys, games and sports requisites; parts and accessories thereof.	1
Total		**920**

Source: Authors' database.

and agreed for Indian ROO formulation of twin criteria that stipulated CTSH plus 35 per cent value addition.

This ROO formulation became a benchmark for subsequent negotiations between Indian and her trading partners – of which, the India–Republic of Korea FTA has been implemented with the same formulation as is evident from Section 5.3 below and Table 5.2.

5.3   ROO in India's RTAs

India is negotiating several RTAs and ROO are also a part of such negotiations. Some of the criteria for determining the "origin" in cases of India's RTAs are summarized in Table 5.2.

Table 5.2 ROO in India's RTAs

Agreement	Qualifying criteria for manufactured products using non-original inputs
India–Nepal Treaty on Trade	CTH + 30% value addition
India–Bhutan Trade Agreement	Goods should be manufactured in Bhutan.
Asia Pacific Trade Agreement (APTA)	45% value addition only.
Global System of Trade Preferences (GSTP)	50% value added only. Negotiations are being held on the threshold of value addition and introducing detailed non-qualifying operations.
SAARC Preferential Trade Area (SAPTA)	40% value addition.
India–Afghanistan Preferential Trade Agreement	CTH + 40% value addition
India–(MERCOSUR PTA)	60% value addition
India Chile PTA	CTH + 40% value addition
India–Sri Lanka FTA (ISLFTA)	CTH + 35%
Agreement on SAFTA	CTH + 40% (30% for LDCs, 35% for Sri Lanka), and PSRs
Comprehensive Economic Cooperation Agreement (CECA) between India and Singapore	CTH + 40%, and PSRs
ASEAN & India FTA	CTSH + 35%
Framework Agreement for establishing Free Trade Area between India and Thailand	Consensus has not been reached.
Framework Agreement on the BIMST-EC FTA	Consensus has not been reached.
India–Mauritius CECPA	A PTA is being negotiated through a positive list approach, negotiations are to be concluded shortly.
India–Korea CECA	CTSH + 35%
India–Japan CECA	Consensus has not been reached.

Source: Ratna (2006).

Table 5.2 illustrates the positive dimensions of ROO in the bilateral context. However, the phenomena of the 'spaghetti-bowl' are also being seen in cases of complexities in ROO. Cases where the same set of countries is participating in more than one agreement with different ROO are becoming the order of the day. Let us examine the same agreement in the context of some other agreements to which India and Sri Lanka are members and thereby exchanging tariff concessions in those agreements also. India and Sri Lanka are members of SAFTA and APTA. In case of SAFTA, the ROO prescribe the criteria for Sri Lanka's exports to India as CTH + 35 per cent, but for India's exports to Sri Lanka it is CTH + 40 per cent. Therefore, while there is no extra burden on Sri Lanka's exporter to export an item to any other SAARC Member, including India; the Indian exporter is required to meet an additional obligation. The same goods on which India can enjoy tariff preference for export to Sri Lanka with CTH + 35 per cent (bilateral FTA ROO), they would now require to undertake an additional 5 per cent value addition for exporting to Sri Lanka under SAFTA (to meet the SAFTA ROO of 40 per cent). This situation is not an ideal one for an Indian exporter as the sourcing pattern of the inputs would need to be re-worked in order to meet this additional 5 per cent value addition threshold. This adds to the transaction cost of the Indian exporter. In this case, therefore, while the Sri Lankan exporter enjoys the benefit of harmonisation, the Indian exporter does not. Coming now to APTA concessions on similar products, both, the Indian and Sri Lankan exporters are required to carry out additional value addition as the APTA ROO provides for 45 per cent value addition. Therefore, they are required to re-work their sourcing patterns to fulfil the ROO criteria, which is burdensome to the exporters. The different rules in different agreements, therefore, either force the exporters to forgo tariff concessions and export on MFN basis or change their sourcing requirements agreement to agreement. Even attracting investments in such cases is difficult as the industry does not know in advance what rules they will be required to follow to export to the same country and under which agreement. The situation becomes more complex if it involves the same set of countries – the tariff concessions and products also vary from one agreement to another agreement at a given time to which they are party. Definitely, the transaction cost increases as the exporter has to suffer for the lack of harmonized ROO.

5.3.1 Trade deflection measurement: case study on some of India's RTAs

In Chapter 2 we discussed the issue of trade deflection and arrived at the following formula:

$$TR = (1 + t_I)/(1 + t_{SL})$$

where t_I is India's external tariff and t_{SL} is Sri Lanka's external tariff. The higher the TR the greater is the possibility of trade deflection. In this scenario it was also discussed that if the TR is greater than 1 the chances are higher that trade deflection will take place. We have examined the same in the case of India–Sri Lanka FTA, especially in the case of India's imports from Sri Lanka during the implementation period. The calculation of TR was done at 6-digit HS as the concessions exchanged by both the countries were at 6-digit HS. We have taken the top items that were exported by Sri Lanka to India during the period 2000–2001, when the FTA commenced, and calculated the TR. We have also analysed the TR for the periods 2003–2004 and 2004–2005, the two consecutive years when India imported goods from Sri Lanka at zero duty. We compared the TRs for different periods and examined how the items have behaved, especially in cases where the TR was higher, and also how many new items were included in the top items of imports from Sri Lanka.

For the period 2000–2001 the top 55 import items (in value terms) from Sri Lanka to India were selected. The list of these items along with their TR is shown in Table 5.3. These items constituted imports worth US$39.61 million, which is 88 per cent of the total imports (US$45.01 million) from Sri Lanka to India in that year. The average TR of the 55 items in year 2000–2001 is 13.53. Overall TR band ranges from 1 to 36. The top 11 items in terms of TR (comprising 12.82 US$ million imports, i.e. 28.48 per cent of total imports from Sri Lanka to India) are given in Table 5.3.

Table 5.3 Trade deflection ratio on selected items: India–Sri Lanka FTA

HS code	Commodity	India's imports from Sri Lanka in 2000–2001 (US$m)	TR for 2001
270799	Other oil & oil products of distillation of high temp coal tar, etc.	5.31	36
720449	Other waste and scrap	4.91	36
740400	Copper waste & scrap	1.33	36
720410	Waste and scrap of cast iron	0.32	36
720430	Waste and scrap of tinned iron or steel	0.28	36
720421	Waste and scrap of stainless steel	0.2	36
401490	Othr hygnc & phrmctl artcls	0.14	36
284910	Carbides of calcium w/n chmcly defined	0.13	36
401511	Surgical gloves, mittens & mitts	0.13	36
391190	Other products in primary forms	0.11	36
581100	Quilted txtl products in the piece cmpsd of one/more layers of txtl matrls assmbld with paddng by stitching, etc. Excpt hdg 5810	0.1	36

Source: Authors' calculations based on Government of India, DGCIS Database (2008).

Among these 55 items, 7 items are in India's negative list, whose TR ranges from 1.71 to 21 and, therefore, no concessions were offered. The imports were made on MFN basis and concessions, if any, would have been offered due to other agreement. On these items there is no trade deflection due to the bilateral FTA (Table 5.4).

In the given scenario, imports from Sri Lanka were higher for items where the chances of deflection were more, except the 7 items mentioned above. The top 35 items in terms of value of imports from Sri Lanka to India were taken for the period 2003–2004. The list of items and their TR is shown in Table 5.5.

During this period India had granted duty-free market access to Sri Lanka. These comprised US$152.3 million of imports, which makes up 78.5 per cent of total imports from the country. Out of these 35 items, only 12 appear among the top items exported during 2000–2001. Out of these 12, the TR has remained at the 2001 level for 7 items (i.e. India's tariff level has remained the same), has increased for 1 item, and decreased for all others (indicating that India has liberalized its tariffs on MFN). These 12 common items comprised US$22.06 million imports in 2000–20–01(which made up 49.01 per cent of total imports in that year), while they comprised US$45.7 million imports in the year 2003–2004 (which made up 23.47 per cent of total). Thus, though there is a decrease in percentage terms of import shares of these items from

Table 5.4 Trade deflection ratio on items in india's negative list

HS code	Commodity	2000–2001 in US$m	TR for 2001
540210	High tenacity yarn of nylon/ other polyamides	0.4	21
540241	Other yarn of nylon/other polyamides, untwisted or with a twist < =50 turms per m single	0.27	21
540231	Textured yarn of nylon or other polyamides measurng per single yarn not more than 50 tex	0.2	21
392690	Other articles of plastics	1.16	6.79
482110	Printed labels	0.38	3.27
400129	Natural rubber in other forms	0.13	2.36
392620	Arts of apprl & clothing accessories (incl. gloves)	0.44	1.71

Source: Authors' calculations based on Government of India, DGCIS Database (2008).

Table 5.5 India's Top 35 import items from Sri Lanka (2003–2004)

S. No.	HS code	Commodity	2003–2004 US$m	TR for 2001	TR for 2004
1	740311	Cathodes & sectns of cathodes of refined copper	56.92	36	2.13
2	740319	Other refined copper, unwrought	8.31	36	2.13
3	90411	Pepper neither crushed nor ground	7.67	1.38	2.49
4	720449	Other waste and scrap	7.23	36	1.5
5	680221	Simply cut/sawn marble travertine & alabaster with a flat or even surface	6.03	1.38	1.38
6	740312	Wire-bars of refined copper	5.89	36	36
7	854419	Winding wires of other metals/ substances	5.66	6	6
8	90700	Cloves (whole fruit cloves & stems)	5.12	1.38	1.38
9	847330	Prts & accssrs of mchns of hdg No. 8471	4.67	16	0.25
10	392690	Other articles of plastics	4.42	6.79	1.93
11	470790	Other incl. unsorted waste and scrap	3.85	16	3.38
12	852812	Receptn aparts for TV, etc. colour	3.37	6	6
13	282410	Lead monoxide (litharge, massicot)	2.57	36	36
14	980100	Project goods	2.25	NA	NA
15	740710	Bars, rods & profiles of refined copper	2.23	36	36
16	152000	Glycerol, crude; glycerol waters & lyes	2.08	3.27	3.27
17	121190	Othr plnts & prts of plnts of hdng 1211	1.86	2.67	2.67
18	740729	Bars rods, etc. of other copper alloys	1.84	36	2.13
19	80111	Coconut desiccated	1.79	2.73	2.49
20	90810	Nutmeg	1.73	1.38	1.09
21	710239	Other non-industrial diamonds	1.64	16	13.5
22	854459	Other elctrc cndctrs for a voltage excdng 80 V but not excdg 1000 V	1.33	2.57	2.57
23	151110	Crude palm oil & its fractns	1.32	2.15	2.15

(*Continued*)

Table 5.5 Continued

S. No.	HS code	Commodity	2003–2004 US$m	TR for 2001	TR for 2004
24	853931	Fluorescent, hot cathode discharge lamps	1.28	10.29	10.29
25	760120	Aluminium alloys	1.26	26	2.13
26	740313	Billets of refined copper	1.16	36	2.13
27	850440	Static converters	1.12	6.7	6.71
28	482110	Printed labels	1.04	3.27	3.27
29	130190	Other natural gums/resins/ balsams	1.03	16	7.75
30	854260	Hybrid integrated circuits	1.03	NA	0.14
31	420212	Trunks suit cases, etc. and smlr contnr with outer surface of plastic/of txtl materials	1.02	1.38	1.38
32	401120	New pneumatic tyres used on buses/lorries	0.95	1.38	1.38
33	151710	Margarine excluding liquid margarine	0.93	1.38	1.53
34	854411	Winding wire of copper	0.86	2.25	0.76
35	740911	Plates, sheets, etc. of refind copper in coils	0.84	36	36

Source: Authors' calculations based on Government of India, DGCIS Database (2008).

2000–2001 to 2003–2004, there has been a rise in imports of these items in value terms. The list of these 12 items is shown in Table 5.6.

Upon further examination it was also found that from the list of the top 35 imports, there are 23 new items that did not appear among the top 55 items of 2000–2001. These 23 items constitute US$106.6m of imports, which makes up 54.73 per cent of the total imports from SL in that year (2003–2004). Thus, the majority of imports in 2003–2004 were items that were not imported in large quantities earlier and were new items. The average TR for the top 35 imports has decreased from 14.49 in 2001 to 7.04 in 2004, which was mainly due to unilateral reduction of tariffs by India on MFN basis and therefore reduced the risk of the trade deflection. However, the TR remained higher than 1 and therefore the chances of deflection could not be ruled out. Out of these 35 items, 2 items were in the negative list of India. There is no trade deflection in their case, as there is no tariff concession given. These 2 items are printed labels (HS 482110) and other articles of plastics (HS 392690).

Table 5.6 India's 12 Common import items from Sri Lanka (2001 and 2004)

HS code	Commodity	2003–2004 USDm	TR for 2001	TR for 2004
130190	Other natural gums/resins/balsams	1.03	16	7.75
470790	Othr incl unsorted waste and scrap	3.85	16	3.38
152000	Glycerol, crude; glycerol waters & lyes	2.08	3.27	3.27
482110	Printed labels	1.04	3.27	3.27
121190	Other plnts & prts of plnts of hdng 1211	1.86	2.67	2.67
90411	Pepper neither crushed nor ground	7.67	1.38	2.49
392690	Other articles of plastics	4.42	6.79	1.93
720449	Other waste and scrap	7.23	36	1.5
680221	Simply cut/sawn marble travertine & alabaster with a flat or even surface	6.03	1.38	1.38
90700	Cloves (whole fruit cloves & stems)	5.12	1.38	1.38
401120	New pneumatic tyres used on buses/ lorries	0.95	1.38	1.38
90810	Nutmeg	1.73	1.38	1.09
847330	Prts & accssrs of machines of hdg No. 8471	4.67	16	0.25

Source: Authors'calculations based on Government of India, DGCIS Database (2008).

The top 74 items (imports in value terms) comprising 91.93 per cent of total imports from Sri Lanka during the period 2005–2006 were considered (Table 5.7).

There were 29 items that were also in the earlier list of top import items comprising imports worth US$363.56 million, which makes up 62.93 per cent of total imports from Sri Lanka to India during the period. Therefore, a majority of imports comprised items that were also top imports in the year 2000–2001 and 2003–2004. Only about 37 per cent of imports were new goods. The 29 common items are shown in Table 5.8.

The average TR for these 74 items has fallen from 16.01 in 2001 to 9.7 in 2005–2006 but is still high enough to make it beneficial for processing in Sri Lanka and exporting to India.

When considering the nature of the items that are on the list, it is evident that there are two pertinent items that have created a lot of criticism among Indian industry. The industry had alleged misuse of the provisions or circumvention of the ROO in the case of copper and vegetable fats, known as Vanaspati in India. It is evident that the TRs on these items are higher and imports on these items have been significantly high. These items were also new items that Sri Lanka started exporting to India after FTA. It is indeed true that the high differential

Table 5.7 India's Top 74 import items from Sri Lanka (2005–2006)

S. No.	Hs code	Commodity	2005–2006	TR for 2001	TR for 2004
1	151620	Vegtbl fats & oils & their fractns	148.81	3.27	4.76
2	740319	Other refined copper, unwrought	61.39	36	36
3	740312	Wire-bars of refined copper	42.96	36	36
4	760511	Aluminium wire-not alloyed – of which the maximum cross-sctnl dimension exceeds 7 mm	35.81	26	0.65
5	294190	Other antibiotics	22.85	36	3.38
6	741300	Stranded wire, cables, plaitd bands & like of copper, not electrically insulated	20.56	1.38	0.47
7	90700	Cloves (whole fruit cloves & stems)	18.82	1.38	1.38
8	151790	Othr edbl mxr/prpns of anml/vegtbl fats/ oils/ of fractns of diffrnt fats/oils	13.46	3.27	3.27
9	760120	Aluminium alloys	10.69	26	26
10	680221	Simply cut/sawn marble travertine & alabaster with a flat or even surface	10.41	1.38	0.47
11	90411	Pepper neither crushed nor ground	10.04	1.38	2.49
12	740819	Other wire of refined copper	7.6	1.38	1.38
13	470790	Othr incl unsorted waste and scrap	6.79	16	16
14	720449	Other waste and scrap	6.33	36	36
15	854411	Winding wire of copper	6.27	2.25	0.76
16	392690	Other articles of plastics	6.22	1.93	1.93
17	854419	Winding wires of othr metls,/substances	5.48	6	6
18	854449	Other elctrc cndctrs for a voltage <=80 v	5.36	1	1
19	441199	Othr fibre board of wood	3.81	36	36
20	282410	Lead monoxide (litharge, massicot)	3.68	36	3.38
21	441111	Fibr bord of density excd 0.8 G/cm3 not mechanicaly workd or surface covrd	3.62	36	3.38
22	790500	Zinc plates, sheets, strip & foil	3.51	36	2.13

155

Table 5.7 Continued

S. No.	Hs code	Commodity	2005–2006	TR for 2001	TR for 2004
23	740321	Copper–zinc base alloys (brass)	3.35	36	36
24	853931	Fluorescent,hot cathode discharge lamps	3.31	10.29	10.29
25	401120	New pnmtc tyres used on buses/lorries	3.09	1.38	1.38
26	470710	Wste and scrp of unblechd kraft papr or paprbord or corgtd papr/paprbord	3.01	16	16
27	847330	Prts & accssrs of mchns of hdg no.8471	2.72	16	0.25
28	400121	Natrl rubr in smkd sheets	2.45	1.62	1.62
29	151190	Refined palm oil & its fractions	2.15	2.9	2.9
30	710239	Other non-industrial diamonds	2.03	16	16
31	940330	Wooden frntr of a knd used in offices	2	1.38	1.38
32	90810	Nutmeg	1.98	1.38	1.38
33	340290	Other washing prpns & cleaning prpns	1.88	4.93	1.34
34	420212	Trunks suit cases etc and smlr contnr wth outer surface of plastic/of txtl matrls	1.85	1.38	0.47
35	262030	Ash & residues contng mainly copper	1.82	36	2.13
36	441129	Other fibre board of density excd 0.5G/cm^3 but not excd 0.8 G/cm^3	1.79	36	36
37	382319	Other industrial monocarboxylic fatty acid	1.67	36	36
38	230220	Bran sharps & other residues of rice	1.62	1.45	1.23
39	482110	Printed labels	1.58	0.47	0.47
40	853710	Bords, etc. for a voltage < =1000 vlts	1.54	3.27	1.04
41	940320	Other metal furniture	1.5	1.38	0.47
42	152000	Glycerol, crude; glycerol waters & lyes	1.46	3.27	2.38
43	294200	Other organic compounds	1.43	36	3.38
44	720429	Waste & scrap of other alloy steel	1.43	36	1.5

(*Continued*)

Table 5.7 Continued

S. No.	Hs code	Commodity	2005–2006	TR for 2001	TR for 2004
45	740811	Wire of refined copper of which maximum cross-sectional dimension exceeds 6mm	1.43	36	2.13
46	680210	Tiles cubes, etc. w/n rectnglr (incl sqr) whose lrgst surface area be enclsd in a sqr measuring	1.38	1.38	1.38
47	780199	Other unrefined lead & lead alloys	1.37	36	36
48	800700	Other articles of tin	1.34	26	3.38
49	130190	Other natural gums/resins/balsams	1.32	16	16
50	520931	Dyed plain weave cotton fabrics weghng more than 200 g per sqm	1.25	36	36
51	730640	Other, welded, of circular cross-section, of stainless steel tubes/pipes	1.2	3.27	1.04
52	780110	Refined lead	1.18	36	1.5
53	90820	Mace	1.14	1.38	1.09
54	740400	Copper waste & scrap	1.12	36	36
55	401519	Other gloves, mittens & mitts	1.1	1.38	1.38
56	90610	Cinnamon & tree flwrs not crshd/grnd	1.07	1.38	1.09
57	721720	Wire of irn/non-alloy steel, pltd/cotd wth zinc	1.07	3.27	0.53
58	281700	Zinc oxide & zinc peroxide	1.05	36	36
59	871639	Other trlrs & semi-trlr for trnsprt of goods	1	3.27	3.27
60	853939	Other discharge lamps, other than ultra violet lamps	0.98	6	1.04
61	382311	Stearic acid	0.94	36	4.95
62	842230	Mchnry for fillng, closing, sealing, capsuling or labelling bottles, cans, boxes, bags/other containers; mchnry for aerating beverages	0.94	11.3	3.38
63	520829	Other cotton fabrics, bleached contng 85% or more by wt of cotton weighing not more than 200 g per sqm	0.93	36	36

157

Table 5.7 Continued

S. No.	Hs code	Commodity	2005–2006	TR for 2001	TR for 2004
64	691110	Tableware and kitchenware of porcelain china	0.93	1.38	1.38
65	441119	Other fibre bord of density excd 0.8 G/cm3	0.92	36	36
66	80290	Other nuts fresh or dried	0.9	2.63	3.05
67	854460	Other elctrc cndctrs for voltage excdg 1000 v	0.9	6	1.93
68	580620	Othr narrow wvn fbrcs cntng by wt 5% or more of elastomrc yarn/rubber thread	0.87	36	36
69	520942	Denim	0.86	NA	NA
70	730890	Other structrs & parts of structrs, etc.	0.82	1.38	0.47
71	401511	Surgical gloves, mittens & mitts	0.81	36	3.38
72	90240	Other blck tea/other prtly frmntd tea	0.73	2.73	2.73
73	151800	Anml veg fats & oils & their frctns, boiled oxid. dehyd. sulphrsd blown polymrsd excl hdg 1516; inedible mixtures	0.71	3.27	3.27
74	151710	Margarine excluding liquid margarine	0.7	1.38	1.53

Source: Authors' calculations based on Government of India, DGCIS Database (2008).

Table 5.8 India's imports from Sri Lanka: comparison of TR

HS code	Commodity	2005–2006	TR for 2001	TR for 2004
740319	Other refined copper, unwrought	61.39	36	36
740312	Wire-bars of refined copper	42.96	36	36
720449	Other waste and scrap	6.33	36	36
740400	Copper waste & scrap	1.12	36	36
281700	Zinc oxide & zinc peroxide	1.05	36	36
760120	Aluminium alloys	10.69	26	26
470790	Othr incl unsorted waste and scrap	6.79	16	16
470710	Wste and scrp of unbleachd craft paper or paperboard or corrugtd. paper/paperboard	3.01	16	16
710239	Other non-industrial diamonds	2.03	16	16

(Continued)

Table 5.8   Continued

HS code	Commodity	2005–2006	TR for 2001	TR for 2004
130190	Other natural gums/resins/balsams	1.32	16	16
853931	Fluorescent, hot cathode discharge lamps	3.31	10.29	10.29
854419	Winding wires of other metals/ substances	5.48	6	6
282410	Lead monoxide (litharge,massicot)	3.68	36	3.38
401511	Surgical gloves, mittens & mitts	0.81	36	3.38
80290	Other nuts fresh or dried	0.9	2.63	3.05
151190	Refined palm oil & its fractions	2.15	2.9	2.9
90240	Other black tea/other prtly frmntd tea	0.73	2.73	2.73
90411	Pepper neither crushed nor ground	10.04	1.38	2.49
152000	Glycerol, crude; glycerol waters & lyes	1.46	3.27	2.38
392690	Other articles of plastics	6.22	1.93	1.93
151710	Margarine excluding liquid margarine	0.7	1.38	1.53
90700	Cloves(whole fruit cloves & stems)	18.82	1.38	1.38
401120	New pneumatic tyres used on buses/ lorries	3.09	1.38	1.38
940330	Wooden furniture of a kind used in offices	2	1.38	1.38
90810	Nutmeg	1.98	1.38	1.38
90820	Mace	1.14	1.38	1.09
854449	Othr electric conductors for a voltage < = 80 v	5.36	1	1
854411	Winding wire of copper	6.27	2.25	0.76
680221	Simply cut/sawn marble travertine & alabaster with a flat or even surface	10.41	1.38	0.47
420212	Trunks suit cases, etc. and smlr contnr wth outer surface of plastic/ of txtl materials	1.85	1.38	0.47
482110	Printed labels	1.58	0.47	0.47
847330	Prts & accssrs of machines of hdg no. 8471	2.72	16	0.25

Source: Authors' calculations based on Government of India, DGCIS Database (2008).

in TR makes it highly desirable for a manufacturer in Sri Lanka to reap the maximum benefit by exporting to India under FTA as his profits will be very high due to higher duties in India. Under this situation, it would be prudent on the part of India to liberalize its tariffs on MFN basis on such high TR items so that the effect of trade deflection is minimized.

5.4 Effect of FTA on actual trade flows: are ROO really trade-restrictive?

With the implementation of SAFTA as a regional agreement, an interesting question arises: whether the bilateral agreements become redundant or whether they continue to play a more prominent role than SAFTA in governing the trade flows. A case study of India was carried out. It was observed that India has more favourable bilateral FTAs with Sri Lanka, as well as with Bhutan and Nepal, on a non-reciprocal basis, and so it is highly likely that India's trade flows with Sri Lanka, Bhutan and Nepal will be governed by these bilateral treaties rather than SAFTA. At the same time, these countries are also providing a better market access to India by these bilateral agreements. Even the timeframe for tariff liberalisation as agreed under SAFTA is much longer when compared to the bilateral agreements and, therefore, has not much of relevance in terms of providing preferential access within the group of countries namely India, Sri Lanka, Nepal and Bhutan. At the same time the size of the sensitive list in SAFTA is larger than those listed in bilateral agreements, so that even when a zero duty preferential regime in SAFTA is established, concessions on more number of items would be available to Bhutan, Nepal and Sri Lanka under their bilateral agreements *vis-à-vis* SAFTA. However, India's trade with Bangladesh, Maldives and Pakistan would to a large extent depend on the concessions offered under SAFTA. There is a commonality; however, on the ROO between SAFTA and these bilateral agreements, with the exception of Bhutan. Therefore, if a product can qualify under one agreement, it can qualify under the SAFTA as well or vice versa. This harmonisation on the ROO is a positive sign for the exporters, who would not be required to maintain separate inventories for qualification of a product for preferences.

India's import from SAARC for the period 2002–2003 to 2007–08 is given in Table 5.9. Though the imports from SAARC increased steadily during the period and have quadrupled, it remained at only around 1 per cent of India's global imports. Despite the fact that most of its neighbours are import-dependent, India's trade with these countries has not been very impressive, both in terms of volume and as a percentage of its global trade. As is evident from Table 5.9, while India has a favourable balance of trade with all countries in the South Asian region, it has a huge trade surplus with Bangladesh, Sri Lanka, Pakistan and Nepal.

Upon examining the bilateral trade patterns, it can be seen that historically Nepal was the largest exporter to India in the region till 2003–2004. This trend was broken by Sri Lanka in 2004–2005, and since then it became the largest exporter to India among the SAARC members. In fact,

Table 5.9 India's trade with SAARC Members

(Value in US$m)

	2002–03		2003–04		2004–05		2005–06		2006–07		2007–08	
	Exports to	Imports from	Exports to	Imports from	Exports to	Imports from	Exports to	Imports from	Exports to	Imports from	Exports to	Imports from
Afghanistan									181.58	34.48	248.86	109.23
Bangladesh	1176	62.05	1740.75	77.63	1631.12	59.37	1664.36	127.03	1,626.58	228.31	2,916.79	257
Bhutan	39.05	32.15	89.49	52.37	84.58	71	99.17	88.77	57.46	141.33	86.65	194.38
Maldives	31.59	0.33	42.34	0.37	47.61	0.61	67.58	1.98	68.67	3.05	89.55	4.15
Nepal	350.36	281.76	669.36	286.04	743.14	345.83	859.97	379.85	927.77	305.73	1,506.05	627.72
Pakistan	206.16	44.85	286.94	57.65	521.05	94.97	689.23	179.56	1,348.55	323.01	1,944.17	287.8
Sri Lanka	920.98	90.83	1319.2	194.74	1413.18	378.4	2024.67	577.7	2,253.82	470.26	2,825.16	631.12

Source: Ratna (2008).

India's imports : FTA effect

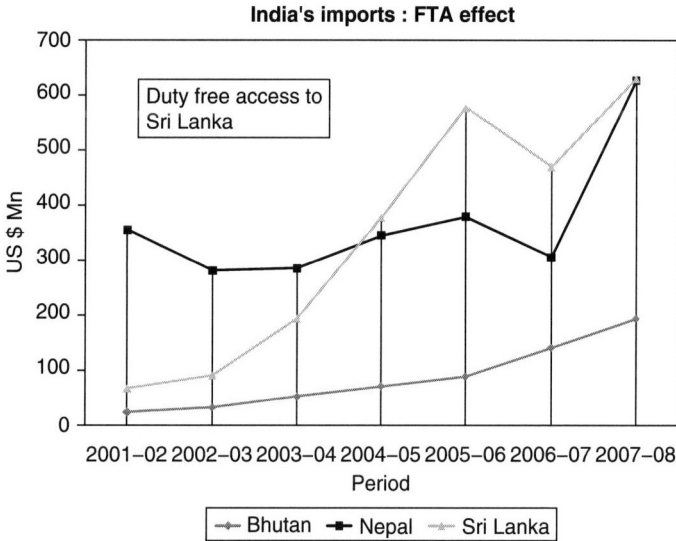

Source: ibid.
Figure 5.1 India's imports: FTA effect.

the sharp rise in their exports to India every year has been observed since 2002–2003 onwards (see Figure 5.1). During 2001–2002, Sri Lanka's exports to India saw a 150 per cent increase over the preceding year. India gave duty free treatment to Sri Lankan goods with effect from March 2003. In another two years Sri Lanka's exports surpassed Nepal's exports to India, making Sri Lanka the largest exporter to India!. This happened even though the size of India's negative list in the Nepal treaty is minuscule compared to that of Sri Lanka's FTA and the ROO for Nepal is more relaxed than the one with Sri Lanka. India definitely reaped the benefits from bilateral FTAs and it had simultaneously allowed Nepal and Sri Lanka, and to some extent Bhutan, to gain effective preferential market access in India. This happened despite the fact that the agreements with Nepal and Sri Lanka were not free from pitfalls. Indian industry has been making several complaints about misuse of some of the provisions of these agreements and the talks continue to resolve these issues to the mutual satisfaction of the respective sides.

The above trends in trade present a very interesting feature of India's trade with SAARC members if one takes into account the history of India's bilateral agreements with SAARC nations, especially with Nepal and Sri Lanka. Under the bilateral trade treaty India has given duty free access to Nepal, which utilized the agreement to its advantage by continuously maintaining its status by being the largest exporter in SAARC to India. Nepal's exports to India in value terms also remained much higher than any other SAARC member. India is one of the largest exporters to Nepal, and it would be inclined to attribute this to the constraints a land-locked country faces. The literature suggests that in such cases the neighbours are the most important natural trading partners and it would have to be assumed that it would not only be the tariff preferences that make India the principal trade partner of Nepal but also the geographical proximity. However, the trade data illustrates the fact that the reverse trend is also true, i.e. Nepal is the largest exporter to India from among the SAARC Member countries. Similarly, Sri Lanka became the largest exporter to India post-bilateral FTA implementation, which again is a small-island country. Therefore, one would be inclined to argue that tariff concessions indeed play a significant role in determining the trade flows, even for a land-locked or small-island neighbouring country.

As has been explained in earlier chapter, the ROO can also play a developmental role. In the case of South Asia, especially in India's agreements this feature is prominent. In SAPTA, which was implemented in 1995, India granted tariff concessions ranging from 10 per cent to 75 per cent to the SAARC LDCs. SAPTA had a value added of 30 per cent for LDCs and did not have detailed minimal or non-qualifying operations. During that time India had a more favourable bilateral treaty with Bhutan and Nepal. In 2002 the ROO for its treaty with Nepal became CTH and 35 per cent (30 per cent in 2003). A significant point is the fact that Nepal's exports to India has continued to increase. This was despite the fact that during 1996 to 2002 the ROO were lax, but they became much more stringent in 2002 where a twin criteria of CTH and value added was applied. This happened only due to the fact that India's investments to Nepal continued and there were more serious players post-2002. The fact that relaxed ROO may increase trade was not proved true in the case of SAARC as it did not lead to serious intra-regional investments under SAPTA. With the simpler or relaxed rules most of the industry's investments were to make the benefit of tariff concessions due to higher duties in India and there was a lack of serious investments flowing to either Bangladesh or Nepal from India. Today India is the leading source of Foreign Direct Investments (FDI) in Nepal, accounting for one-third of foreign investments in Nepal. There are

295 Indian Joint Ventures in Nepal with total Indian investments of IRS 6 billion.

Similarly, in the case of Sri Lanka, India has only invested there in a more meaningful way after the bilateral FTA was signed. In this case too, though significant tariff concessions were given to Sri Lanka under SAPTA the Indian investments in Sri Lanka were not meaningful or significant. Post-FTA India became the largest invester in Sri Lanka. This happened, again, with the stringent ROO of CTH and a value added content requirement of 35 per cent. This fact has even been reported by UNCTAD (see Box 5.1).

Even in the other regional agreement, it can be observed that if the ROO are slightly restricted, the intra-regional trade and investment flows will be enhanced and will be sustainable, as in the above cases. In examining the case of NAFTA, the dislocation of industries from USA to Mexico happened in the case of textiles and clothing, and automobile sector. It is again a well-known fact that the ROO for these sectors were more restricted than the overall ROO of NAFTA.

Box 5.1 The Sri Lanka FTA and FDI

Free Trade Agreement gives duty-free market access to India and Sri Lanka on a preferential basis. Covering 4,000 products, it foresaw a gradual reduction of import tariffs over three years for India and eight years for Sri Lanka.

To qualify for duty concessions in either country, the Rules of Origin criteria spelled out value added at a minimum of 35% for eligible imports. For raw materials sourced from either country, the value-added component would be 25%.

The effect? Sri Lankan exports to India increased from $71 million in 2001 to $168 million in 2002. And India's exports to Sri Lanka increased from $604 million in 2001 to $831 million in 2002. Although the agreement does not address investment, it has stimulated new FDI for rubber-based products, ceramics, electrical and electronic items, wood-based products, agricultural commodities and consumer durables. Because of the agreement, 37 projects are now in operation, with a total investment of $145 million.

Source: UN, *World Investment Report* (2003).

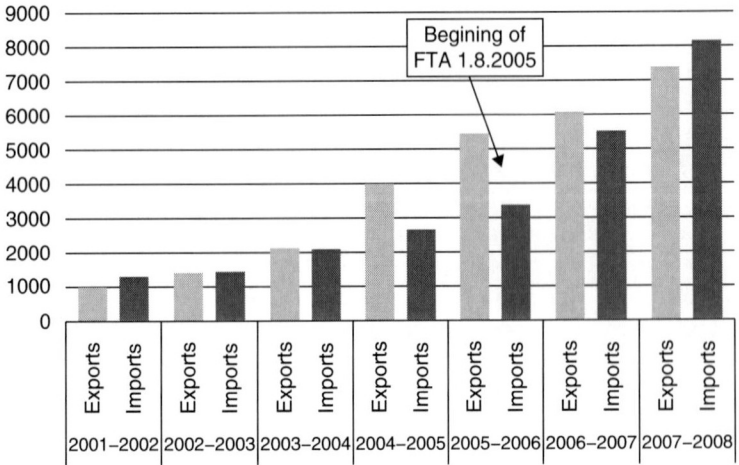

Source: Authors' calculations based on Government of India, DGCIS Database (2009).
Figure 5.2   India–Singapore CECA.

The India–Singapore CECA, which included FTA in trade on goods, commenced on 1 August 2005. The bilateral trade between India and Singapore has been increasing since then as is evident from Figure 5.2.

India had a favourable balance of trade with Singapore till 2006–2007 and the balance shifted in favour of Singapore in 2007–2008. This is despite the fact that Singapore has duty free imports on MFN basis and the ROO prescribe for the criteria of CTH and 40 per cent value added content. The bilateral investments have also increased post-FTA.

5.5   India's FTAs: exploring restrictiveness and developmental indices

As discussed in the earlier chapters, several studies have tried to gauge the ROO in terms of the restrictive index. While a vast body of literature is available on the subject, the model put forth by the authors in terms of development index for the ROO is a new concept and therefore there is no empirical evidence to establish the success or the failure of the model. Therefore, it was felt that the developmental index should be tested through a negative test of restrictive index. In this regard, two FTAs of India, namely India–Sri Lanka FTA and India–Singapore FTA were put to the test. The results were compared to see if the results converge or not. At this stage, it is pertinent to mention that the restrictiveness index is not exactly the converse of the developmental index evolved by us.

5.5.1 Empirical estimation of the effects of ROO on trade in an FTA: gravity model estimation

One area of the literature on the subject focuses on assessing the degree of market access in the context of ROO. These approaches entailed creating an index to assess the degree of restrictiveness of ROO (see Estevadeordal, 2000; Brenton, 2003b; Manchin, 2002; Augier *et al.*, 2003; Australian Productivity Commission, 2004; Estevadeordal and Suominen, 2004,). Indexes developed in these studies have focused on particular provisions of ROO – for example, whether a change in tariff classification is at the level of tariff items (HS 8-digit), sub-heading (6-digit), heading (4-digit) or the Chapter (2-digit). Factors affecting the restrictiveness of ROO have included tariff phase-out schedules, cumulation, duty drawback, tolerance, and outward processing provisions in an FTA. Some of them have expanded the list of factors by inducting regional value added content requirements and those influencing market access while calculating the index.

Studies have also estimated gravity equation with ROO Restrictiveness Index as an explanatory variable (e.g. Estevadeordal and Suominen 2004; Cadot *et al.*, 2006; Carrere *et al.*, 2006).

Bilateral exports of one country to another country of the grouping are taken as the dependent variable. The independent variables that have been used to explain the dependent variable include GDP of the importing partner (GDP), value added by each industry (VA), number of employees in each industry (LAB), wages and salaries of employees (WAG) and level of investment in each industry (INV) and ROO Restrictiveness Index (RI).

For each bilateral, for instance India–Sri Lanka FTA and India–Singapore FTA, there is industry-level data on each of the variables for the years 2007. Trade data was taken at HS 6-digit level and industry data at International Standard Industrial classification (ISIC) 3-digit level. Thus, we have a pooled cross-section data and the empirical estimation is carried out using the pooled regression method through the equation:

$$X_{ijk} = \alpha + \beta_1 (GDP)_j + \beta_2 (RI)_{ik} + \beta_3 (VA)_{ik} + \beta_4 (LAB)_{il} + \beta_5 (WAG)_{ik} + \beta_6 (INV)_{ik} + \mu_{ik}$$

where, X_{ijk} is exports from country i (e.g. Sri Lanka) to country j for the 3-digit level industry k.

Table 5.10 Role of ROO in determining trade in India–Sri Lanka: no. of observations: 138

Independent variables	Coefficient (fixed effects)	t-statistic
C	–4343.558	–0.130353
GDP	33.051	4.693041
ROO Index	1998.447	0.293372
No. of employees	0.051	2.639633
Value added	2.34E-07	2.636760
Wages and salaries	–9.67E-07	2.087725
Level of investment	6.44E-09	0.083412
R-squared	0.749640	
Adjusted R-squared	0.717430	

The results of the pooled estimation for fixed effects are presented in Table 5.10 for India–Sri Lanka and in Table 5.11 for India–Singapore FTA. For choosing fixed effects, the Hausman Test was applied and the Breusch-Pagan Test for assessing heteroskedasticity in the alternative scenarios.

As can be observed from Table 5.10, the coefficient of the ROO Index is positive (though not significant). Positive but insignificant importance of ROO is possibly due to the fact that bilateral trade levels are still at modest levels, nevertheless, it supports our argument that ROO could act as a catalyst to trade in an FTA like India–Sri Lanka given its near-optimal formulation.

All the other variables are as expected with partner country's GDP, employment and values added being significant determinants of trade. This is also expected as trade within South Asia is in labour-intensive products and it is important to note that trade is being determined by value added activities. In an indirect sense, this is also a reflection that ROO focusing on value addition either through change in tariff heading or local content requirements have a determining role in trade.

The developmental role of ROO is amplified by the fact that the process of India–Sri lanka trade is employment-based. Conversely, this is also corroborated by the insignificant investment variable as the tradeables could be less capital-intensive.

Similar observations can be made in the context of the India–Singapore FTA (Table 5.11), with the ROO formulation being CTH plus 40 per cent value-addition.

5.5.2 ROO Development Index

On the basis of the RDI value as calculated in Chapter 2, an analysis of ROO provisions of some of the important RTAs was carried out by

Table 5.11 Role of ROO in determining trade in India–Singapore FTA: no. of observations: 145

Independent variables	Coefficient (Fixed Effects)	t-statistic
C	–19533.800	–0.432187
GDP	41.902	4.044
ROO Index	4543.354	0.500335
No. of employees	–1.642771	–1.602320
Value added	5.58E-05	1.058396
Wages and salaries	2.14E-06	1.460819
Level of investment	4.14E-06	0.321571
R-squared	0.795577	
Adjusted R-squared	0.75135	

the authors. Figure 5.3 reflects the developmental-orientation of ROO formulations in these RTAs. Using this methodology, it was found that the highest degree of possibility in meeting the developmental objectives is present in RTAs such as India–Sri Lanka FTA, India–Thailand EHS, India–Singapore CECA and SAFTA. Similarly, RTAs that exhibit a relatively lesser possibility to meet development objectives because of their respective ROO formulations include AFTA, China–ASEAN and South Korea–ASEAN.

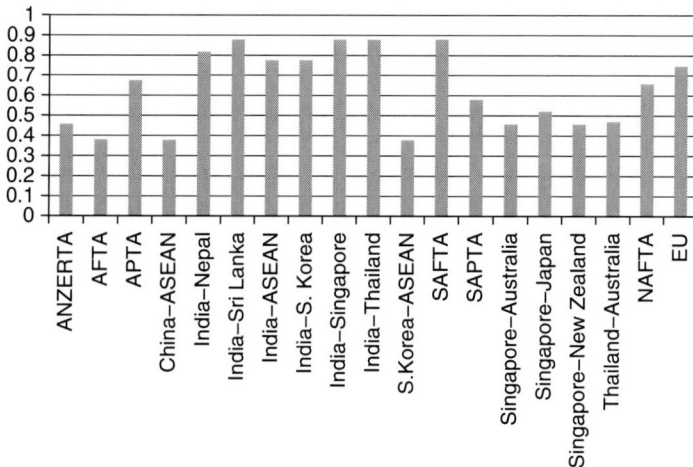

Source: Authors' own calculations based on information of RTAs obtained from UNECAP (2009).
Figure 5.3 ROO Development Index (RDI) of select RTAs.

It needs to be highlighted that two of the most important and deeper regional groupings outside the Asian region, namely. NAFTA and EU GSP display an RDI value that is development-oriented as they are in the range of RDI 0.6–0.8. The relatively lower RDI for NAFTA as compared to the EUS GSP is a result of detailed product /sector-specific ROO with bilateral cumulation, whereas the EU GSP scheme allows for the region-specific cumulation (Figure 5.3).

It can be safely concluded that the RTAs in the South Asian region have evolved a ROO framework that appears to be more development-oriented than several other regions. This is further corroborated by the analysis presented of the trade flows in the South Asian region and especially India's RTAs with Sri Lanka, Thailand and Singapore as well as the estimations made with the help of the gravity model.

5.6 Industry perception

With its increasing engagements for FTAs, India views the ROO as a tool to address the trade deflection or circumvention of goods coming from non-RTA partners under the ambit of its PTA/FTA. The chances of mis-declaring and circumvention of the ROO to achieve preferential market access in Indian market are greater due to much higher customs duty of India than its RTA partners. The Indian industry has expressed several concerns and complaints regarding misuse of the provisions of ROO.

As has been shown by the trends of trade practices under few agreements, there is a distinct possibility of third country goods being diverted to India with minimal processing, or no processing, causing a serious threat to domestic industry. Hence, the industry has demanded that ROO should be 'strong' and implemented vigorously to deter such trade diversion and fraudulent practices. Since India is providing a huge market, hence, the ROO should be to meet industry's concerns of trade deflection. The industry also suggested that the application of diverse origin criteria under RTAs should be avoided. This would minimize the complications in account-keeping and compliance of origin certification requirements. They indicated their preference for having a single general rule for all the RTAs.

The Indian industry suffers from serious disadvantages because of the lack of adequate infrastructure and high cost of power and other utilities. Further, the cost of borrowing is also high due to high interest rates. Given these constraints, the industry finds itself in a vulnerable position except in the case of certain industries that are well established, enjoy the benefits of economies of scale and have an assured domestic market. Therefore, the ROO should be such that it facilitates the greater value addition in the region and the provision for cumulation is built in all the agreements.

To sum up, this chapter highlights the fact that ROO can definitely determine the trade as well as investment flows in any RTA. Contrary to the general belief that relaxed rules will enhance greater opportunities this is not always true especially if the duties in one oRTA partner is higher and the other partner is economically much weaker (as in case of India Nepal, India–Sri Lanka or USA–Mexico). It is only when the rules are carefully crafted or designed, which at times could be stringent or more onerous, that the overall developmental goals could be achieved through the trade and intra-investment flows. Under these circumstances a dislocation or reorientation of industries happens, which leads to optimising the benefits of relative strengths or utilisation of resources as per the comparative advantages. The integration through a backward–forward linkage of industries could happen in these cases thereby leading to a win–win situation for both the partners as it also provides a wider and larger economic space for the business entrepreneurs and they can utilize the benefits of the agreements to their mutual advantages.

The discussion in this chapter on the increase in trade flows in different RTAs of India in the post-RTA implementation phase raises the question whether ROO formulation in RTAs under consideration is really trade-restrictive? In other words, it can be concluded that the ROO formulation in India's RTAs with different countries has helped rather than acting as a trade barrier, as often perceived by experts.

Appendix: India's RTA Agreements

Agreement	Current stage of negotiations
India – Nepal Treaty on Trade	India and Nepal have signed three treaties /agreement, namely (1)Treaty of Trade to regulate bilateral trade – last revised and renewed for five years with effect from 06.03.2002, (2) Treaty of Transit to facilitate each other's trade with third countries through territory of the other – last renewed and signed on 05.01.1999 for a period of seven years, and (3) Agreement of Cooperation to control Unauthorized Trade between the two countries – last renewed for a period of five years with effect from 06.03.2002.
	Under Treaty of Trade, primary products from each other are allowed duty-free access without quantitative restrictions. Under this Treaty, India, on non-reciprocal basis, grants duty free access to Nepalese goods subject to fulfilling the stipulated 30% value addition and change of tariff heading at four-digit level. Duty free facility is, however, restricted to annual quotas on four sensitive items, namely Vanaspati (10,000 lakh MTs), Copper Products (10,000 MTs), Acrylic Yarn (10,000 MTs), Zinc Oxide (2,500 MTs).
India – Bhutan Trade Agreement	India-Bhutan trade relations are governed by Agreement on Trade and Commerce, a free trade agreement. Under this Agreement, Government of India allows transit facilities for Bhutan's trade with third countries, through the Indian territory. The movement of goods under this provision is to be allowed through specified entry / exit points. The ten year validity of the Agreement expired on 1.3.2005. *The validity of the Agreement has been extended till a new Agreement comes into force.* Bilateral discussions on the amendments have been completed and the revised agreement is expected to be notified soon.
Asia Pacific Trade Agreement (APTA)	APTA, previously known as Bangkok Agreement, is a PTA signed in July, 1975 among Bangladesh, Republic of Korea, Sri Lanka and India. China has acceded to this Agreement in 2001. Three rounds of negotiations have been concluded under this Agreement. The third Round concessions have been implemented w.e.f. 1 September, 2006. At the first Ministerial Council meeting held on 2 November, 2005, the Bangkok Agreement was renamed as Asia Pacific Trade Agreement (APTA) and signed by member countries. APTA provided for the first time a common rules of origin for the Members, which prescribes for 45% local value added content. Currently the new round of negotiations are being held and services and investment framework agreements are under negotiation.

(Continued)

Appendix Continued

Agreement	Current stage of negotiations
Global System of Trade Preferences (GSTP)	The Agreement establishing the Global System of Trade Preferences (GSTP) among Developing countries was signed on 13 April, 1988 at Belgrade following conclusion of the First Round of Negotiations. The Agreement entered into force in April, 1989 after a long process of negotiations which started in 1976. Till date Forty-four countries have ratified the Agreement and have become participants. The GSTP establishes a framework for the exchange of trade concessions among the members of the Group of 77. It lays down rules, principles and procedures for conduct of negotiations and for implementation of the results of the negotiations. The coverage of the GSTP extends to arrangements in the area of tariffs, para-tariff, non-tariff measures, direct trade measures including medium and long-term contracts and sectoral agreements. One of the basic principles of the Agreement is that it is to be negotiated step by step improved upon and extended in successive stages. So far only two Rounds of negotiations have been concluded under GSTP. The number of products covered for tariff concessions is very limited and so was the number of countries which participated in negotiations. Third round of negotiations have been launched in June, 2004 and are expected to conclude at end of 2009.
SAARC Preferential Trade Area (SAPTA)	Four rounds of negotiations have been concluded under SAPTA. Bangladesh, Bhutan, India, Maldives, Nepal, Pakistan and Sri Lanka are participants in the Agreement signed in April, 1993. Concessions exchanged during the four rounds of SAPTA have already been implemented.
India-Afghanistan Preferential Trade Agreement	A Preferential Trade Agreement (PTA) between India and Afghanistan was signed on 6 March, 2003. India has granted concessions on 38 products mainly fresh and dry fruits in return for concessions on 8 items for exports to Afghanistan.
India – MERCOSUR Preferential Trade Agreement (PTA)	A PTA was signed between India and MERCOSUR (Brazil, Argentina, Uruguay and Paraguay) in January, 2004 in New Delhi. The annexes to the PTA have been signed in March, 2005 in New Delhi. The PTA has been implemented in 2009.
India – Sri Lanka Free Trade Agreement (ISLFTA)	India-Sri Lanka Free Trade Agreement was signed in December, 1998 and is in operation since March, 2000. FTA provided for tariff reduction/elimination in a phased manner on all items except the negative list and tariff rate quota (TRQ) items. While India has already completed the tariff elimination programme in March 2003, Sri Lanka is scheduled to reach zero duty by 2008. The two countries have since initiated negotiations in August 2004 on Comprehensive Economic Partnership Agreement (CEPA) which covers trade in services and investment.

(Continued)

Appendix   Continued

Agreement	Current stage of negotiations
Agreement on SAFTA	The Agreement on South Asia Free Trade Area (SAFTA) was signed during the 12th SAARC Summit on 6 January, 2004 in Islamabad, Pakistan. Since then negotiations on four annexes, viz., Rules of Origin, Sensitive Lists, Revenue Compensation for LDCs and Technical Assistance to LDCs have been completed and the tariff liberalization programme under the Agreement has been implemented from 1 July 2006.
Comprehensive Economic Cooperation Agreement (CECA) between India and Singapore	India-Singapore CECA has been signed on 29 June, 2005. The Agreement came into force on 1st August, 2005. The Agreement provides for Early Harvest scheme, phased reduction/elimination of duties by India by 1 April 2009, on products other than those in the negative list, whereas Singapore eliminated duties on all products originating from India from 1 August 2005. CECA also covers Investment, Services, Mutual Recognition Agreement, customs cooperation.
Framework Agreement on Comprehensive Economic Cooperation between ASEAN & India	The Framework Agreement between ASEAN and India for Comprehensive Economic Cooperation was signed on 8 October, 2003 in Bali, Indonesia. The Trade Negotiating Committee (TNC) is negotiating FTA in goods. Implementation is likely to start in January 2010.
Framework Agreement for establishing Free Trade Area between India and Thailand	The Framework Agreement for establishing Free Trade Area between India and Thailand was signed on 9 October, 2003 in Bangkok. The Early Harvest Scheme covering 82 items for exchange of concessions between India and Thailand has been implemented with effect from 1 September, 2004. The Trade Negotiating Committee is already negotiating FTA in goods; and negotiations on services and investment are still at preliminary stage. The deadlines to conclude negotiations have ended. Negotiations are being held to conclude the negotiations as soon as possible.
Framework Agreement on the BIMST-EC FTA	The Framework Agreement on BIMSTEC (Bay of Bengal Initiative for Multi-sectoral Technical & Economic Corporation) Free Trade Area was signed in February, 2004 at Phuket, Thailand. Bangladesh, Bhutan, India, Myanmar, Nepal, Sri Lanka and Thailand are members of the grouping. The Framework Agreement provides for implementation of FTA on Goods with effect from 1 July 2006. Negotiations are being held by the BIMSTEC Trade Negotiating Committee (TNC) on FTA in goods, services and investment. The deadlines to conclude negotiations have ended. Negotiations are being held to conclude the negotiations as soon as possible.

(Continued)

Appendix   Continued

Agreement	Current stage of negotiations
India-Chile Framework Agreement on Economic Cooperation	A Framework Agreement on Economic Cooperation was signed between India and Chile on 20 January 2005. The Agreement envisages a PTA between the two sides. The negotiations on PTA have been concluded and the Agreement was signed on 8 March 2006. Implemented in 2009.
India-Korea Joint Task Force (JTF)	Based on the recommendations of the JSG, India and Korea constituted as Joint Task Force for having negotiations on FTA in goods, services and investment. The negotiations are likely to be concluded by end of 2009.
India-China Joint Task Force (JTF)	A Joint Task force between India and China has been set up to study in detail the feasibility of, and the benefits that may derive from the possible China-India Regional Trading Arrangement and also give its recommendations regarding its content.
India-Gulf Cooperation Council (GCC) FTA	A Framework Agreement on Economic Cooperation was signed between India and GCC on 25 August, 2004. The first round of negotiations on India-GCC FTA was held in Riyadh in March 2006 wherein both sides agreed to include Services as well as Investment and General Economic Cooperation, along with Goods, in the proposed FTA.

6
Trade in Services

The number of bilateral and regional free trade agreements (FTAs) involving members of the Asian region is increasing at a very fast pace and now most of these agreements seek the liberalization of trade in services at a faster pace than was foreseen under the WTO's General Agreement on Trade in Services (GATS). The commitments anticipated in these agreements are expected to be wider and deeper than the latest offers made under the Doha Round negotiations.

One of the questions that needs to be addressed in these RTA negotiations covering services is to what extent non-members benefit from the trade preferences that are negotiated among members? This question is resolved through *ROO* also referred to as *denial of benefits* under which the conditions relating to market access are determined under different modes. Unlike in the case of goods, it is the ROO in services trade that primarily determines the extent of market access opportunities and their ultimate economic effects. Notwithstanding the conclusion of many new FTAs, hardly any research is available that can guide policy-makers on the economic implications of different ROO.

In this chapter we first try to bring out as to how services trade is distinct from trade in goods, thereby underscoring the point that the approaches to ROO with respect to the former would also have to be distinct from the latter. In so doing, this chapter highlights the uniqueness of trade in services followed by the distinct approaches towards ROO in trade in services as evolved in different RTAs. This has been undertaken by setting in place a conceptual framework for ROO relating to trade in services in RTAs. Subsequently, dimensions of ROO in the Asian context including India's RTAs are analysed and in the end certain policy suggestions are made to improve the efficacy of ROO for services trade.

Trade in services has distinct features as compared to those in goods and therefore it needs to be analysed and approached differently. Services possess three main features that make them very different from goods: first, they are intangible although often incorporated in tangible products; secondly, they are non-storable; and thirdly, they involve a simultaneous action between the service provider and the service consumer. Further, unlike production of goods, ownership of a service is often not transferred during the process of service provision. Instead, the service supplier stores the capacity to provide the service to be rendered at a time when there is a demand for that service. The inability to store means that services mostly are produced and consumed simultaneously.

If service providers in one country possess a desired service, then they must somehow interact with service consumers in other countries for trade to take place. For services trade to occur, the means of transporting the services often have to be allowed to cross national boundaries, with the result of making international transaction in services more complex conceptually than international transactions in goods. Services have in fact often been characterized as non-tradables in the sense that they involve movement in factors of production. For instance, provision of services to global markets often necessitates the movement of capital (economic activities generated through foreign direct investment) or labour (personnel to manage such activities or to provide different types of expertise, including basic labour).

According to Stern and Hoekman (1988) services can be (a) complementary to trade in goods, (b) substitute for trade in goods or (c) unrelated to goods. Depending on these, implications for services trade would change. The intangibility and non-storability of services imply that in order for them to become tradable, services have to be embodied in objects, information flows or persons. When services are globally traded through crossing borders they are embedded into products such as in the case of computer programs in CD-ROMs, air transport through aircraft, music in digital products, films in videotapes, etc. Some services may be transmitted via the telecommunications networks.

Due to these features, trade in services assumes a special character. The simultaneous nature of service transaction impacts upon the modalities of international transactions in services. It is for this reason that international transactions in services have been defined according to four modalities (Sampson and Snape, 1985) and later set out in Article I of the GATS, namely Cross border supply, Consumption abroad, Commercial presence, and Supply through movement of natural persons (see Box 6.1 for definitions).

Box 6.1 Different modes of services

Trade in services can take place under any of the following four modes defined under GATS:

Cross border supply (Mode 1)

Cross-border supply refers to a situation where the service flows from the territory of one Member country into the territory of another Member county. For example, architects can send their architectural plans through electronic means; teachers can send teaching material to students in any other country; doctor sitting in Germany can advise theirs patients in India through electronic means. In all these cases, trade in services takes place and this is equivalent to cross-border movement of goods.

Consumption abroad (Mode 2)

Consumption abroad refers to a situation where consumer of a service moves into the territory of another Member country to obtain the service. For example, a tourist using hotel or restaurant services abroad; a ship or aircraft undergoing repair or maintenance services abroad.

Commercial presence (Mode 3)

Commercial presence implies that service suppliers of a Member country establish a territorial presence (a legal presence) in another Member country with a view to providing their services. In this case, the service supplier establishes a legal presence in the form of a joint venture/subsidiary/ representative/ branch office in the host country and starts supplying services.

Movement of natural persons (Mode 4)

Presence or movement of natural persons (this only refers to export of manpower) covers situations in which a service is delivered through persons of a Member country temporarily entering the territory of another Member country. Examples include independent service suppliers (e.g. doctors, engineers, Individual consultants, accountants, etc.) However, GATS covers only temporary movement and not citizenship, residence or employment on a permanent basis in the foreign country.

6.1 Rules of origin in services: conceptual issues

Due to the reasons explained above there has not been much research carried out on conceptual as well as empirical issues relating to ROO in trade in services under RTAs.

Cadot *et al.* (2006) have explored the issues of ROO in trade in services by advancing a few thoughts on a range of economic and legal considerations. They take a number of economic considerations that relate to the design of ROO for services trade by analysing adverse effects of trade and investment diversion and their protectionist effects that limit the benefits of accession. The empirical evidence provided by them on subsidiaries of transnational corporations points to the fact that liberal origin rules for service producers will increasingly imply liberal rules for their products and further divergence of the treatment of goods and services. Beviglia-Zampetti and Sauvé (2004) have offered a detailed overview of ROO in services encountered in existing investment and trade agreements.

Mattoo and Fink (2004) have analyzed the economic effects of preferential versus MFN liberalization in services. Their conclusions from the viewpoint of the *importing* FTA member are summarized in Box 6.2.

Box 6.2 Analysis of effects of preferential versus MFN liberalization in services

Economic implications

- First, relative to the status quo, preferential liberalization in services brings about static welfare gains. This finding differs from the more ambiguous conclusion drawn in the goods case. The key difference is that protection in services does not generate fiscal revenue, as do tariffs on imported goods. Thus, trade diversion effects associated with preferential liberalization in services do not lead to any loss in government revenue that can lead to negative welfare effects in the case of goods.
- Second, MFN liberalization yields greater welfare gains than preferential liberalization. Non-discriminatory market opening does not bias competition from abroad and therefore promotes entry of the most efficient service providers. Additional gains from trade, associated with greater economies of scale and knowledge spillovers, are also likely to be greater if liberalization proceeds on

---

(Continued)

Box 6.2 Continued

an MFN basis. There is one exception to this conclusion. If 'learning by doing' effects are important, preferential liberalization may enable domestic service suppliers from member countries to become more efficient, as they face some competition from within the FTA territory, but are not yet exposed to global competition. In theory, preferential liberalization can thus prepare infant domestic suppliers for competition at the global level.

• Third, there is a special long-term trade diversion effect to worry about. Preferential liberalization may offer a first-mover advantage to potentially second-best service providers from within the FTA territory. Since many service industries are characterized by high location-specific sunk costs, first-best providers from outside the FTA territory may be deterred from entering the market when trade is eventually liberalized on an MFN basis. Thus, even if preferences are temporary, they may have long-term implications for a country's ability to attract the world's most efficient service providers.

What do these conclusions imply for the choice of rules of origin? Unless preferential FTAs are specifically designed to promote learning-by-doing, a liberal rule of origin is in economic terms *more desirable*. Even though a liberal rule of origin does not fully eliminate discrimination against non-member countries, it does away with some discrimination and therefore enlarges the pool of foreign suppliers competing for access to the domestic market. By contrast, if policy-makers believe that their domestic service industries are at an infant stage and cannot be immediately exposed to global competition, a restrictive rule of origin may be a prerequisite for governments to commit to market opening in an FTA.

From the viewpoint of the *exporting* FTA member, additional considerations apply. The choice of rule of origin determines *who* will benefit from an FTA. One can broadly distinguish from three groups of beneficiaries: national service suppliers, foreign suppliers already established, and foreign suppliers not yet established (more on how these suppliers are defined below). This raises the following issues:

• If service suppliers take the form of firms (juridical persons), a restrictive rule of origin would limit export and associated employment gains to national suppliers (or, more broadly, already established

Box 6.2 Continued

suppliers). This outcome may be sought for non-economic reasons, such as the promotion of certain ethnic groups. In addition, a restrictive rule of origin could also underpin possible 'learning-by-doing' effects mentioned above.

By contrast, a liberal rule of origin may attract new FDI from outside the FTA territory. Indeed, a country with liberal entry conditions for suppliers from outside the free trade area may specifically seek to become a hub for companies to access markets within the free trade area. The benefits from this form of FDI would depend on the modes through which services are exported to other FTA members. In the case of Modes 1 and 2, there may be significant employment gains in the exporting country. In the case of Mode 3, employment gains may be small, but governments may still benefit from higher tax revenues. Depending on the nature and purpose of FDI, there may also be important spillover externalities for the host economy.

- If service suppliers take the form of individuals (natural persons), a restrictive rule of origin again limits export gains to nationals, which may be sought for non-economic reasons (see above). However, the effects of a liberal rule of origin are trickier. Hypothetically, if service workers from outside the FTA territory merely used the exporting FTA member as a transit point to other FTA markets, a liberal rule of origin would yield little benefit to this member (unless this type of transit were taxed). Benefits would only arise if service providers from outside the FTA territory had an *economic interest* in the exporting member—that is, if they spent at least part of their income in the exporting FTA member. From an economic perspective, the center of an individual's economic interest thus seems a more important criterion for a rule of origin than the individual's nationality.

In sum, from an economic perspective, the choice of rule of origin depends on the objectives attached to an FTA. A liberal rule of origin promotes greater economic efficiency by reducing discrimination and can attract FDI from outside the FTA territory, but it can undermine learning-by-doing externalities sought after in an FTA.

(Continued)

Box 6.2 Continued

Bargaining implications

There are various reasons why countries engage in bilateral or regional trade negotiations, rather than pursuing liberalization on an MFN basis at the WTO. One is that bargaining may be more productive among a smaller set of countries. The WTO now has 149 members at all levels of development and the multilateral trade agenda has much expanded since the GATT days. Trade negotiations at the multilateral level therefore tend to be complex and time-consuming. For countries ready to commit to market opening in services, a bilateral or regional forum may deliver quicker results.

Another handicap of multilateral negotiations is that countries can free-ride on the bargaining efforts of others. Multilateral services negotiations proceed on a bilateral request and offer basis, but eventual commitments are made on an MFN basis. Thus, even though one WTO member may be interested in improved market access in another member, it may be reluctant to engage in reciprocal bargaining if there are third members interested in the same market access. The end result is a less ambitious negotiating outcome. In principle, FTAs offer a way out, as the smaller number of players reduces the scope for free-riding on the bargaining efforts of others. However, this assumes that countries not party to an FTA do not benefit from deeper market access negotiated under the FTA. In other words, for free-rider problems to be less severe in a bilateral or regional context, FTAs need to adopt a *restrictive* rule of origin.

This argument has an important upshot, which is of current relevance to the bargaining situation of several ASEAN countries. Suppose a country negotiates sequentially two or more bilateral FTAs. If it commits to liberal market access in the first FTA and this FTA adopts a liberal rule of origin, the trading partner for the second FTA may be unwilling to 'pay' for making the same commitment in the second FTA. In other words, with a liberal rule of origin, it may not be possible to 'sell' the same market access commitment twice.

In sum, a liberal rule of origin may undermine the bargaining advantages that FTAs offer relative to multilateral trade negotiations.

Box 6.2 Continued

> As a final note, the GATS imposes certain disciplines on rules of origin that WTO members entering into FTAs may adopt. In particular, WTO members are required to extend trade preferences to commercially established service suppliers from third countries that engage in substantive business operations within an FTA territory (Article V.6). However, in the case of FTAs involving *only* developing countries, preferential treatment may, in addition, be limited to companies *"owned or controlled by natural persons of the parties"* to an FTA (Article V.3b). Interestingly, the GATS does not create any discipline on the rule of origin FTA members may adopt for individual service providers.
>
> *Source*: Mattoo and Fink (2004).

Broadly, the existing literature on ROO relating to trade in services analyse its effects in terms of trade and investment diversion; the 'learning by doing' effects in the context of infant domestic suppliers; long-term trade diversion effects; and their protectionist effects that limit the benefits of accession and often rules of origin under this framework are termed as 'denial of benefits'. On each of these dimensions we offer an alternative economics of services trade as determined by the ROO.

6.2 Alternative conceptual understanding: development perspective

As with the argument for the ROO in trade in goods in this case as well the ROO could play a developmental role for trade in services. The objective of ROO is to prevent the deflection of service suppliers of non-RTA members and to reap the benefits for the RTA members only. While doing so, the ROO would play the developmental role even in case of preferential agreement on trade in services. Generally, a majority of RTAs in services have followed the GATS-plus approach through the liberalisation of services sector on the basis of positive list approach. We firmly believe that the purpose of ROO is not to deny the market access to the RTA members, contrary to what has been argued in the literature on the subject. The best option to protect the vulnerable/sensitive industry from the external competition under RTA is not to offer market access on those sectors rather than building trade-restrictive ROO. The detailed explanations in this regard follows.

6.2.1 Trade and investment diversion: efficiency vs sustainability

As is evident from the preceding section, the existing literature argues that the restrictive ROO cause long-term trade and investment diversion effects. It also points to preferential liberalization offering a first-mover advantage to potentially second-best service providers from within the RTA territory due to high location-specific sunk costs; hence the first-best providers from outside the FTA territory may be deterred from entering the market. It has also been argued that a liberal ROO may attract new FDI from outside the RTA territory.

The arguments relating to trade and investment diversion need to be viewed from a developmental perspective due to which the economic considerations and their outcomes in any preferential services trade liberalisation may change.

So far as the issue of first-mover advantage is concerned, no service provider from the rest of the world or from an RTA member, will be able to gain market access, especially in those sectors where the domestic service provider is already present, even if the foreign service provider is more efficient. It is thus quite obvious that the issue of 'first-mover advantage' has hardly any practical relevance. In other words, the first-mover advantage will always be with the domestic service provider. In fact, with trade in services liberalisation in RTAs would exert competitive pressures on domestic service suppliers for becoming more efficient, which might otherwise be difficult in the case of multilateral trade liberalisation due to which the domestic industry would face the risk of being driven out of business. The very liberal ROO will also have effects on the domestic industry similar to multilateral trade liberalisation. Due to these concerns, even GATS negotiations are based on a positive list approach as opposed to trade in goods (negative list approach), and almost in all RTAs even the members have followed the GATS-plus formula but with a positive list approach.

Given the arguments above, furthermore there is a potential developmental effect that can accrue in an RTA through origin rules via the positive spill-over and demonstration effects of service provider of an RTA member on domestic service providers. Also, if the domestic service providers could sustain their business operations due to enhanced efficiency within the liberalized RTA framework, at a later stage, they may even be ready to face the challenges relating to multilateral trade liberalisation.

Thus, the issue of trade and investment diversion in the context of ROO pertaining to trade in services liberalisation under an RTA need to be approached from a developmental angle of sustainability rather than merely from an efficiency angle.

6.2.2 Learning by doing: restrictiveness vs infant service supplier

As observed above, the literature perceives restrictiveness of ROO having 'learning-by-doing' effects. According to which, 'learning by doing' effects under an RTA may enable domestic service suppliers from member countries to become more efficient, as they face some competition from RTA members, but are not yet exposed to global competition. In theory, preferential liberalization can thus prepare infant domestic suppliers for competition at the global level.

Our simple argument is that rather than perceiving ROO in terms of restrictiveness it needs to be viewed from a developmental perspective where the infant service suppliers are exposed first to limited competition from the more efficient RTA service providers so that they can be better prepared to face the global competition at a later stage. This is consistent with our earlier assertion that the purpose of ROO is not to protect the infant service provider from the external competition under RTA by making restrictive ROO. On the contrary, it is to expose the infant service suppliers to limited competition under RTA prescribing such ROO that can meet these objectives.

6.2.3 Denial of benefits: challenging the nomenclature

Most of the literature has perceived the ROO as an instrument by which preferential market access can be denied, thus commonly termed as 'denial of benefits'. In this regard, one would need to explore the basic objective of the ROO. We would like to reiterate that the purpose of ROO is not to deny the preferential market access rather only prevent the trade deflection taking place whereby the non-RTA members can gain market access.

This becomes even more important in case of trade in services *vis-à-vis* trade in goods as the negative spill-over effects will be of greater magnitude as the trade in services are often intangibles. Services trade involves movement of capital under mode 3, hence, even financial security/non-economic considerations also call for proper tracing of capital movements that can best be addressed through appropriate ROO. Likewise, since trade in services also entails temporary movement of natural persons under mode 4, building such ROO, which can allow non-RTA members' natural persons to get similar market access opportunities, is neither desirable nor warranted due to sensitive immigration issues.

In trade in services, therefore, ROO cannot be looked at purely from the perspective of denial of benefits in terms of restrictiveness vs liberal, as it they have much broader developmental perspective, often going beyond the economic considerations.

6.3 Determining criteria for ROO in trade in services

Just as in the case of trade in goods, even in trade in services certain criteria are prescribed for determining the origin of the service providers for granting preferential market access under RTAs. These criteria are prescribed as a part of ROO in trade in services and they vary according to the modes of services trade. For modes 1 and 3, the criteria are prescribed for defining the service providers, which is considered as originating in terms of companies /juridical persons, however, for mode 4 it is defined in terms of natural persons. In the case of mode 2, determination of ROO is not clearly spelt out because of the nature of services trade transactions.

Based on practices in different RTAs some of the key criteria for determining the ROO under modes 1 and 3 include:

(i) One of the requirements may relate to a service supplier to be incorporated under the laws of the exporting RTA member. The criterion thus applied in this case is called 'incorporation'.

(ii) Another criterion that is applied relates to the condition that the service supplier possesses a business or service licence in the territory of the exporting RTA member. In addition, conditions relating to a minimum number of years of establishment; the payment of national taxes; a minimum domestic sales requirement; owning, leasing or renting of land /dwellings; and a requirement that the export of services within the RTA territory may be the same as the services supplied in the exporting RTA member. The criterion thus applied in this case is called 'substantive business operations.'

(iii) Criterion relating to originating status of a service provider is also expressed in terms of it's ownership. In this case, it is through the condition of owning/controlling of the firm or company, either by the nationals of the exporting RTA member or cumulated ownership and control criterion within the RTA members. This criterion is usually defined through the equity share in a company or the voting rights controlled by domestic/RTA members' shareholders. The criterion thus applied in this case is called 'domestic ownership and control.'

(iv) Often conditions relating to grant originating status are also linked to a minimum number of domestic employees that are employed in the firm or company. The criterion thus applied in this case is called 'domestic employment'.

For service suppliers under mode 4, described as natural persons, the criteria for determining ROO in general are:

(i) The most straightforward and easy way of determining origin of a service provider is by way of his/her nationality in the passport. The criterion thus applied in this case is called 'nationality'.

(ii) Another approach for determining the origin through nationality relates to a much broader residency approach. According to which the foreign nationals present in the exporting RTA members are also included. For instance, the market access benefits can be accorded to the permanent residents including the foreign nationals; however the temporary residents are excluded from the coverage. The criterion thus applied in this case is called 'residency'.

In view of the above, it is easily discernible that the focus of ROO in services trade agreements has been different from that in the case of goods as rather than defining the origin of a 'service', agreements have sought to accord the origin to a 'service supplier'.

6.4   ROO as practised in some important RTAs

As trade in services has increased in recent times, various trade policy measures are being devised to facilitate it. Since trade in services is not always similar to trade in goods the need for evolving trade policies specific to the services sector is increasingly realized. The academic research as well as the policy-making process on ROO has primarily focused mainly on ROO for goods. However, with increasing cross border trade in services and some of the global and regional trading arrangements focusing on the liberalisation of services markets, determination of the origin of service providers has become important. As integration of service markets often necessitates physical presence of service-suppliers in the country that is seeking services, any preferential treatment to them within a regional trading arrangement would require setting in place of origin norms for services.

Most of the agreements pertaining to trade in services adopt a nationality-cum-incorporation based origin norms. However, the US – Canada Free Trade Agreement uses the criterion of ownership and control rather than incorporation. On the other hand, in the NAFTA services and investment rules are more liberal as it covers investments made by any resident or incorporated entity in a member country of NAFTA, regardless of country of ownership or control. In the case of GATS, juridical persons are defined as entities constituted under the law of contracting party and engaged in substantial business operations in the contracting state or is owned or controlled by natural persons who are nationalized under the law of contracting party.

The China–Hong Kong Closer Economic Partnership Agreement which came into force on 1 January 2004, provides very clear criteria for granting preferences for services trade (Box 6.3).

Box 6.3 ROO in the China–Hong Kong Closer Economic Partnership Agreement

The China–Hong Kong Closer Economic Partnership Agreement is in many ways a special trade agreement. It grants Hong Kong-based service providers preferential access to China's market, in advance of the liberalization schedule to which China committed as part of its accession package to the WTO. China's offer to Hong Kong under CEPA had little to do with classical arguments of trade bargaining. Hong Kong, being one of the most open economies in the world, had little to give in terms of improved market access for Chinese suppliers. Rather, the Agreement was intended to promote deeper integration between the Mainland and Hong Kong and has to be understood in the context of the "one country, two systems" formula.

If CEPA had adopted a liberal rule of origin and given Hong Kong's liberal entry policies, service suppliers from outside of Hong Kong would have had a way to enter the Chinese market

Box 6.3 Continued

in advance of the WTO schedule. This was not the intention of the Chinese and Hong Kong governments. Thus, CEPA has an annex on the definition of service suppliers, which translates into one of the most detailed rule of origin so far seen in a trade agreement. In particular, for Hong Kong companies to enjoy preferential treatment under CEPA, they must have had substantive business operations for 3-5 years in Hong Kong for the services they intend to provide in the Mainland; they must have paid profit tax in Hong Kong; they must own or rent premises for business operations in Hong Kong; and more than 50 per cent of employees must be Hong Kong residents (or Chinese people staying in Hong Kong on a one way permit). Additional rules exist for law firms, which require the sole proprietor and all partners of a firm to be registered as practicing lawyers. In the case of individuals (natural persons), eligibility for preferential treatment is confined to Hong Kong permanent residents.

In order to be certified as Hong Kong Service Suppliers under CEPA, interested service suppliers must submit an application to Hong Kong's Department of Trade and Industry, along with documentation which verifies that suppliers meet the above criteria.

Source: Information provided on the website of Hong Kong's Department of Trade and Industry (http://www.tid.gov.hk/english/cepa/fulltext.html)

6.4.1 ASEAN

A research project of the ASEAN Economic Forum research network focussed on the ROO for juridical persons in selected service subsectors. National research studies were conducted in the following five ASEAN countries: Lao PDR, Malaysia, the Philippines, Thailand, and Vietnam (Arunanondchai and Nikomborirak, 2006, Avila and Manzano, 2006, Douangboupha *et al.*, 2006). A core element of these studies is in assessing which service providers would or would not be eligible for preferences negotiated under a region-wide FTA (Box 6.4).

So far as India is concerned, as of today, it is only the India–Singapore CECA that covers preferential market access for trade in services. The exact definitions of ROO criteria are given in Box 6.5.

Box 6.4 ROO in services: a case study of five ASEAN countries

The Thailand–Australia Free Trade Agreement stipulates that either Party may deny the benefits of pre-establishment national treatment to *"an investor of the other Party that is a juridical person of such Party and to investments of such an investor where the Party establishes that the juridical person is owned or controlled by persons of a non-Party"*. That is, foreign owned or controlled companies incorporated under Australian Law may be denied benefits under the TAFTA. A similar rule of origin is embedded in the India-Singapore Economic Cooperation Agreement, but only for services supplied through commercial presence. Domestic ownership and control is also required in the Treaty of Amity signed between Thailand and the United States in 1966. The Treaty grants benefits only to American or Thai owned or controlled companies engaging in substantial business operations in either country. Consequently, American companies applying for benefits under the Treaty to invest in a businesses restricted to foreigners would have to prove that the majority of their "ultimate beneficial owners" are indeed American citizens.

Aside from these two agreements, all other services agreements involving ASEAN countries have adopted a rule requiring only substantial business operations in the territory of a Party. In other words, a non-party service supplier which engages in substantial business operations may also benefit from the bilateral free trade agreement. Most FTAs, including the AFAS and FTAs involving the United States and Japan, adopt this rule of origin with only small deviations. It should be noted, however, that even though this broader rule of origin extends trade preferences to third-Party service suppliers, it still discriminates between Party and non-Party suppliers in that the latter can be denied benefits in the absence of proof of substantial business operation, while the former is entitled to the benefit regardless of the size of its business operation in territory of the Party. For example, a subsidiary of an American company operating in a third country, say Citibank operating in Brazil, may also benefit from the Singapore–US Free Trade Agreement (SUSFTA), while a German company, say Siemens, can take advantage of the agreement only through its subsidiary operating in the United States.

None of the FTAs in the ASEAN region defines the term "substantial business operations" more closely – for example, along the lines of

Box 6.4 Continued

the China – Hong Kong CEPA discussed earlier. Implementation is left to FTA parties and, so far, there has not been any jurisprudence on this question. The term "owned and controlled" is also not clearly defined in FTAs. In the Japan–Singapore Economic Partnership Agreement (JSEPA), a company is "owned" by persons of a party if more than 50 percent of the equity interest in it is *"ultimately owned?] by the persons of that party"*. As for the issue of control, JSEPA stipulates that a company is "controlled" by persons of a Party if such persons have the power to name the majority of its directors or otherwise legally direct its actions. Presumably, this refers to the nationality of the person who can legally represent the company or who is the designated official whose signature must accompany the company's seal on all legal documents.

Finally, most agreements extend benefits to incorporated and non-incorporated legal entities, as long as the substantial business criterion is met. In other words, branches and representative offices of enterprises incorporated in non-parties are typically eligible for FTA preferences.

Source: Carsten and Nikomborirak (2007), World Bank Policy Research Working Paper 4130.

Box 6.5 India–Singapore CECA: ROO definitions

juridical person means any legal entity duly constituted or otherwise organised under applicable law, whether for profit or otherwise, and whether privately-owned or governmentally-owned, including any corporation, trust, partnership, joint venture, sole proprietorship or association; cooperative or society;

juridical person of the other Party means a juridical person which is either:

(i) constituted or otherwise organised under the law of the other Party or
(ii) in the case of the supply of a service through commercial presence, owned or controlled by:

(*Continued*)

Box 6.5 Continued

(1) natural persons of the other Party; or

(2) juridical persons of the other Party identified under paragraph (e)(i);

Provided, however, that for the purposes of supply of audio-visual, education, financial and telecommunications services through commercial presence, except as otherwise agreed by the Parties, a "juridical person of the other Party" means a juridical person that is owned or controlled by:

(i) the other Party; or

(ii) natural persons of the other Party; or

(iii) juridical persons constituted or organized under the laws of the other Party that are owned by natural persons of the other Party or the other Party, whether directly or indirectly, or controlled by natural persons of the other Party or the other Party;

Provided, further, that for the purposes of supply of financial services through commercial presence in India, except as otherwise agreed by the Parties, a "juridical person of the other Party" includes DBS Group Holdings Limited, United Overseas Bank Limited and Oversea-Chinese Banking Corporation Limited (hereinafter collectively referred to as "Singapore Banks"), each of which may, respectively, nominate not more than one legal entity from among its holding companies, successors in title that it may designate, or entities which it owns or controls, or itself, to enter into the financial services sector in India, provided that any such entry by each of the Singapore Banks will be by means of incorporation of a separate legal entity in India, and will be restricted respectively to one legal entity each in respect of banking, asset management and insurances services; except that in respect of the remaining financial services, the restriction to one entity will not apply and in respect of bank branches, incorporation in India will not be required.

measure means any measure by a Party, whether in the form of a law, regulation, rule, procedure, decision, administrative action, or any other form;

Box 6.5 Continued

measures by Parties means measures taken by:

(i) central, regional, or local governments and authorities; and
(ii) non-governmental bodies in the exercise of powers delegated by central, regional or local governments or authorities;

measures by Parties affecting trade in services include measures in respect of:

(i) the purchase, payment or use of a service;
(ii) the access to and use of, in connection with the supply of a service, services which are required by the Parties to be offered to the public generally;
(iii) the presence, including commercial presence, of persons of a Party for the supply of a service in the territory of the other Party;

monopoly supplier of a service means any person, public or private, which in the relevant market of the territory of a Party is authorised or established formally or in effect by that Party as the sole supplier of that service;

natural person of a Party means a natural person who resides in the territory of the Party or elsewhere and who under the law of that Party:

(i) is a national of that Party; or
(ii) has the right of permanent residence in that Party;

a *juridical person* is:

(i) *owned* by persons of a Party if more than 50 per cent of the equity interest in it is beneficially owned by persons of that Party;
(ii) *controlled* by persons of a Party if such persons have the power to name a majority of its directors or otherwise to legally direct its actions;
(iii) *affiliated* with another person when it controls, or is controlled by, that other person, or when it and the other person are both controlled by the same person;

person means either a natural person or a juridical person;

services means all services except services supplied in the exercise of governmental authority;

(*Continued*)

Box 6.5 Continued

service consumer means any person that receives or uses a service;

service of the other Party means a service which is supplied:

(i) from or in the territory of the other Party, or in the case of maritime transport, by a vessel registered under the laws of the other Party, or by a person of the other Party which supplies the service through the operation of a vessel and/or its use in whole or in part; or

(ii) in the case of the supply of a service through commercial presence or through the presence of natural persons, by a service supplier of the other Party;

Source: Department of Commerce, Government of India.

6.5 Policy issues in ROO relating to trade in services

Against the backdrop of the preceding discussions it is possible to lay down a menu of policy issues relating to ROO for services trade that need consideration.

6.5.1 Ownership and control

These concepts are still not well developed in RTAs as far as the criteria accord to origin for services, trade is concerned. This is also due to the fact that information on the ownership of service provider companies is of not disclosed and on several occasions details of foreign nationals and their ownership are unavailable.

It has been highlighted that a similar problem arises in the case of service suppliers whose equity is publicly traded since share ownership may be diffused across a large number of countries, may change hands frequently, and no single shareholder may exercise control over the company.

6.5.2 Free-rider's problem

Another issue relates to the extent of strictness of origin rules. In the case of a liberal regime of rules, there is always the risk of non-RTA members enjoying the benefits of preferential market access without reciprocating the same – commonly known as free-riders, the equivalent of *trade deflection* in trade in goods. However, if the regime of origin rules is such that it may limit such an effect; the same would foster regional cumulation in services as well. As a long term effect investment inflows from non-RTA members would come to the most efficient service provider RTA member. The ROO therefore can also play a developmental role in services as well.

6.5.3 Tax obligations

Since different countries have different structure of tax regimes, the tax obligations by exporting services from RTA member by a subsidiary firm/company may vary from tax obligation of the parent firm/company situated in non-RTA member. The exports from a subsidiary may thus entail higher or lower tax obligations. The movement of companies through commercial presence under mode 3 would be largely dependent on the extent of tax obligations through *ownership criteria* prescribed under ROO.

6.5.4 Business transaction costs

The conditions prescribed under the ROO in the form of *substantial business operations* for getting preferential market access entry may add to the transaction costs for a firm or company for establishing and maintaining a commercial presence in RTA member. Additionally, the ROO criteria in services under modes 1 and 3 relating to 'domestic ownership and control' and 'domestic employment' would also entail significant transaction cost.

In this chapter different features of trade in services as distinct from trade in goods have been highlighted so as to emphasize that ROO for the former would need a different approach than the latter. Having done so, an attempt was made to understand the criteria relevant for according originating status to service providers in an RTA under different modes. Further, the ROO practised in various RTAs were documented. Based on the above, certain issues that warrant policy attention, as they stand unresolved, were laid down.

7
Policy Issues

The framework of ROO being an integral part of multilateral trading system has remained without a set of actual harmonized rules in place. Secondly, the plethora of RTAs has emerged as one of the most controversial issues in any trade negotiations, especially due to the complexity of ROO proposals in negotiations.

Various divergent views have emerged in academic and policy circles in terms of the efficacy of ROO. Generally, the local industry is apprehensive about trade deflection and has voiced its concerns. Local industries often advocated formulation of ROO in such a manner that it becomes a non-trade barrier.

Therefore, in this chapter, the following policy recommendations are offered in order to make ROO serve the dual objective of stopping trade deflection on the one hand, and playing a developmental role on the other:

- Need for consistency and harmonisation: a myth or reality
- Issues for implementation
- Trade in services
- Investment
- GIs
- Labelling requirements through ROO
- A trade policy instrument or tools for development

7.1 Need for consistency and harmonisation: a myth or reality

Against the backdrop of the analysis presented in the previous chapters, one important policy implication that emerges is in terms of harmonising different provisions of ROO under different trading arrangements. Since this is not an easy task, the need for envisaging consistency and harmonisation among different formulations of ROO emerges as a question in terms of its feasibility. It is also popularly believed that one of the most important contributors to the *spaghetti bowl* phenomenon is the multiplicity of ROO. In this section, therefore, we explore the possibility of consistency and harmonisation of ROO and if so in what manner a policy-maker may approach it. In this regard, three scenarios of rules of origin harmonisation are considered: (i) within ROO harmonisation: non-preferential; (ii) within ROO harmonisation: preferential; and (iii) between ROO harmonisation: non-preferential and preferential. Each is being discussed below.

7.1.1   Within-ROO harmonisation: non-preferential

We have emphasized the importance of transparent and non-burdensome procedures relating to the ROO in earlier chapters. In our view, the imposition of ROO should be approached purely as a technical and neutral matter. But because there are no common global standards, it has been observed that increasingly the ROO are being formulated in isolation by countries. To address the complications that this might entail, countries are now in the process of formulating harmonized NPROO under the terms outlined in the WTO Agreement on ROO.

The lack of harmonization of NPROO in the WTO has given enough flexibility to each of its members to prescribe its own set of ROO. This has even given rise to disputes. It has already been illustrated that in the WTO, while some Members have notified their NPROO, some have notified that they do not have any and the rest have not stated their position. This has thus created a complex situation and an exporter, therefore, has to comply with differing ROO even to trade on MFN-basis where no tariff preferences are given which adds to its cost, depending on the market.

Therefore, we recommend that the harmonization of NPROO should be finalized and implemented without further delay. This, however, will not be possible unless the entire proposal relating to ROO is agreed by all the members. Reportedly, the present status of rules of origin harmonization is already complete on around 90 per cent of total tariff lines at HS 6-digit level. The entire harmonization programme is being delayed because of a lack of consensus on the remaining 10 per cent of tariff lines. Therefore, to break the stalemate we recommend that the WTO members decide to implement the NPROO at this stage on the 90 per cent of tariff lines where harmonization has been achieved. This would contribute to removing the complexities associated with different

NPROO implemented by individual countries and help facilitate freer flows of trade and reduce exporters' cost of adhering to different ROO.

7.1.2 Within-ROO harmonisation: preferential

So far there has not been any standard framework that could be used as a reference-point by the policy-makers in devising origin criteria in a regional grouping. It is evident that there has been very little work done at the analytical or empirical levels in terms of assessing the economic effects of ROO, despite the fact that such an assessment would form the very basis of evolving the origin system.

In view of the above, there is doubt whether harmonization of PROO will be possible? To answer to this question, one would need to look at the common elements as well as the major differences in some of the important PROO. While it may not be a gigantic problem to attempt harmonization of the common elements, it may be difficult, if not impossible, to harmonize such elements where differences exist. Narrowing these differences may be difficult as each member of RTA would have different objectives for framing such rules and in some cases there could be some conflicting interests too.

On the one hand, it is not uncommon for a single country to have to apply several different sets of rules, depending on the RTAs to which the country belongs. For instance, certain types of goods produced in Mexico, both a NAFTA member and a partner in the EU–Mexico agreement, may be subject to two rather different origin determination mechanisms depending on whether they are shipped to North America or Europe.

However, within ROO harmonization among PTAs is not a complete impossibility. In this regard, an encouraging example relates to the Mexican Authorities who have also realized the problems and complexities relating to different ROO in their agreements with EU and NAFTA and have made sure that similar principles are applied in the context of both RTAs.

Likewise, the recent consolidation of bilateral trade agreements among the Southern European countries and a replacement by the common rules as part of an amended Central European Free Trade Agreement (CEFTA) deal is another positive example in the direction of reducing complexities of rules. The new CEFTA consolidates 32 bilateral free trade agreements into a single regional trade agreement which improves conditions to promote trade and investment by means of fair, clear, stable and predictable rules.

Looking at India's ROO, which have been discussed in previous chapters, it can be seen that India's ROO with her different trading partners in various RTAs broadly follow the same origin criteria, with some exceptions due to varying negotiating outcomes.

On the other hand, it appears that the same basic mechanisms or criteria are used by all RTAs, although in varying combinations. As RTAs proliferate, a small number of models, initially formulated by major trading partners such as the US or the EU, are replicated in the new agreements concluded between them and third countries. Cumulation provisions further expand the coverage of these models and promote harmonization among participants. Most of Europe now benefits from the effects of the European cumulation area and similar benefits with respect to preferential access, should probably be expected in the Americas once the FTAA process is concluded.

As has been elaborated in earlier chapters, having a closer look at PROO, it can be easily identified that broader commonality is found on several elements of these ROO and it would be easier to attempt harmonizing these elements (Ratna 2007). They include: General definitions; list of wholly obtained or produced goods; Insufficient or minimal operations or processes that do not confer origin; neutral elements; consignment criteria; Certificate of Origin; denial of preferential tariff treatment; claim for preferential tariff treatment; administrative arrangements relating to issuance and verification of Certificate of Origin, etc. It has been observed that there are very little differences between these elements and any attempt to harmonize them would yield the desired result.

Given the diverse treatments that are specified in different agreements, the elements that would require greater understanding and lengthy discussions relating to harmonization include: qualifying criteria for not-wholly obtained or produced goods; cumulation; no drawback rule; treatment of profits by local traders; and PSRs.

Of these elements, the most difficult task would relate to harmonization of PSRs. For the latter, one would need to learn lessons from the WTO Harmonization Work Programme. Hence, instead of an overly ambitious harmonization programme, a more realistic, i.e. step-by-step approach would be desirable.

It would be further important to understand that while harmonization is important, the final result should not be too cumbersome or burdening. Any attempt for harmonized PROO should not lose sight of the following objectives (Ratna, 2007, p. 89):

(i) *Trade Deflection/circumvention*: The basic objective of the harmonized rules should be to prevent trade deflection. It should also be framed in a manner that it facilitates and creates trade among the members.

(ii) *Simple*: The harmonized rules should be simple to operate and easy to follow. They should be transparent and predictable.

(iii) *Cost-effective*: For improved market access, it is necessary that the rules are made such that the cost of proving the origin of product for procuring the Certificate of Origin is not high. This will have a greater impact on the small and medium enterprises, as a higher cost will nullify their market access margins.

(iv) *Cumulation*: The Cumulation rule be made such that it allows greater integration among RTA members and facilitates intra-regional trade and investment flows.

(v) *Trade facilitation*: Complex rules of origin place a greater burden on customs procedures which may compromise progress on trade facilitation. The process of verification be also made simpler as the cost/burden of proof lies with the producer.

(vi) *Sensitivity*: Restrictive rules of origin targeted at sensitive products are not an effective mechanism for protecting domestic industry. Therefore, RoO should not be devised in a manner which has been formulated for nullifying the tariff concessions.

(vii) *PSRs*: The most difficult task will be the harmonization of these. Therefore, in the Harmonized Rules the PSRs should be avoided.

(viii) *Special & Differential Treatment*: Rules of Origin should be devised by taking into account the differential levels of development of the ESCAP members.

7.1.3   Between-ROO harmonisation: non-preferential and preferential

As a result of the series of multilateral trade negotiations for trade liberalization under the auspices of GATT/WTO, the average tariffs are now much lower. However, the lack of uniformity in ROO as discussed earlier causes unnecessary delay and imposes additional cost, not only to the customs authorities, but also to business and trading communities. This situation will be improved only when the implementation of harmonization of NPROO takes place.

In the case of RTAs a question that arises is whether expected benefits from preferential access in other partners' markets will outweigh the inconvenience. Related production and sourcing decisions by companies already established or considering investing in participating countries may vary accordingly. Viewed from the perspective of RTA members the proliferation and overlapping of differing systems of ROO is perhaps less a problem of systemic incompatibility than of increased transaction costs for involved traders.

From the perspective of non-participating countries the stakes are obviously different than for participating countries. Most of the PROO allow minimal or no third country inputs, producers in RTA members have a strong incentive to avoid such inputs so as to preserve the preferential status of their own products. In this case third country supplies are not only denied the preferential access provided for by the RTA, in practice they often lose access altogether.

The above presents a strong case for the harmonization of NPROO and PROO. The establishment of a single set of ROO brings about a number of benefits to public and private sectors. It will certainly reduce the time and costs required thus facilitating trade. It will equally contribute to the international trading system by strengthening certainty, predictability, and consistency of origin determination. It will also reduce number of trade dispute cases by implementing a single set of origin rules. As a resultant, to obtain the maximum global welfare on account of global trade flows, the harmonization of origin rules between non-preferential and preferential is of paramount importance.

In view of the above arguments, we tend to argue strongly in following the step-by-step approach whereby the implementation of harmonization of NPROO start without further waiting to reach a consensus on all the items that are pending for the decision. Steps should then be taken to harmonize PROO and the process can be started at any inter-governmental forum which can provide a theoretical framework for this exercise. This would ultimately lead to only two sets of global ROO – preferential and non-preferential. The last step would be to complete the exercise of harmonization of PROO and NPROO. However, to achieve the global welfare, the authors feel that the initiation of work programme for this harmonization should not wait for conclusion of the two sets of rules, rather it can start as soon as the theoretical framework for harmonizing PROO has been completed. The work may be initiated by multilateral and regional institutions like the WCO, WTO, UNCTAD, UNESCAP, ADB, OECD, etc. where a Tripartite Task Force by drawing experts from policy circles, businesses and academia could be constituted to prepare a global framework of harmonized ROO.

7.2 Issues for implementation

The issues relating to rules of origin implementation and enforcement are of crucial importance both in the preferential and non-preferential contexts. Efforts geared towards minimization of cost of compliance through procedural simplifications also warrant priority-attention. It has been argued earlier, often the enforcement costs of rules of origin are quite high and thereby the utilization ratios for RTA preferences are low. In order to improve the efficacy of ROO implementation the following policy-measures could be considered (Das, 2008):

7.2.1   E-ROO

A web-based system could be installed and developed wherein clients could fill the requisite forms online. The facilities should allow online-clearance of requests, subject to inspection. This could be a part of a broader frame of e-governance. A ROO Web-clearance Portal (RWP) could be established. It could have three components of ROO: (i) Online Application System (OAS); (ii) Online Tracking System (OTS); and (iii) Online Clearance System (OCS). In addition, the Programme could focus on developing and instituting a common regional ROO certification software. Regional IT connectivity among certificate-issuing Institutions/authorities and customs check-posts to facilitate online clearance of consignments needs to be evolved.

7.2.2   Validity-period for Certificate of Origin

Once inspection is completed and a certificate of origin is issued, it should have a certain period of validity. It may be made valid for one or two years to begin with, because the technologies needed to produce an item are not changed by enterprises in a shorter period than this. By introducing validity in origin certificates not only would the businesses find a hassle-free operational compliance of ROO but it would also build trust and goodwill among different stakeholders and the government officials.

7.2.3   Capacity-building and technical cooperation

Capacity-building modules for personnel handling certification and for customs officials need to be carried out. These could be customized, covering dimensions such as conceptual, empirical and operational.

7.2.4   Penalties and surveillance

Whenever there is any infringement of any rule or circumvention of ROO, an argument is put forth that the rules need to be modified or dispensed with. It must be highlighted that violation of a particular rule need not necessarily be a poor reflection on the rule per se. Any circumvention of even a well-formulated rule could be a reflection on the enforcement of the particular rule. For infringement of ROO, heavy penalties need to be imposed along with internal surveillance and monitoring.

7.3 Trade in services

Though global trade in services has increased in recent times, with the contribution of both the developed and developing countries, it may be reiterated that trade in services is not always similar to trade in goods. With the increasing trend of inclusion of trade in services in several regional trading arrangements, the determination of the ROO of service providers has become equally important.

As we have discussed earlier, most of the regional trade agreements pertaining to trade in services adopt a nationality-cum-incorporation based origin norms, however, some of them use the criterion of ownership and control rather than incorporation. Some others cover investments made by any resident or incorporated entity in a member country, regardless of country of ownership or control or a rule requiring only substantial business operations in the territory of a Party. In other words, a non-party service supplier that engages in substantial business operations may also benefit from the bilateral free trade agreement.

On the other hand, GATS juridical persons are defined as entities constituted under the law of contracting party and engaged in substantial business operations in the contracting state or is owned or controlled by natural persons we are nationalize under the law of contracting party.

Therefore, it is possible to lay down a menu of policy issues relating to ROO for services, trade that addresses the three, namely information, systemic issues and developmental concerns.

7.3.1 Database and information sharing on ownership and control

Since full information on the ownership of service provider companies is often not disclosed and details of foreign nationals and their ownership are unavailable, the concepts of ownership and control linked to ROO are not well developed in RTAs. A similar problem arises in the case of service suppliers whose equity is publicly traded. Since share ownership may be diffused across a large number of countries, companies may change hands frequently, and no single shareholder may exercise control over the company. Therefore, countries must cooperate to share information and build databases on that ROO in services trade can be adhered to and implemented in an efficacious way.

7.3.2   Policy coherence on definitions pertaining to services providers

As highlighted earlier, various concepts, definitions and rules according originating status to service providers are used in different RTAs, which include nationality-cum-incorporation; ownership and control; and substantial business operations. This causes arbitrariness and has the potential of restricting services trade. One policy prescription, thus, could be to aim at policy coherence across RTAs in terms of different concepts relating to trade in services.

7.3.3   Balanced formulation of Rules of Origin for trade in services

The liberal approach to ROO is another issue that needs to be addressed, especially with regard to the risk of non-RTA members enjoying the benefits of preferential market access without reciprocating the same – commonly known as free-riders. On the other hand, if the rules are such that they limit such an effect, the same would foster regional cumulation in services. As a long-term effect, investment inflows from non-RTA members would come to the most efficient service provider RTA member. However, any set of rules governing services trade should also be not trade-restrictive. Thus, it is imperative that the policies according originating status to service providers are formulated in a balanced manner, being neither too liberal nor too stringent.

7.4   Investment

In case of conventional FTA in goods the linkage between trade and investment is weak as there are no explicit undertakings on investments, unlike comprehensive agreements where commitments are made in services as well as investments. However, we have also illustrated in earlier chapters that even when there is the sole commitment relating to goods, the possibility of intra-regional investment flows is high (case of India–Sri Lanka FTA and NAFTA). One possible explanation for this relates to the backward and forward linkage between the industries that emanates from the provisions of ROO. In the case of trade in services the intra-regional investment flows take place through the commitments made under mode 3. Here again the definition of juridical persons under rules of origin plays a very important role.

In case of trade in goods the RTA partners commit to provide market access on the basis of value-added criteria on the export product. In other words, preferential tariffs can be extended to the goods where imported inputs have been used. In this scenario, the ownership criteria of the factory which has produced such goods have not been taken into consideration. One of the important lessons that one can draw from past experiences as a policy option is to explore the possibility of determining the origin of goods produced in a partner country by factories in which the partner countries' nationals are holding substantial or more than 50 per cent equity of the factories. This could well turn out to be a novel policy recommendation that would strengthen intra-regional trade and investment linkages.

Another policy suggestion in this context could be in terms of devising regional cumulation provisions to attract extra-regional FDI inflows into the regional grouping, just as it has been successfully implemented in groupings like the NAFTA. This is a policy avenue that has not been harnessed in the developing world and needs adequate policy focus.

7.5 Geographical indications

As has been discussed earlier, the basic objective of ROO is to determine the origin of a product; and the products are classified into different categories depending on use of inputs. Issue of what will entail 'substantial transformation' is also discussed. In this regard, a new dimension that can be explored for determining the ROO relates to the provisions of GI.

Here we have tried to discuss if there is any necessity to have any criteria on any product that has been registered in one of the RTA members as a GI product. In general, in RTAs such provisions are silent, thereby making it imperative for the GI products to go through the test of criteria for determining the origin. GI products are not only 'wholly obtained' instead they are a step ahead as they are not only country-specific but location-specific in a particular country.

Since GI status is accorded to products after necessary examination and registration formalities they need to be exempt from ROO tests for determining origin. This would make the implementation of ROO on GI products time- and cost-saving and simple. This would further facilitate meeting the developmental objectives of ROO. Given the above, one would need to explore if GI products in different countries such as French Champagne, Indonesian Batik-printed garments and made-ups, Indian Darjeeling Tea, Banarasi Sarees, Kashmiri Pashmina Shawls, Bangladeshi Silk, etc. can be treated as originating in respective countries on the basis of their GI certification.

7.6 Labelling requirements through Rules of Origin

As discussed earlier, in recent times, the issues relating to meeting the labelling requirements on food products through origin certification have been debated and it has been considered whether ROO could be used to serve as an important human role in food and health safety. The debate has further tried to explore if such measures act as a barrier to trade either through their stipulations or their implementation. An important policy perception, therefore, is whether they are essential or it is possible to meet these objectives through other instruments.

7.7 Rules of Origin as a development policy tool

It is often understood that ROO would be redundant once a country, which is a member of different trade agreements, reduces its MFN-tariffs considerably, to very low levels. In fact, there is evidence to suggest that stringent ROO and liberal tariff regimes are inversely related. This however, may not be the case if one looks at the existing disputes among the WTO members under ARO. In fact, the disputes relating to ROO in case of textiles (post-ATC) of USA on one hand with EU and India on the other, as has been analysed in this book, suggest that even when the sector is liberalized both in terms of tariffs and quotas, disputes still arise on ROO.

An explanation to such a phenomenon possibly lies in the fact that ROO are not just trade policy instruments. From the legal interpretation of the WTO Panel on ROO, it has been clearly explained in this book that they are meant to support trade policy.

The authors need not over-emphasize the developmental role that ROO can play. The developmental role is easily explained in terms of the effects of ROO on trade, investment, industrialization process and welfare, at large. It is, therefore, highly recommended that the policy-makers look into devising such rules that facilitate the developmental role that those components can play. This aspect has an empirical bearing as brought out in the context of a new developmental index of ROO.

7.8 Policy suggestions based on the development index

There are several factors of the ROO that influence the origin of the product and the economic activity of the RTA member country, thereby influencing the trade flows. These factors relate to the level of CTC at which the substantial transformation should take place (HS 2-, 4-, 6-, 8-digit), local/regional value added content, minimal operations, cumulation provisions, tolerance or *de minimis* thresholds, provisions relating to drawback allowed and outward processing not allowed.

In order to optimize the developmental roles that the above factors can play we have prescribed earlier that the provisions should be neither too stringent nor too liberal. Therefore, the maximum developmental objectives can only be met if an overall balance is envisaged between the two extremes. It is with this reason that our development-oriented ROO index has important, long-term and sustainable policy implications.

In view of the above, to attain the maximum developmental objectives, the following policy conceptions are prescribed.

7.8.1 Change in tariff classification

The change in tariff classification at the HS 2-digit level provides the highest order of processing and at the HS 8-digit level the processing requirements are too liberal. In either case, the developmental effect of ROO is negated. The change in tariff classification at the HS 4-digit level entails the maximum degree of 'substantial transformation' as also recognized by the WTO ROO Agreement in the case of even non-preferential trade flows.

7.8.2 Local/regional value-added content

Any ROO provisions that prescribe value added being greater than 70 per cent may though entail achieving higher degree of the developmental objectives due to greater economic activity, however this may not be a realistic proposition in the present age of global production chains and networks. Therefore, a 51 per cent value added would be the most ideal in terms of developmental effects while providing considerable degree of flexibility to source other materials from non-members of RTA and thereby making it logically '*made in the particular RTA member*'.

7.8.3 Minimal or non-qualifying criteria

The stipulations of minimal criteria filter out those processes that cannot be considered as those contributing to 'substantial transformation' and development. Therefore, it has an important policy relevance that is often not given adequate policy-importance.

7.8.4 Cumulation

The provisions of cumulation in different forms allow the RTA members to count materials purchased from other members as originating within that RTA for the purpose of determining origin. In our view, the most important policy device that can have the maximum developmental effects is full cumulation, as in this the extent of value added contribution made in another RTA member is also taken even if the material as a whole does not originate.

7.8.5   Tolerance/*de minimis* provisions

The Tolerance or *de minimis* rules allow certain percentage of non-originating materials that could be used in manufacturing a product that is otherwise not accepted ROO. A maximum ceiling (*de minimis*) is prescribed for treating the product as originating. This assumes policy relevance in terms of an important dimension relating to the developmental needs of an RTA member. This is so because this provision provides for flexibility in terms of preventing a substantial manufacturing process from being excluded from getting preferential tariff treatment due to the use of a very small fraction of non-originating input in an RTA member.

7.8.6   Duty drawback

Another important policy recommendation is to allow for the refund of government taxes or duties in terms of duty drawback provisions in the ROO framework as it has a developmental effect; whereas their denial would have no development effect on account of duty drawback.

***

Summing up, in this chapter we have discussed the importance of policy prescriptions that are needed to be taken into account while negotiating the rules of origin provisions either in the multilateral or the regional/bilateral context. If a policy-maker is looking for achieving long-term sustainable developmental goals for a country through the trade policy formulations including the ROO, the above policy prescriptions cannot be ignored.

8
Summing Up

Given that the global trading regime has witnessed a proliferation of RTAs in both the developed and developing worlds, and the fact that the framework of ROO as an integral part of RTAs has emerged as one of the most controversial issues in any trade negotiations, this book demonstrates how India has adopted a comprehensive approach thus far, in terms of laying down originating criteria for its preferential imports.

Given also that divergent views have emerged in the academic and policy circles in terms of the efficacy of ROO because the industry is generally apprehensive of trade deflection, the book has presented an objective viewpoint of the ROO. This is particularly important as the industry in India and the Asian region has voiced its concerns and advocated for ROO as a possible safeguard instrument against deflected imports. This has been done by critically examining the analytical debate on the subject and the associated economic rationale for keeping or dispensing with ROO. In a nutshell, this book has made an objective assessment of analytical arguments along with empirical exploration into the issues, which could help to provide policy insights in order to facilitate a consensus on the Indian framework of ROO to be applied during the economic engagements of India with her partner countries. It may also be useful in deriving similar inferences on the subject in a broader context of RTA negotiations in other parts of the world.

In Chapter 1 the subject was introduced and the context for the analysis was set by highlighting the conceptual ambiguity that envelopes this trade policy instrument in developing countries, in general, and India, in particular. In a somewhat novel way, Chapter 2 built a conceptual economic basis for ROO. It underscores the importance of ROO and argues how if properly formulated they can play a developmental role in the context of RTAs, an aspect often omitted from the analysis on the subject. The economic effects of ROO are considered for varying dimensions of trade flows, especially of goods in different categories. This has been argued and conclusions drawn by including in the analysis the positive effects of ROO through three channels, namely (i) preventing trade deflection, (ii) facilitating value addition, and (iii) augmenting intra-regional trade. The chapter also refers to the aspects of balancing export interests and preventing undue import competition.

This chapter also contributes to laying the foundations of ROO analysis with the help of the gravity model and also offers new methodologies to measure trade deflection. In this context, the book presents a new concept of a development index of ROO as opposed to the well-known restrictiveness index on the subject.

An index approach is one way to assess the degree of restrictiveness of government interventions where price and quantity measures of the impact of those interventions, such as ROO, are not readily available. An index quantifies prevailing restrictions into a summary measure to facilitate comparisons on a common basis across RTAs.

As has been discussed earlier, very little work has been done to examine the developmental dimension of ROO as the entire focus was to look at them as an impediment to trade. However, the RTA without any ROO has no meaning and while at one point of time it eliminates the circumvention of trade taking place through non-members, it subsequently enforces a certain degree of linkages among RTA members thereby facilitating the intra-regional trade and investment flows. The developmental dimensions of ROO therefore cannot be neglected. In the above background based on the commonly followed practices of some of the important ROO, an attempt has been made to quantify the development index of ROO. Additionally, the quantification of the ROO development index is also imperative, given the fact that the restrictiveness index fails to capture the realities associated with RTAs in the developing world, especially in the Asia-pacific region.

As has also been discussed earlier, the basic objective of ROO is to determine the origin of a product and the products are classified into different categories depending on the use of inputs. The issue of what will entail 'substantial transformation' is also discussed. In this regard, a new dimension that can be explored for determining the ROO relates to the provisions of GI. Here the book has tried to discuss whether there is any necessity to have any criteria on any product that has been registered in one of the RTA members as a GI product. In general, in RTAs such provisions are absent, thereby making it imperative for the

GI products to go through the criteria for determining origin. GI products are not only 'wholly obtained' but also country-specific and location-specific. Since GI status is accorded to products after the necessary examination and registration formalities, they need to be exempt from ROO tests for determining origin. This would make the implementation of ROO on GI products time- and cost-saving, and simple. This would further facilitate meeting the developmental objectives of ROO.

In Chapter 3 the merits and demerits of ROO are assessed in detail. The intricacies surrounding the concepts of wholly owned and not wholly owned criteria are explained along with the imperatives of understanding the nuances of CTH with respect to the level of determination of 'substantial transformation'. Against this background, the chapter offers new insights by answering the rarely asked question of whether CTH and CTSH are substitutes or complements? Similarly, the chapter examines the various contentious dimensions of the percentage test and the specific process test and concludes that an optimum mix is needed of these tests in a country-specific context. Further, the ambiguities relating to the minimal processes and different types of cumulation are addressed.

In Chapter 4, ROO as practised in different RTAs are analysed before embarking upon presenting an objective analysis of ROO in India's RTAs in Chapter 5. Apart from tracing the evolution of ROO in India's RTAs, the chapter dwells upon some of the case studies of infringement of ROO in the India's RTAs; assesses Indian industry's perception; and analyses the trade effects of ROO formulation with the help of detailed data analysis, gravity modelling and calculating trade deflection ratio. It is worth highlighting that the empirical analysis has been undertaken with the help of the developmental index that the book conceptualizes afresh in an earlier chapter.

Among one of the few attempts, Chapter 6 provides a comprehensive treatment of ROO regarding trade in services, which are assuming greater importance and are being increasingly included in RTAs without being fully understood.

Finally, in Chapter 7, some of the important policy issues are dealt with including those relating to consistency in ROO, negotiating aspects, interface between domestic imperatives and international commitments. On the basis of analysis, both conceptual and empirical, this book concludes that ROO, if properly formulated, could not only serve as an important trade policy instrument but also as a crucial tool for development.

Appendix: WTO Agreement on Rules of Origin

Members,

Noting that Ministers on 20 September 1986 agreed that the Uruguay Round of Multilateral Trade Negotiations shall aim to "bring about further liberalization and expansion of world trade", "strengthen the role of GATT" and "increase the responsiveness of the GATT system to the evolving international economic environment";

Desiring to further the objectives of GATT 1994;

Recognizing that clear and predictable rules of origin and their application facilitate the flow of international trade;

Desiring to ensure that rules of origin themselves do not create unnecessary obstacles to trade;

Desiring to ensure that rules of origin do not nullify or impair the rights of Members under GATT 1994;

Recognizing that it is desirable to provide transparency of laws, regulations, and practices regarding rules of origin;

Desiring to ensure that rules of origin are prepared and applied in an impartial, transparent, predictable, consistent and neutral manner;

Recognizing the availability of a consultation mechanism and procedures for the speedy, effective and equitable resolution of disputes arising under this Agreement;

Desiring to harmonize and clarify rules of origin;

Hereby *agree* as follows:

PART I

DEFINITIONS AND COVERAGE

Article 1

Rules of Origin

1. For the purposes of Parts I to IV of this Agreement, rules of origin shall be defined as those laws, regulations and administrative determinations of general application applied by any Member to determine the country of origin of goods provided such rules of origin are not related to contractual or autonomous trade regimes leading to the granting of tariff preferences going beyond the application of paragraph 1 of Article I of GATT 1994.

2. Rules of origin referred to in paragraph 1 shall include all rules of origin used in non-preferential commercial policy instruments, such as in the application of: most-favoured-nation treatment under Articles I, II, III, XI and XIII of GATT 1994; anti-dumping and countervailing duties under Article VI of GATT 1994; safeguard measures under Article XIX of GATT 1994; origin marking requirements under Article IX of GATT 1994; and any discriminatory

quantitative restrictions or tariff quotas. They shall also include rules of origin used for government procurement and trade statistics.[7]

PART II

DISCIPLINES TO GOVERN THE APPLICATION OF RULES OF ORIGIN

Article 2

Disciplines During the Transition Period

Until the work programme for the harmonization of rules of origin set out in Part IV is completed, Members shall ensure that:

(a) when they issue administrative determinations of general application, the requirements to be fulfilled are clearly defined. In particular:
  (i) in cases where the criterion of change of tariff classification is applied, such a rule of origin, and any exceptions to the rule, must clearly specify the subheadings or headings within the tariff nomenclature that are addressed by the rule;
  (ii) in cases where the ad valorem percentage criterion is applied, the method for calculating this percentage shall also be indicated in the rules of origin;
  (iii) in cases where the criterion of manufacturing or processing operation is prescribed, the operation that confers origin on the good concerned shall be precisely specified;
(b) notwithstanding the measure or instrument of commercial policy to which they are linked, their rules of origin are not used as instruments to pursue trade objectives directly or indirectly;
(c) rules of origin shall not themselves create restrictive, distorting, or disruptive effects on international trade. They shall not pose unduly strict requirements or require the fulfilment of a certain condition not related to manufacturing or processing, as a prerequisite for the determination of the country of origin. However, costs not directly related to manufacturing or processing may be included for the purposes of the application of an ad valorem percentage criterion consistent with subparagraph (a);
(d) the rules of origin that they apply to imports and exports are not more stringent than the rules of origin they apply to determine whether or not a good is domestic and shall not discriminate between other Members, irrespective of the affiliation of the manufacturers of the good concerned[8];
(e) their rules of origin are administered in a consistent, uniform, impartial and reasonable manner;

---

[7] It is understood that this provision is without prejudice to those determinations made for purposes of defining "domestic industry" or "like products of domestic industry" or similar terms wherever they apply.

[8] With respect to rules of origin applied for the purposes of government procurement, this provision shall not create obligations additional to those already assumed by Members under GATT 1994.

(f) their rules of origin are based on a positive standard. Rules of origin that state what does not confer origin (negative standard) are permissible as part of a clarification of a positive standard or in individual cases where a positive determination of origin is not necessary;

(g) their laws, regulations, judicial decisions and administrative rulings of general application relating to rules of origin are published as if they were subject to, and in accordance with, the provisions of paragraph 1 of Article X of GATT 1994;

(h) upon the request of an exporter, importer or any person with a justifiable cause, assessments of the origin they would accord to a good are issued as soon as possible but no later than 150 days[9] after a request for such an assessment provided that all necessary elements have been submitted. Requests for such assessments shall be accepted before trade in the good concerned begins and may be accepted at any later point in time. Such assessments shall remain valid for three years provided that the facts and conditions, including the rules of origin, under which they have been made remain comparable. Provided that the parties concerned are informed in advance, such assessments will no longer be valid when a decision contrary to the assessment is made in a review as referred to in subparagraph (j). Such assessments shall be made publicly available subject to the provisions of subparagraph (k);

(i) when introducing changes to their rules of origin or new rules of origin, they shall not apply such changes retroactively as defined in, and without prejudice to, their laws or regulations;

(j) any administrative action which they take in relation to the determination of origin is reviewable promptly by judicial, arbitral or administrative tribunals or procedures, independent of the authority issuing the determination, which can effect the modification or reversal of the determination;

(k) all information that is by nature confidential or that is provided on a confidential basis for the purpose of the application of rules of origin is treated as strictly confidential by the authorities concerned, which shall not disclose it without the specific permission of the person or government providing such information, except to the extent that it may be required to be disclosed in the context of judicial proceedings.

Article 3

Disciplines after the Transition Period

Taking into account the aim of all Members to achieve, as a result of the harmonization work programme set out in Part IV, the establishment of harmonized rules of origin, Members shall ensure, upon the implementation of the results of the harmonization work programme, that:

(a) they apply rules of origin equally for all purposes as set out in Article 1;

(b) under their rules of origin, the country to be determined as the origin of a particular good is either the country where the good has been wholly obtained

---

[9] In respect of requests made during the first year from the date of entry into force of the WTO Agreement, Members shall only be required to issue these assessments as soon as possible.

or, when more than one country is concerned in the production of the good, the country where the last substantial transformation has been carried out;

(c) the rules of origin that they apply to imports and exports are not more stringent than the rules of origin they apply to determine whether or not a good is domestic and shall not discriminate between other Members, irrespective of the affiliation of the manufacturers of the good concerned;

(d) the rules of origin are administered in a consistent, uniform, impartial and reasonable manner;

(e) their laws, regulations, judicial decisions and administrative rulings of general application relating to rules of origin are published as if they were subject to, and in accordance with, the provisions of paragraph 1 of Article X of GATT 1994;

(f) upon the request of an exporter, importer or any person with a justifiable cause, assessments of the origin they would accord to a good are issued as soon as possible but no later than 150 days after a request for such an assessment provided that all necessary elements have been submitted. Requests for such assessments shall be accepted before trade in the good concerned begins and may be accepted at any later point in time. Such assessments shall remain valid for three years provided that the facts and conditions, including the rules of origin, under which they have been made remain comparable. Provided that the parties concerned are informed in advance, such assessments will no longer be valid when a decision contrary to the assessment is made in a review as referred to in subparagraph (h). Such assessments shall be made publicly available subject to the provisions of subparagraph (i);

(g) when introducing changes to their rules of origin or new rules of origin, they shall not apply such changes retroactively as defined in, and without prejudice to, their laws or regulations;

(h) any administrative action which they take in relation to the determination of origin is reviewable promptly by judicial, arbitral or administrative tribunals or procedures, independent of the authority issuing the determination, which can effect the modification or reversal of the determination;

(i) all information which is by nature confidential or which is provided on a confidential basis for the purpose of the application of rules of origin is treated as strictly confidential by the authorities concerned, which shall not disclose it without the specific permission of the person or government providing such information, except to the extent that it may be required to be disclosed in the context of judicial proceedings.

PART III

PROCEDURAL ARRANGEMENTS ON NOTIFICATION, REVIEW, CONSULTATION AND DISPUTE SETTLEMENT

Article 4

Institutions

1. There is hereby established a Committee on Rules of Origin (referred to in this Agreement as "the Committee") composed of the representatives from each of

the Members. The Committee shall elect its own Chairman and shall meet as necessary, but not less than once a year, for the purpose of affording Members the opportunity to consult on matters relating to the operation of Parts I, II, III and IV or the furtherance of the objectives set out in these Parts and to carry out such other responsibilities assigned to it under this Agreement or by the Council for Trade in Goods. Where appropriate, the Committee shall request information and advice from the Technical Committee referred to in paragraph 2 on matters related to this Agreement. The Committee may also request such other work from the Technical Committee as it considers appropriate for the furtherance of the above-mentioned objectives of this Agreement. The WTO Secretariat shall act as the secretariat to the Committee.

2. There shall be established a Technical Committee on Rules of Origin (referred to in this Agreement as "the Technical Committee") under the auspices of the Customs Co-operation Council (CCC) as set out in Annex I. The Technical Committee shall carry out the technical work called for in Part IV and prescribed in Annex I. Where appropriate, the Technical Committee shall request information and advice from the Committee on matters related to this Agreement. The Technical Committee may also request such other work from the Committee as it considers appropriate for the furtherance of the above-mentioned objectives of the Agreement. The CCC Secretariat shall act as the secretariat to the Technical Committee.

Article 5

Information and Procedures for Modification and Introduction of New Rules of Origin

1. Each Member shall provide to the Secretariat, within 90 days after the date of entry into force of the WTO Agreement for it, its rules of origin, judicial decisions, and administrative rulings of general application relating to rules of origin in effect on that date. If by inadvertence a rule of origin has not been provided, the Member concerned shall provide it immediately after this fact becomes known. Lists of information received and available with the Secretariat shall be circulated to the Members by the Secretariat.

2. During the period referred to in Article 2, Members introducing modifications, other than *de minimis* modifications, to their rules of origin or introducing new rules of origin, which, for the purpose of this Article, shall include any rule of origin referred to in paragraph 1 and not provided to the Secretariat, shall publish a notice to that effect at least 60 days before the entry into force of the modified or new rule in such a manner as to enable interested parties to become acquainted with the intention to modify a rule of origin or to introduce a new rule of origin, unless exceptional circumstances arise or threaten to arise for a Member. In these exceptional cases, the Member shall publish the modified or new rule as soon as possible.

Article 6

Review

1. The Committee shall review annually the implementation and operation of Parts II and III of this Agreement having regard to its objectives. The Committee

shall annually inform the Council for Trade in Goods of developments during the period covered by such reviews.

2. The Committee shall review the provisions of Parts I, II and III and propose amendments as necessary to reflect the results of the harmonization work programme.

3. The Committee, in cooperation with the Technical Committee, shall set up a mechanism to consider and propose amendments to the results of the harmonization work programme, taking into account the objectives and principles set out in Article 9. This may include instances where the rules need to be made more operational or need to be updated to take into account new production processes as affected by any technological change.

Article 7

Consultation

The provisions of Article XXII of GATT 1994, as elaborated and applied by the Dispute Settlement Understanding, are applicable to this Agreement.

Article 8

Dispute Settlement

The provisions of Article XXIII of GATT 1994, as elaborated and applied by the Dispute Settlement Understanding, are applicable to this Agreement.

PART IV

HARMONIZATION OF RULES OF ORIGIN

Article 9

Objectives and Principles

1. With the objectives of harmonizing rules of origin and, *inter alia*, providing more certainty in the conduct of world trade, the Ministerial Conference shall undertake the work programme set out below in conjunction with the CCC, on the basis of the following principles:

   (a) rules of origin should be applied equally for all purposes as set out in Article 1;

   (b) rules of origin should provide for the country to be determined as the origin of a particular good to be either the country where the good has been wholly obtained or, when more than one country is concerned in the production of the good, the country where the last substantial transformation has been carried out;

   (c) rules of origin should be objective, understandable and predictable;

   (d) notwithstanding the measure or instrument to which they may be linked, rules of origin should not be used as instruments to pursue trade objectives directly or indirectly. They should not themselves create restrictive, distorting or disruptive effects on international trade. They should not pose unduly strict requirements or require the fulfilment of a certain condition not relating to manufacturing or processing as a prerequisite for the determination of the country of origin. However, costs not directly related to manufacturing or processing may be included for purposes of the application of an ad valorem percentage criterion;

(e) rules of origin should be administrable in a consistent, uniform, impartial and reasonable manner;

(f) rules of origin should be coherent;

(g) rules of origin should be based on a positive standard. Negative standards may be used to clarify a positive standard.

Work Programme

2. (a) The work programme shall be initiated as soon after the entry into force of the WTO Agreement as possible and will be completed within three years of initiation.

(b) The Committee and the Technical Committee provided for in Article 4 shall be the appropriate bodies to conduct this work.

(c) To provide for detailed input by the CCC, the Committee shall request the Technical Committee to provide its interpretations and opinions resulting from the work described below on the basis of the principles listed in paragraph 1. To ensure timely completion of the work programme for harmonization, such work shall be conducted on a product sector basis, as represented by various chapters or sections of the Harmonized System (HS) nomenclature.

(i) *Wholly Obtained and Minimal Operations or Processes*

The Technical Committee shall develop harmonized definitions of:

– the goods that are to be considered as being wholly obtained in one country. This work shall be as detailed as possible;

– minimal operations or processes that do not by themselves confer origin to a good.

The results of this work shall be submitted to the Committee within three months of receipt of the request from the Committee.

(ii) *Substantial Transformation – Change in Tariff Classification*

– The Technical Committee shall consider and elaborate upon, on the basis of the criterion of substantial transformation, the use of change in tariff subheading or heading when developing rules of origin for particular products or a product sector and, if appropriate, the minimum change within the nomenclature that meets this criterion.

– The Technical Committee shall divide the above work on a product basis taking into account the chapters or sections of the HS nomenclature, so as to submit results of its work to the Committee at least on a quarterly basis. The Technical Committee shall complete the above work within one year and three months from receipt of the request of the Committee.

(iii) *Substantial Transformation – Supplementary Criteria*

Upon completion of the work under subparagraph (ii) for each product sector or individual product category where the exclusive use of the HS nomenclature does not allow for the expression of substantial transformation, the Technical Committee:

– shall consider and elaborate upon, on the basis of the criterion of substantial transformation, the use, in a supplementary or exclusive manner,

of other requirements, including ad valorem percentages[10] and/or manufacturing or processing operations[11], when developing rules of origin for particular products or a product sector;
- may provide explanations for its proposals;
- shall divide the above work on a product basis taking into account the chapters or sections of the HS nomenclature, so as to submit results of its work to the Committee at least on a quarterly basis. The Technical Committee shall complete the above work within two years and three months of receipt of the request from the Committee.

Role of the Committee

3. On the basis of the principles listed in paragraph 1:
  (a) the Committee shall consider the interpretations and opinions of the Technical Committee periodically in accordance with the time-frames provided in subparagraphs (i), (ii) and (iii) of paragraph 2(c) with a view to endorsing such interpretations and opinions. The Committee may request the Technical Committee to refine or elaborate its work and/or to develop new approaches. To assist the Technical Committee, the Committee should provide its reasons for requests for additional work and, as appropriate, suggest alternative approaches;
  (b) upon completion of all the work identified in subparagraphs (i), (ii) and (iii) of paragraph 2(c), the Committee shall consider the results in terms of their overall coherence.

Results of the Harmonization Work Programme and Subsequent Work

4. The Ministerial Conference shall establish the results of the harmonization work programme in an annex as an integral part of this Agreement.[12] The Ministerial Conference shall establish a time-frame for the entry into force of this annex.

ANNEX I

TECHNICAL COMMITTEE ON RULES OF ORIGIN

Responsibilities

1. The ongoing responsibilities of the Technical Committee shall include the following:
  (a) at the request of any member of the Technical Committee, to examine specific technical problems arising in the day-to-day administration of the rules of origin of Members and to give advisory opinions on appropriate solutions based upon the facts presented;

---

[10] If the ad valorem criterion is prescribed, the method for calculating this percentage shall also be indicated in the rules of origin.

[11] If the criterion of manufacturing or processing operation is prescribed, the operation that confers origin on the product concerned shall be precisely specified.

[12] At the same time, consideration shall be given to arrangements concerning the settlement of disputes relating to customs classification.

(b) to furnish information and advice on any matters concerning the origin determination of goods as may be requested by any Member or the Committee;

(c) to prepare and circulate periodic reports on the technical aspects of the operation and status of this Agreement; and

(d) to review annually the technical aspects of the implementation and operation of Parts II and III.

2. The Technical Committee shall exercise such other responsibilities as the Committee may request of it.

3. The Technical Committee shall attempt to conclude its work on specific matters, especially those referred to it by Members or the Committee, in a reasonably short period of time.

Representation

4. Each Member shall have the right to be represented on the Technical Committee. Each Member may nominate one delegate and one or more alternates to be its representatives on the Technical Committee. Such a Member so represented on the Technical Committee is hereinafter referred to as a "member" of the Technical Committee. Representatives of members of the Technical Committee may be assisted by advisers at meetings of the Technical Committee. The WTO Secretariat may also attend such meetings with observer status.

5. Members of the CCC which are not Members of the WTO may be represented at meetings of the Technical Committee by one delegate and one or more alternates. Such representatives shall attend meetings of the Technical Committee as observers.

6. Subject to the approval of the Chairman of the Technical Committee, the Secretary-General of the CCC (referred to in this Annex as "the Secretary-General") may invite representatives of governments which are neither Members of the WTO nor members of the CCC and representatives of international governmental and trade organizations to attend meetings of the Technical Committee as observers.

7. Nominations of delegates, alternates and advisers to meetings of the Technical Committee shall be made to the Secretary-General.

Meetings

8. The Technical Committee shall meet as necessary, but not less than once a year.

Procedures

9. The Technical Committee shall elect its own Chairman and shall establish its own procedures.

ANNEX II

COMMON DECLARATION WITH REGARD TO PREFERENTIAL RULES OF ORIGIN

1. Recognizing that some Members apply preferential rules of origin, distinct from non-preferential rules of origin, the Members hereby *agree* as follows.

2. For the purposes of this Common Declaration, preferential rules of origin shall be defined as those laws, regulations and administrative determinations of general application applied by any Member to determine whether goods qualify for preferential treatment under contractual or autonomous trade regimes leading to the granting of tariff preferences going beyond the application of paragraph 1 of Article I of GATT 1994.

3. The Members *agree* to ensure that:

   (a) when they issue administrative determinations of general application, the requirements to be fulfilled are clearly defined. In particular:

      (i) in cases where the criterion of change of tariff classification is applied, such a preferential rule of origin, and any exceptions to the rule, must clearly specify the subheadings or headings within the tariff nomenclature that are addressed by the rule;

      (ii) in cases where the ad valorem percentage criterion is applied, the method for calculating this percentage shall also be indicated in the preferential rules of origin;

      (iii) in cases where the criterion of manufacturing or processing operation is prescribed, the operation that confers preferential origin shall be precisely specified;

   (b) their preferential rules of origin are based on a positive standard. Preferential rules of origin that state what does not confer preferential origin (negative standard) are permissible as part of a clarification of a positive standard or in individual cases where a positive determination of preferential origin is not necessary;

   (c) their laws, regulations, judicial decisions and administrative rulings of general application relating to preferential rules of origin are published as if they were subject to, and in accordance with, the provisions of paragraph 1 of Article X of GATT 1994;

   (d) upon request of an exporter, importer or any person with a justifiable cause, assessments of the preferential origin they would accord to a good are issued as soon as possible but no later than 150 days[13] after a request for such an assessment provided that all necessary elements have been submitted. Requests for such assessments shall be accepted before trade in the good concerned begins and may be accepted at any later point in time. Such assessments shall remain valid for three years provided that the facts and conditions, including the preferential rules of origin, under which they have been made remain comparable. Provided that the parties concerned are informed in advance, such assessments will no longer be valid when a decision contrary to the assessment is made in a review as referred to in subparagraph (f). Such assessments shall be made publicly available subject to the provisions of subparagraph (g);

   (e) when introducing changes to their preferential rules of origin or new preferential rules of origin, they shall not apply such changes retroactively as defined in, and without prejudice to, their laws or regulations;

   (f) any administrative action which they take in relation to the determination of preferential origin is reviewable promptly by judicial, arbitral or

---

[13] In respect of requests made during the first year from entry into force of the WTO Agreement, Members shall only be required to issue these assessments as soon as possible.

administrative tribunals or procedures, independent of the authority issuing the determination, which can effect the modification or reversal of the determination;

(g) all information that is by nature confidential or that is provided on a confidential basis for the purpose of the application of preferential rules of origin is treated as strictly confidential by the authorities concerned, which shall not disclose it without the specific permission of the person or government providing such information, except to the extent that it may be required to be disclosed in the context of judicial proceedings.

4. Members *agree* to provide to the Secretariat promptly their preferential rules of origin, including a listing of the preferential arrangements to which they apply, judicial decisions, and administrative rulings of general application relating to their preferential rules of origin in effect on the date of entry into force of the WTO Agreement for the Member concerned. Furthermore, Members agree to provide any modifications to their preferential rules of origin or new preferential rules of origin as soon as possible to the Secretariat. Lists of information received and available with the Secretariat shall be circulated to the Members by the Secretariat.

Notes

Chapter 2

1. Recent accession of new members to EU has reduced the total number of RTAs (source: WTO, 2009).
2. Source: WTO (2009).
3. This section draws to an ongoing work on this theme by the authors.
4. At the same time, the Kyoto Convention (1973) was revised in 1999, but it failed to address the issue of determining the origin of goods that are produced by using multi-country inputs.
5. Common Declaration with regard to Preferential Rules of Origin, Annex II of the Agreement.
6. It is understood that this definition is without prejudice to members' rights and obligations who are not States Parties to the United Nations Convention on the Law of the Sea.

References

ACCI (2003), 'Rules of Origin', Australia Chambers of Commerce and Industry, Australia.

Alan, K., Powers, W. and Winston A. (2008), 'Textile and Apparel Barriers and Rules of Origin: What's Left to Gain after the Agreement on Textile and Clothing? *Journal of Economic Integration,* 23(3), pp. 656–84.

Anson, J. and Cadot O. (2003), ules of Origin in North–South Preferential Trading Arrangements with an Application to NAFTA', University of Lausanne.

'Area with Rules of Origin, NBER Working Paper No.6857.

Arunanondchai, J. and Nikomborirak, D. (2006), 'Thailand's Rules of Origin in Services in Regional and Bilateral Trade Agreements', mimeo.

Augier, P., Gasiorek, M. and Lai-Tong, C. (2003), 'The Impact of Rules of Origin on Trade Flows' *Economic Policy,* 20(43) pp. 567–624.

Australian Productivity Commission (2004) *Restrictiveness Index for Rules of Origin,* Supplement to the Productivity Commission Research Report, Canberra.

Avila, J.L. and Manzano, G. (2006), 'Rules of Origin in Services: A Philippine Perspective', mimeo.

Beniglia-Zampetti, A. and Sauvé. P. (2006), 'Rules of Origin for Services: A Review of Current Practice', in Estevadeordal, A. *et al.,* (eds), *The Origin of Goods.* (London: Oxford University Press and CEPR), pp. 114–45.

Bhagwati, J. (2002), *Free Trade Today,* Princeton: Princeton University Press.

Brenton, P. (2003a), *Rules of Origin in Free Trade Agreements,* Trade Note 4, World Bank Group. URL: http://siteresources.worldbank.org/INTRANETTRADE/Resources/

Brenton, P. (2003b), Notes on Rules of Origin with Implications for Regional Integration in South East Asia: Poverty Reduction and Economic Management: International Trade Department, The World Bank, Washington DC.

Brenton, P. and Manchin, M. 2002, *Making EU Trade Agreements Work: the Role of Rules of Origin,* Working Document No. 183, Centre for European Policy Studies. URL: http://shop.ceps.be/BookDetail.php?item id=93

Cadot, O., de Melo, J. and Perez, A.P. (2006), *Rules of Origin for Preferential Trading Arrangements: Implications for the ASEN and Free Trade Area of EU and US Experience,* Working Paper Series 4016, The World Bank.

Cadot, O., Estevadeordal, A., Suwa-Eisenmann, A. and Verdier, T. (2006), Rules of Origin for services: economic and legal considerations, The Origin of Goods, February, pp. 114–147(34), Oxford Scholarship Online Monographs.

Carrere, C., de Melo, J. and Pondrad, E. (2006), *Are Different Rules of Origin Equally Costly? Estimates from NAFTA,* CERDI Working Paper 12/2004.

Cornejo, R. (2005), 'New Challeges in Rules of Origin', Word Bank, Washington, DC, 16 June.

Dang, N.-V., Nguyen C.-T., and Vu, H.-D., (2006), 'Rule of Origin in Services: Selected Sectors in Vietnam's Case', mimeo.

Das, R.U. (2004a), 'Rules of Origin Need Proper Perspective Under Trade Pacts', *The Financial Express,* Monday, 10 May.

Das, R.U. (2004b), 'Identification of Items at 6-digit HS Level of Trade Classification that would not Qualify for Change at 4-digit HS Level'', study conducted for Ministry of Commerce and Industry, Government of India.

Das, R.U. (2007), 'Developing a Comprehensive View on Rules of Origin', *Indian Engineering Exports*, September.

Das, R.U. (2008), 'Proliferation of Rules of Origin under Bilateral Free Trade Agreements among South Asian Countries and BIMSTEC FTA: Implications for South Asian Free Trade Area (SAFTA)', Manila: ADB.

Das, R. U. (2009), 'Regional Trade–FDI–Poverty Alleviation Linkages: Some Analytical and Empirical Explorations', Discussion Paper 18, Bonn, Germany: German Development Institute (GDI).

Das, R. U. (2010), 'Rules of Origin under Regional Trade Agreements', Discussion Paper # 163, New Delhi: RIS

Das, R.U. and Ratna, R.S. (forthcoming), 'Quantifying the Developmental Role of Rules of Origin in Regional Trade Agreements'.

Douangboupha, L., Thiengthepvongsa, T. and Vilavong, B. (2006), 'Rules of Origin in Services Regional Trade Agreements: The Practices in Laos', mimeo.

Duttagupta, R. and Panagariya, A. (2003) 'Free Trade Areas and Rules of Origin: Economics and Politics', IMF Working Paper, WP/03/229.

Estevadeordal, A. (2000), 'Negotiating Preferential Market Access: The Case of the North American Free Trade Agreement', *Journal of World Trade*, vol. 34, no. 1, pp. 141–66.

Estevadeordal, A. and Suominen, K. (2003), *Measuring Rules of Origin in the World Trading System and Proposals for Multilateral Harmonization*, Integration, Trade and Hemispheric Issues Division, Integration and Regional Programs Department, Inter-American Development Bank.

Estevadeordal, A. and Suominen, K. (2004), Rules of Origin: A World Map and Trade Effects, In Cadot, O., Estevadeordal, A. Suwa-Eisenmann, A. and Verider, T. eds. *The Origin of Goods: A Conecptual and Empirical Assessment of Rules of Origin in PTA.s* Washington: IADB-and CEPR.

European Commission (2003), 'Green paper on the future of rules of origin in preferential trade arrangements', COM(2003) 787 final, Brussels.

Falvey, R. and Reed, G. (2002), 'Rules of Origin as Commercial Policy Instruments', *International Economic Review*, XXXXIII (2), pp. 303–407.

Fink, C. and Nikomborirak, D. (2007), 'Rules of Origin in Services: A Case Study of Five ASEAN Countries', World Bank Policy Research Working Paper 4130, WPS4130.

Gelb, B.A. (2003), 'Textile and Apparel Rules of Origin in International Trade', CRS Report for Congress, RL31934, May.

Ghoneim, A.F. (1992), 'Rules of Origin and Trade Diversion: The Case of the Egyptian–European Partnership Agreement', Cairo University.

Ghoneim, A.F. (2003), 'Rules of Origin and Trade Diversion: The Case of the Egyptian–European Partnership Agreement, *Journal of World Trade*, XXXVII (3), pp. 597–621.

Gretton, P. and Gali, J. (2005) 'The Restrictiveness of Rules of Origin in Preferential Trade Agreements', Paper presented at the 34th Conference of Economists University of Melbourne 26–28 September.

224 *References*

Grossman, G.M. (1981), 'The Theory of Domestic Content Protection and Content', The Quarterly Journal of Economics, Vol. 96, No. 4, pp. 583–603.
Herin, J. (1986), *Rules of Origin and Differences in Tariff Levels in the EFTA and in the EC*, EFTA Occasional Paper No. 13, Geneva.
Hirsch, M. (2002), 'International Trade Law, Political Economy and Rule of Origin', *Journal of World Trade*, XXXVI, (2), pp. 171–88.
Hoekman, B. (1993a), 'Developing Countries and the Uruguay Round Negotiations on Services Rules of Origin for Goods and Services: Conceptual Issues and Economic Considerations', Discussion Paper Nos 821–2, October, IT.
Hoeckman, B. (1993b), 'Rules of Origin for Goods and Services: Conceptual and Economic Considerations', *Journal of World Trade*, XXVII (4), pp. 82–99.
Inama, S. (1995), 'A Comparative Analysis of the Generalized System of Preferences and Non-preferential Rules of Origin in the Light of the Uruguay Round Agreement', *Journal of World Trade*, XXIX(1), pp. 77–111.
James, W.E. (1997), 'APEC Preferential Rules of Origin: Stumbling Blocks for Liberalization of Trade?', *Journal of World Trade*, 31 (3), pp. 113–34.
James W.E. (2006), 'Rules of Origin in Emerging Asia-Pacific Preferential Trade Agreements: Will PTAs Promote Trade and Development?', Consultative Meeting on Trade Facilitation and Regional Integration, Bangkok, Thailand.
Ju, J. and Krishna K. (1998), 'Firm Behaviour and Markey Access in a Free Trade Area with Rules of Origin', Canadian Journal of Economics, Canadian Economics Association, Vol. 38(1), pp. 290–308.
Kalirajan, K. (2000), *Restrictions on Trade in Distribution Services*, Productivity Commission Staff Research Paper, AusInfo, Canberra.
Kawai, M. and Wignaraja, G. (2008), 'EAFTA or CEPEA: Which Way Forward?', *ASEAN Economic Bulletin*, Vol. 25, No. 2, pp. 113–139.
Koskinen, M. (1983), 'Excess Documentation Costs as a Non-Tariff Measure: An Empirical Analysis of the Effects of Documentation Costs', Swedish School of Economics and Business Administration Working Paper.
Krishna, K. (2005), *Understanding Rules of Origin*, Pennsylvania State University and National Bureau of Economic Research (NBER).
Krishna, K. and Krueger, A. (1995), *Implementing Free Trade Areas; Rules of Origin and Hidden Protection*, Working Paper No. 4983, NBER.
Krueger, A.O. (1993), *Free Trade Agreements as Protectionist Devices: Rules of Origin*, Working Paper No. 4352, National Bureau of Economic Research (NBER).
LaNasa, J.A. (1995), 'An Evaluation of the Uses ad Importance of Rules of Origin, and the Effectiveness of the Uruguay Round's Agreement on Rules of Origin in Harmonizing and Regulating Them', Working Paper, Harvard Law School.
Leow, E. (2003),' Business Perspectives on Rules of Origin in Singapore's Concluded Free Trade Agreements', PECC Trade Forum, Brunei Darussalam.
Low, L. (2003), 'Singapore's Bilateral Free Trade Agreements: Institutional and Architectural Issues', PECC Trade Forum, Institute for International Economics, Inter-American Development Bank, Washington, DC.
Mattoo, A. and Fink, C. (2004), 'Regional Agreements and Trade in Services: Policy Issues', *Journal of Economic Integration*, Vol. 19, No. 4,pp. 742–79.
Mattoo, A., Rathindran, R. and Subramanian, A. (2001), 'Measuring Services Liberalization and Its Impact on Economic Growth', Policy Research Working Paper, No. 2655, World Bank.

Mattoo, A., Roy, D. and Subramanian, A. (2002), 'The Africa Growth and Opportunity Act and Its Rules of Origin: Generosity Undermined', World Bank Policy Research Working Paper 2908.

Nikomborirak, D. (2004). "An Assessment of the Investment Regime: Thailand Country Report." Available at www.iisd.org/pdf/2004/investment_country_report_thailand.pdf.

Nikomborirak, D. and Tawannakul, S. (2006),'The Face of Foreign Companies in the Thai Economy', paper presented at the Mid-year Conference of the Thailand Development Research Institute, 25 August 2006.

NZFIA (2003), 'The Rules of Origin for the closer Economic Relationship (The Cer) Between Australia And New Zealand', Submission to Australian Productivity Council.

OECD (2002), 'The Relationship Between Regional Trade Agreements And Multilateral Trading System: Rules of Origin', Working Party of the Trade Committee, TD/TC/WP) 33.

Palmeter, N.D. (1993), 'Pacific Regional Trade Liberalization and Rules of Origin', *Journal of World Trade*, XXVII (50), pp. 49–62.

Panchamukhi, V.R. and Das, R.U. (2001), 'Conceptual and Policy Issues in Rules of Origin: Implications for SAPTA and SAFTA'", *South Asia Economic Journal*, Vol. 2, No. 2, July–December, Sage, New Delhi.

Productivity Commission (2004), *Restrictiveness Index for Rules of Origin*, Supplement to the Productivity Commission Research Report, Australia.

Ratna, R.S. (2006), 'GSTP Rules of Origin', Geneva, UNCTAD.

Ratna, R.S. (2007), 'Rules of Origin: Diverse Treatment and Future Development in the Asia and Pacific Region', *Towards Coherent Policy Framework, Understanding Trade & Investment Linkages*, ST/ESCAP/2469, Bangkok, UNESCAP.

Ratna, R.S. (2008), 'Making SAFTA a Success: The Role of India', Commonwealth Secretariat, London and CUTS International, Jaipur.

Ratna, R.S. and Ramanan, P.R.V. (2005). 'India's approach towards preferential RoO FTA negotiations with ASEAN', paper presented in the Workshop on India ASEAN FTA RoO, 17–18 October 2005, Jakarta, ASEAN Secretariat.

Rodriguez, P. L. (2001), 'Rules of Origin with Multistage Production', *The World Economy*, Vol. 24, No. 2, pp. 201–20.

Roy, M., Marchetti, J. and Hoe, J.L. (2006–07), 'Services Liberalization in the New Generation of Preferential Trade Agreements (PTAs): How Much Further than the GATS?', World Trade Organization: Staff Working Paper ERSD.

Rugman, M.A. (1998), 'The Rules for Foreign Investment in NAFTA', *Latin American Business Review*, Vol. 1 (1) 1998, pp. 77–94

Sampson, G. P. and Snape, R. H. (1985), 'Identifying the Issues in Trade in Services'. *The World Economy*, 8 (2) : 171–182.

Satapathy, C. (1998), 'Rules of Origin: New Weapon against Free Trade in Textiles?', *Economic and Political Weekly*, 2336, pp. 2336–7.

Sauvé, P., and Beviglia-Zampetti, A. (2006), 'Rules of Origin for Services: A Review of Current Practice', in Estevadeordal, A., Cadot, O. and Verdier, T. eds, *The Origin of Goods*. London: Oxford University Press and Centre for Economic Policy Research.

Shibata, H. (1967), 'The Theory of Economic Unions: A Comparative Analysis of Customs Unions, Free Trade Areas, and Tax Unions', in C.S. Shoup (ed.), *Fiscal Harmonization in Common Markets*, Columbia University Press, New York.

Stephenson, S.M. and James, W.E. (1995), "Rules of Origin and the Asia-Pacific Economic Cooperation', *Journal of World Trade*, Vol. 29, No. 2, April, pp. 77–103.

Stephenson, S. and Nikomborirak, D. (2002), 'Regional Liberalization in Services', in Sherry Stephenson, Christopher Findlay and Soonhwa Yi (eds), *Services Trade Liberalisation and Facilitation*, Asia Pacific Press at Australian National University.

Stern, R.M. and Hoekman, B. 1988. "Conceptual Issues Relating to Services in the International Economy," in C.H. Lee and S.F. Naya (Eds.), *Trade and Investment in Services in the Asia-Pacific Region*, Boulder, Colorado: Westview Press, pp. 7–26.

Stevens, C. and Kennan, J. (2000), *Post-Lomé WTO-Compatible Trading Arrangements*, Institute of Development Studies.

Suominen, K. (2000), *Rules of Origin in FTA: A World Map*, University of California, San Diego.

Tepp, S. 2007. *Understanding Rules of Origin: A Critical Review of the Literature*, Working Paper 2007-05, Department of Finance.

Thailand – Australia Free Trade Agreement (2004), 'Rules Of Origin: Australian Customs', Notice No. 2004/51.

Siew Yean T. and Abidin, M.Z. (2006). 'Rules of Origin in Services: Case of Malaysia', mimeo.TradeNote4.pdf.

Ujiie, T. 2006. Trade Facilitation. ERD Working Paper Series No. 78, Economics and Research Department, Asian Development Bank, Manila.

UNCTAD (1998), *Handbook on the Scheme of Norway: UNCTAD Technical Cooperation Project on Market Access, Trade Laws and Preferences*, UNCTAD/ITCD/TSB/Misc.29.

UNCTAD. 1999. *Digest of GSP Rules of Origin*. UNCTAD Technical Cooperation Project on Market Access, Trade Laws and Preferences, United Nations Conference on Trade and Development, Geneva.

United States Trade Representative (USTR). 2006. "North American Free Trade Agreement." (available: at http://www.nafta-sec-alena.org)

US (2002), United States – Rules Of Origin For Textiles And Apparel Products, Oral Statement of the United States at the First Meeting of the Panel with the Parties, *WT/DS243*.

Vermulst, E. (1992), 'Rules of Origin as Commercial Policy Instruments – Revisited', *Journal of World Trade*, Vol. 26, No. 6, pp. 61–102.

Viner, J. (1950), *The Customs Union Issue*, New York: Carnegie Endowment for International Peace.

WTO (2002), 'Rules of Origin Regimes in Regional Trade Agreements', Committee on Regional Trade Agreements, WT/REG/W/45.

WTO (2006), 'Report of the Committee on Rules of Origin', G/L/790.

WTO (2009), 'Regional Trade Agreements: Facts and Figures', WTO Secretariat (http://www.wto.org/english/tratop_e/region_e/regfac_e.htm)

Index